Rationality and Moral Theory

D1611525

Routledge Studies in Ethics and Moral Theory

Rationality and Moral Theory

How Intimacy Generates Reasons

Diane Jeske

Routledge
Taylor & Francis Group
New York   London

Acknowledgments

This book would never have been written without the immense and unflagging support and encouragement of my colleague and friend Richard Fumerton. Richard's greatest gift as a philosopher is his ability to get inside views that he himself rejects, and see how those views should be developed and defended. As a colleague and mentor, he has always been extraordinarily generous with his time and abilities. Knowing Richard has been, and continues to be, the best philosophical education for which one could hope. More importantly, he has been one of a few people who have shaped my views on friendship by helping me to experience it.

David Brink introduced me to ethics when I was a graduate student at MIT, and inspired me to pursue it. Thomas Williams and Sarah Buss provided extremely helpful comments on and discussion of various portions of the book manuscript, while audiences at Washington University and Bowling Green State University challenged me when I read portions of the book as talks at their departments.

Tracy Isaacs has been a steadfast friend, encouraging philosophical interlocutor, and intrepid shopping companion—she has sustained me through many difficult times and celebrated the good ones with me.

Finally, my parents, Ron and Barbara Franke, and my grandparents, William and Olga Jerman, to whom this book is dedicated, and my brother, Jerry Jeske, have provided me with a model of how family can become friends. To them I owe more than words can ever express.

Introduction
Agents and Their Reasons

If there is one truth about reasons to which all ethicists would most likely assent, it is that we each have an awful lot of them. At every moment of our lives, we have reasons for many actions and against many others. Disagreement enters when we start to ask *which* actions we have reasons to perform or to refrain from performing, and when we ask *what makes it the case* that we have the reasons that we do. Take, for example, an action such as making monthly contributions to an animal shelter. Not only will there be disagreement as to *whether,* for any given individual, she has reason to make that monthly contribution, but there will also be disagreement as to *why* she has such a reason: is it because doing so will minimize pain and/or maximize pleasure, because doing so will cultivate the virtue of generosity or the virtue of benevolence, because doing so is required by a right on the part of the animals themselves or on the part of some persons appropriately related to the animals, because the agent has a desire that puppies and kittens be safe and happy, or because of something else altogether?

Disagreement will also reign when we ask, *what is it* for a person to have a reason? *What are reasons?* Even if all can agree that, whatever reasons are, we have a lot of them, there will be plenty of disagreement as to whether all of the reasons that we have are the same sort of thing. Are there different types of reasons, as opposed merely to reasons that support different types of actions (or refrainings from actions)? Worse yet, there will be no agreement as to how we ought to go about settling these questions: what one of us takes as a compelling argument, another will regard as altogether irrelevant to settling the matter.

Many works in ethics attempt to answer the so-called metaethical questions concerning what reasons are and what it is for an agent to have a reason in isolation from the so-called normative question concerning what makes it the case that an agent has a reason (or, what grounds an agent's reasons).[1] I am going to take as my starting point the 'commonsense' intuition that at least one of the things that makes it the case (or grounds the fact) that we have reasons are our intimate relationships. We believe ourselves to have reasons to care for our intimates—friends, family members, colleagues, lovers—that we do not have to care for persons who are not our intimates. I do not mean that we do not take ourselves to have reasons to care for strangers or for mere acquaintances, but that we take ourselves to have *further* or *extra* reasons to care for those who stand in various sorts of special relationships to us. And those further or extra reasons—what I call *reasons of intimacy*—seem to arise *in virtue of* those special relationships. So we have reasons to care for our intimates, and it is our intimate relationships themselves that make it the case that we have, i.e., that ground, those reasons. These claims seem to be part of our *commonsense* understanding of our reasons: they are widely accepted and just seem right, even obvious, to those untutored in philosophy.

But those tutored in philosophy know that 'common sense' can lead us astray. So I will subject our 'commonsense' understanding of reasons of intimacy to philosophical scrutiny, and that will involve seeing whether we can fit that understanding into a general account of what reasons are and what it is for an agent to have a reason. Thus, the normative and meta-ethical will serve to reinforce one another: one account of the grounds of our reasons will offer support for an account of the nature of reasons, and vice versa. I will not, of course, defend every aspect of the view that I will ultimately put forth: the length of such a book would exhaust the patience of even the most dedicated of readers. So some claims and points of methodology will be presupposed, leaving the reader to assess the overall plausibility of the resultant picture of the nature of reasons. I have been a professional philosopher long enough to have no expectation of convincing very many of my readers—but I do hope that I will make my theory of both the grounds and the nature of reasons appear attractive enough that you will see why it needs to be taken seriously as an alternative.

Chapter 1 will provide the basic framework in which I will be working, setting forth concepts and definitions that we will need in our attempt to understand the nature of reasons of intimacy. The second half of the chapter will be devoted to an exposition and defense of the two types of reasons—what I will call the subjective agent-relative and the objective agent-neutral—that I will be using as a foil for reasons of intimacy. Chapter 2 is devoted to showing how and why reasons of intimacy, as understood by 'common sense,' cannot be assimilated to either of these two types of reasons. In Chapter 1 I will explain what I take the basic normative properties to be and how I understand them. I hope that the characterization and defense of reasons of intimacy that follows will lend support and weight to that metaethical view about the nature of reasons and what it is for agents to have reasons.

Once I have in place a general framework (Chapter 1) and have shown how our understanding of reasons of intimacy does not fit comfortably into that framework's categories (Chapter 2), I will proceed to an exploration of the nature of intimacy in Chapter 3. Chapter 4 will show how reasons of intimacy are analogous to our reasons to keep our promises—what I call our reasons of fidelity—and how we need to understand both types of reasons to fit them into the framework of Chapter 1. Chapter 4 will expand on that framework, by offering a defense of an intuitionist epistemology motivated by reasons of fidelity and reasons of intimacy. There have been many objections to intuitionism and I devote Chapters 5 and 6 to addressing two of those objections: (i) intuitionism is unable to give a plausible conception of moral reasoning, and (ii) intuitionism is unable to provide anything like a decision procedure for deciding disputed issues in ethics. I will approach (ii) via a case study, i.e., I will show how intuitionism allows us to make progress on the issue of a deontological constraint against killing or torturing the innocent, i.e., how that epistemology allows us to make progress on a specific normative issue. Finally, in Chapter 7 I will consider whether the account of reasons of intimacy and of reasons of fidelity that I gave in Chapter 4 can be extended into other contexts, in particular, whether it can be extended to cover duties of gratitude and special obligations to family members and compatriots. I will argue that consideration of gratitude, family, and political community should lead us to adopt a voluntarist constraint on our special obligations. Thus, we will end with a so-called normative issue, just as we began with one, but defense of the various normative claims that I make will be interwoven throughout the book with defense of and appeal to a moral epistemology and a moral ontology, i.e., to metaethics.

There is no better place to start our investigation of our understanding of reasons of intimacy and of intimacy itself than with an example, an example to which many of us have already reacted, both intellectually and emotionally . . .

1   Situating the Project

Imagine that you discover that your best friend has been involved, and continues to be involved, in illegal activities that involve selling useless concoctions under the guise of medication. As a result of your friend's activities, hundreds of children have been seriously harmed or have died. If your friend is not stopped, more children are likely to suffer and to die. When faced with the choice of either killing your friend or allowing him to escape from the police, what ought you to do?

The above case sounds like a standard philosophical thought experiment designed to tease out our 'intuitions' about what we think that we ought to do in certain kinds of circumstances. But it is also the description of the choice faced by Holly Martins (played by Joseph Cotton), the central character in *The Third Man*. At the end of that film, Holly faces his friend Harry Lime (Orson Welles) and must choose: 'loyalty' to his best friend, or action in accord with what some would call 'abstract justice.' The power of Carol Reed's film is crystallized in the tension of that final scene as Martins and Lime look at one another, in full recognition of what is at stake. Martins, of course, chooses—rightly, to my mind—'abstract justice.' The power of the film, however, derives from its recognition that, even if Martins does in fact make the right choice, there were significant considerations in support of his letting Harry get away. And those considerations seem clearly to derive from the fact that Lime was Holly's friend. Great art brings into sharp focus a, or perhaps, *the* crux of the ethical life: when 'personal' and 'impersonal' considerations conflict, how ought we to weigh these considerations and to respond?

Before we can address that question in any productive manner, we need to make clear exactly what our inquiry is about and what it is not about. We need to make clear the questions we are attempting to answer, or we may not recognize the answers when we chance upon them. So we must begin with some philosophical ground-clearing: distinctions must be made, definitions set forth.

I. LOCATING REASONS

Justification vs. Explanation

If Holly had had a 'cool moment' to reflect on the choice that he had to make, he would have tried to sort out and to weigh against one another his *reasons* for and against both shooting Harry Lime and letting Harry escape safely. Holly would have been concerned with his *justificatory reasons*, not with his *explanatory reasons*.

An explanatory reason for a person H's performing an action p is an internal psychological state(s) of H that was either the cause or part of the cause of H's doing p.[1] So, for example, one explanatory reason for my eating an entire pizza is my state of anxiety, because, in combination with the belief that a comfort food such as pizza will make me feel better, that state of anxiety caused me to eat the pizza.[2] Various philosophers have put forward theses about what sorts of states can possibly function as explanatory reasons, i.e., can possibly move an individual to action. Famously, David Hume claimed that only one sort of mental state, namely desires or passions, can possibly act as explanatory reasons for action.[3] Given that Hume claims that causal connections are not necessary connections, it is odd that he defends any claim about what could *possibly* cause human conduct. Anyone who thinks that the causal, including causation in the psychological realm, is an empirical matter, will not, *qua* philosopher, have much, if anything, to say about explanatory reasons.[4]

Justificatory reasons, on the other hand, are clearly philosophical territory, and they are also clearly the subject matter of Holly's deliberations when he asks himself whether he ought to shoot Harry Lime. Holly is not looking for a prediction as to whether he will be so moved, but, rather, he wants to know whether he is justified in shooting or in refraining from shooting Harry. When we justify a course of action, we are not (or, at least, not *merely*) explaining that action: it is quite possible for an explanation of a person's action to have nothing to do with any justification of that action. After all, it is quite possible for a person to act in an unjustified manner and, further, for her to believe, even at the time of acting, that she was unjustified in doing what she did. Pettiness, lust, greed, laziness, and too much alcohol can all be factors that *explain* our behavior, but rarely, if ever, do such factors *justify* our behavior.

To justify our behavior is to show it to be rational, supported by *good* reason, immune from (at least some forms of) criticism, etc. But justifying our *actions*, in the sense with which I will be concerned with that activity, is different from some ways of justifying our *beliefs*.[5] While the former is the concern of the ethicist, the latter are the concern of the epistemologist. I have *epistemic* reason for having a belief when there are considerations available (in some sense) to me that support the truth of that belief. But even with a belief for which an agent has few or no epistemic reasons, we can still ask whether she is justified, in the nonepistemic sense, in holding that belief. For example, suppose that Greg is suffering from depression due, in part, to his belief that he will never get married. In trying to help Greg recover from his depression, his friends try to convince him that he has no reason to give up on finding a spouse. Recognizing what his friends are trying to do, Greg might acknowledge that he has a nonepistemic reason to believe that he in fact is likely to get married because his having that belief would be instrumental to his overcoming his depression. So he has reason to believe that he will get married that is not an epistemic reason. Similarly, an agent might have epistemic reasons for a particular belief that it is irrational in the nonepistemic sense for her to have. For example, Emma might have very good evidence for the belief that her fiancé has slept with many women before becoming involved with her. Emma, however, would be troubled by such a belief, troubled in a way that will undermine her ability to have a meaningful long-term relationship with her fiancé. It would be best for Emma if she is able to bring herself to believe that her fiancé has had only very limited sexual experience. So Emma's epistemic and nonepistemic reasons will diverge in this case.

My project in this book is located in the territory of the nonepistemic justificatory. From now on, whenever I use the term 'reason,' unless I indicate otherwise, I will be referring to nonepistemic justificatory reasons. Also, unless I indicate otherwise, when I use 'reason,' I am to be understood to be talking about *prima facie* nonepistemic justificatory reasons: for any course of action supported by one or more reasons, it is always a possibility that that course of action is not supported by the agent's overall balance of reasons, i.e., by an all-things-considered reason. Whether a reason is *prima facie* or all-things-considered is a matter of its relations to other reasons, not a matter of its intrinsic nature: a *merely prima facie* reason is one such that it is outweighed by stronger reasons in the case at hand, where an all-things-considered reason is one such that it outweighs all competing reasons in the case at hand.[6]

The 'Possession' of Reasons

In the case of epistemic reasons, we need to distinguish between S's having reason to believe that p, and S's believing that p on the basis of those reasons. Suppose that the government actually has been hiding aliens who landed at Roswell in the 1950s. My grandfather has been investigating the government cover-up ever since he witnessed government agents loading the aliens into trucks in the New Mexico desert. He has often presented his findings to me, including photographs of the aliens. So I have epistemic reason to believe that aliens landed at Roswell. However, my belief that the government has been covering up the alien landing is based not on my grandfather's evidence as presented to me, but, rather, is the result of my suffering from paranoid schizophrenia: my illness causes me to be prone to believe any conspiracy theory, especially if it involves the United States government. So, while I *have* epistemic reasons to believe that aliens landed at Roswell, it is not the case that I believe in the alien landing *on the basis of* the reasons that I have.

We can make a similar distinction in the case of nonepistemic justificatory reasons: S may have justification for doing p, while it is not the case that she does p on the basis of her justification. Suppose that I am justified in giving a certain portion of my income to charity, insofar as doing so promotes the well-being of needy persons. Also suppose that I give to charities not in order to contribute to the well-being of the needy, but, rather, because I think that giving to charities is the only way to keep the government from getting my money, money that they will use to fund their various cover-ups and conspiracies. I have justification for my action, i.e., my action is supported by justificatory reasons for action, but it is not the case that I act on the basis of the justification. In what follows, I am concerned with the reasons that agents have for various courses of action, not with whether or when they act on the basis of those reasons. The latter task is one for the psychologists, not for the philosophers.

'Ought' Judgments

Normative judgments are often expressed in terms of what a given agent *ought* to do. Typically, we use 'ought' when we are making judgments about an agent's all-things-considered reasons for action, rather than a judgment about her *prima facie* reasons for action. So I will take the claim that S ought to do p as having the same meaning as the claim that S has an all-things-considered reason to do p.

However, it is certainly the case that in everyday discourse, 'ought' has more than one sense. We 'issue' such judgments when we are engaging in the performative utterance activity of criticism. If I say to Daniel, "You ought not spend so much money on clothes," I may be trying to tell him what his all-things-considered reason for action is. But I may be using the 'ought' judgment to criticize his behavior from some particular perspective. Thus, I may be trying to indicate to him that better consequences would result from an alternative use of his money. Or perhaps I simply do not like the way that he uses his money, so the 'ought' judgment may be my way of expressing or stating my own preferences regarding how Daniel uses his money. It may very well be these different uses of 'ought' judgments that have motivated some who have opted for noncognitivism: overemphasis on one function of 'ought' judgments led to a failure to see other uses.[7] But, while 'ought' judgments can have different uses in everyday discourse, this should not trouble the ethicist any more than the epistemologist should be troubled by or interested in the fact that 'know' has a cognitive sense, a 'biblical' sense, and an 'interpersonal' sense ("You know Tracy, don't you?").

II. DISTINCTIONS AMONG REASONS

When we imagine Holly Martins deliberating about whether to shoot Harry Lime, we will imagine his deliberations proceeding differently from the way that they would proceed if Holly and Harry were not good friends. If the film had ended with a police officer being confronted with the options of either shooting Harry or letting him go, that last scene would not have had the power of the actual last scene in the film, because the police officer does not seem to have the considerations supporting letting Harry go that Holly has. We seem, intuitively, to regard Holly as having certain reasons in virtue of being Harry's friend that an agent who is not friends with Harry would not have. This feature of reasons of intimacy—usually labelled 'agent-relativity'—needs to be at the center of any attempt to offer an account of how we actually seem to understand these reasons. A large part of my project is to sort out the notion of agent-relativity implicit in our understanding of reasons of intimacy. I will then show how we can make philosophical sense of this notion, thereby preserving our commonsense understanding of our reasons of intimacy.

Relativity vs. Neutrality

Suppose that the charity Doctors Without Borders sends out a mass mailing requesting funding for a project aimed at AIDS treatment and prevention in the areas of Africa that have been hit hardest by the AIDS epidemic. This mailing will reach many American middle-, upper-middle-, and upper-class households. In such households, let us suppose, at least twenty-five dollars is spent each week on new, nonessential clothing purchases. Does the head of each of these households have a reason to redirect twenty-five dollars from clothing purchases to the AIDS project?

The answer to this question seems clearly to be, yes. Of course, with the information that I have provided, we can conclude only that each head of household has *a* reason to send the money to Doctors Without Borders, not that each has a *decisive* or *all-things-considered* reason to send the money. After all, other reputable charities may have sent out mailings requesting donations for other projects aimed at helping the needy, and each household head may not be in a position to respond to all such requests. Nonetheless, it does seem that the information that I have given is sufficient to support the conclusion that each head of household has at least *prima facie* reason, and the *same type* of *prima facie* reason, to send twenty-five dollars to Doctors Without Borders.

Notice what information I did *not* provide about any of the heads of well-off American households: I did not say that any of these people stand in any relation to the AIDS-afflicted persons in Africa, other than the relation of a person able to provide aid to relieve their suffering. Neither did I point to any specific past actions of the Americans in order to support my claim that each of them had reason to send money to support the AIDS project. Only two facts seemed relevant to the claim that the Americans have a reason to support the project: they have the means to do so, and the project will relieve suffering (relief of which, I take it we all agree, is good).

Now imagine a different case: Tracy sends out invitations to her party, a party celebrating her recent job promotion. She is very excited about this promotion, for which she has worked very hard for several years. Thus, she is really looking forward to a celebration at which she can bask in the glow of accomplishment and pride. Due to a recent malfunction in postal sorting machines, some of the invitations have arrived at the wrong addresses. Susan receives an invitation. Does Susan have a reason to attend Tracy's promotion celebration?

Of course, our answer to this question depends on more than merely the information that Susan has the means to attend Tracy's party, and that Tracy wants a good turnout at her party. Did Susan receive the invitation by mistake? If so, she may not know Tracy from Eve. So why would she have reason to attend a stranger's party?[8] But now suppose that Susan is Tracy's best friend: Susan and Tracy went to graduate school together and have supported each other through the early, stressful years of their careers. Susan knows that Tracy wants her to attend and would be very hurt if she did not attend. Surely, in this case, Susan has a very strong reason to attend the party and to do everything that she can in order to insure that the party is a success.

So the fact that Susan and Tracy are friends seems very relevant to Susan's reasons, just as the fact that Martins and Lime were friends seemed to be very relevant to the former's reasons as he faced Lime in the sewer at the end of the film. We can imagine similar cases in which further information about the relationship between two persons seems relevant to their reasons to perform certain actions, cases in which person S has made a promise to person Q, cases in which S has done numerous favors for Q in the past, cases in which S is Q's colleague, etc. These sorts of reasons are typically referred to as *agent-relative reasons*.

It is, however, quite difficult to specify precisely what distinguishes agent-relative from agent-neutral reasons. One common way of doing so is in terms of the statement of the reason as requiring an essential reference to the agent whose reason it is. The idea is that Susan's reason to attend Tracy's party is derivative from a more fundamental reason, namely Susan's reason to take care of *her, Susan's,* friends. In order to specify Susan's reasons we need to refer to those persons who stand in a certain special relationship to Susan, namely, the friendship relation. But now suppose that Susan is one of those well-off Americans who received the mailing from Doctors Without Borders, and, so, has a reason to send twenty-five dollars to support the AIDS project in Africa. Her reason to send the money is derivative from her more fundamental reason to prevent suffering when *she, Susan,* is in a position to do so. This also seems to be an essential reference to the agent who has the reason: Susan has reason to promote value (e.g., by relieving suffering) in so far as *she* is in a position to do so.

Another attempt to preserve this characterization of agent-neutral reasons in virtue of the nature of their statement would be to say that for all agents S, S has a reason to relieve suffering when S is in a position to do so. Here, we can substitute any S and still have a true statement. But, unfortunately, we can get a parallel formulation of supposedly agent-relative reasons: S has a reason to take care (in certain ways) of person Q when S is in a position to do so and when S is Q's friend. We can preserve the truth of the claim for any S that we substitute. Of course, if we were to drop the condition 'when S is Q's friend,' then the claim would only be true if the S that was substituted were Q's friend. But something similar is true about supposedly neutral reasons: if we drop the condition 'when S is in a position to do so,' then the statement of the reason does not remain true for any S that we substitute in.

What this discussion points out, I think, is that there is an important sense in which a reason is always a reason *for a particular person:* I acquire reasons to relieve suffering when I stand in the appropriate causal relation to those persons who are suffering, and I acquire reasons to care for certain persons when I stand in the appropriate intimate relation to those persons requiring such care. Given this fact, then, all reasons are, in some sense, agent-relative: they are reasons for a particular agent given her situation.[9]

The relevant difference between agent-neutral and agent-relative reasons seems to be the type of 'situation' that determines whether a particular agent has a certain type of reason. In the case of donating to the AIDS project, it seems that any agent has a reason to do so, *as long as she has the causal power to do so.* But the relevant situation described by S's being Q's friend is something other than a causal relationship between S and the state of affairs that she has reason to promote in virtue of being Q's friend. So the fact that a state of affairs T is intrinsically valuable, for example, grounds a reason for any S such that S is in a causal position to promote T.[10] But the fact that a state of affairs would constitute, for example, the keeping of a promise, does not ground a reason for any S such that S is in a causal position to promote it: it is also relevant whether the promise to be kept is S's promise.

The following, then, is how I will understand neutral vs. relative reasons:

> *Agent-Neutral Reason:* S's reason to do or to promote p is an agent-neutral reason if and only if, necessarily, for any Q, Q would also have a reason to do or to promote p if Q were in a causal position to do or to promote p. All other reasons are agent-relative.

For any alleged agent-relative reason, then, we need to specify the further features of a person's 'situation,' beyond her causal powers, that are partly constitutive of the grounds of her reason to do or to promote p.[11] In the case of agent-relative reasons to keep promises—if we do in fact have such reasons—the grounds of the agent's reason to perform action p (the content of her promise), i.e., to promote the situation that constitutes her promise being kept, involves in part that *she* made a promise to do p. Any agent that did not make such a promise does not have a reason *of the same sort* to perform p (there might be agent-neutral reason to do p).

So our reasons of intimacy seem not to be agent-neutral: my reasons to care for my friends seem to be grounded, at least in part, by my relationship to my friends. Any person who is not friends with those people does not have a reason *of the same sort* to care for my friends (there might be agent-neutral reasons to take care of them). The claim that this aspect of reasons of intimacy is central to our commonsense understanding of them will be defended in Chapter 2.

Fundamental vs. Derivative Reasons

The distinction between fundamental and derivative reasons is easier to make than that between agent-relative and agent-neutral reasons. Our well-off Americans have reason to send their twenty-five dollars to support the AIDS project. But, clearly, this is not a fundamental reason, but, rather, it is derived from their reason to promote intrinsically valuable states of affairs in conjunction with the empirical facts regarding the role of the AIDS project in relieving human suffering and, thereby, promoting intrinsic value.

Consider another example: Richard promises Diane that he will give her comments on her book manuscript. Richard then has reason to provide Diane with comments on her book manuscript. But Richard's reason to provide Diane with comments is not a fundamental reason: it is derivative from his reason to keep his promises in conjunction with the fact that he has made a promise to give Diane comments.

These examples illustrate the following distinction:

Fundamental Reason: S's reason R to do p is a fundamental reason if and only if S's reason to do p is not constituted in whole or in part by some other reason R*, where R is not identical to R*. Any reason that is not a fundamental reason is a derivative reason.

So, in the examples, the well-off American's reason to donate to the AIDS project is not fundamental because that reason is constituted, in part, by her reason to promote value, and Richard's reason to provide Diane with comments is not fundamental because that reason is in part constituted by his reason to keep his promises. The well-off American's reason to make the donation of twenty-five dollars is constituted by the conjunction of her reason to promote value and her causal ability to do so, while Richard's reason to give Diane comments on her manuscript is constituted by the conjunction of his reason to keep his promises and his having promised to give her comments on her manuscript.

As I will show in Chapter 2, attempts to construe reasons of intimacy as derivative rather than fundamental do not seem to capture our ordinary understandings of the nature of such reasons, just as our ordinary understanding of reasons to keep promises seems to construe such reasons as fundamental. Utilitarians, of course, understand all reasons as derivative from our reason to promote intrinsic value. The unity and theoretical simplicity of such an account is what makes it particularly pressing for the preservation of the commonsense understanding of reasons of intimacy that we find some coherent philosophical account of such reasons as fundamental.

Objective vs. Subjective Reasons

The terms 'objective' and 'subjective' get used in a lot of different ways, both in philosophy and in everyday discourse, so I want to be very clear as to how I will be using them. Let's begin by considering Humean reasons, i.e., reasons grounded on an agent's desires (or, on an agent's awareness of her desires; see Section IV). If Hume was right, then my desire to eat a Twix grounds a reason for me to eat a Twix. Notice that the grounds of my reason in this case is a subjective psychological state—my desire to eat the Twix—and nothing else.

But I have at least one other reason to eat the Twix. If my eating of the Twix would give me pleasure, and if pleasure is intrinsically valuable (as I take it to be), then I have reason to eat the Twix insofar as my doing so is instrumental to my promotion of intrinsic value. This latter reason, however, is not grounded by the mere fact of my desire, but, rather, by the fact that the consequences of my eating of the Twix would be intrinsically valuable. This reason, then, unlike my Humean reason, is not a subjective reason:

> *Subjective Reason:* S's reason R to do p is a subjective reason if and only if R is grounded by, and only by, the fact that S takes some interest in (or cares about) p or some causal consequence of p (and S's awareness of that fact). All other reasons are objective reasons.

Notice that I have stated the definition of a subjective reason in terms of S's *current* interests or concerns. Suppose that Sally knows that she will want to have a garden when she is sixty years old, although now she has no desire to have a garden. If Sally now wants to insure that her sixty-year-old self will be able to satisfy her desires, then she has a subjective reason to plan ahead for her later gardening interests. However, some philosophers would insist that Sally has a reason to insure that her sixty-year-old self will be able to satisfy her desires even if Sally now has no desire to promote that state of affairs. According to my definition of subjective reasons, Sally's reason of prudence would be objective, not subjective.[12] Of course, my definition is purely stipulative—I am not claiming to be doing any sort of conceptual analysis. However, I hope to show in what follows how my distinction between subjective and objective reasons helps to order the realm of reasons in helpful ways.

III. FUNDAMENTAL OBJECTIVE AGENT-RELATIVE REASONS?

My project in the following chapters is to present and to defend a conception of reasons of intimacy that is, I argue, the conception that is embedded in our ordinary, commonsense notion of such reasons. According to this conception, reasons of intimacy—our reasons to care for our friends and other intimates—are *fundamental, agent-relative,* and *objective.* They share the feature of being fundamental with our reasons to promote intrinsic value, our reasons to keep our promises, and our reasons to satisfy our desires. They share the feature of agent-relativity with only the latter two reasons, but they share the feature of being objective with only the former two. So they seem to be most like our reasons to keep our promises. Unfortunately, reasons of intimacy have the same sorts of philosophical objections to contend with as do reasons of promise-keeping. Thus, my defense of fundamental agent-relative objective reasons of intimacy will also be a defense of the very notion of fundamental agent-relative objective reasons. However, I will argue that we ought not include within the category of fundamental objective agent-relative reasons certain familiar contenders, such as a constraint against killing or torturing the innocent (Chapter 6) and political obligations (Chapter 7).

The Consequentialist Challenge

Consequentialism offers an alternative to understanding reasons of intimacy as fundamental agent-relative reasons. This consequentialist alternative is attractive, simple, and quite compelling. Thus, any account of reasons of intimacy as fundamental agent-relative reasons must meet the challenge of consequentialism head-on.

According to the consequentialist, there is one and only one fundamental reason:

> *Consequentialist Reason:* S has a fundamental reason to promote intrinsic value. Thus, for any action p, S has a derivative reason to do p if and only if the doing of p is a logical or causal means to the production of intrinsic value.[13]

Given the nature of consequentialist reasons, then, all fundamental reasons are agent-neutral: for any intrinsically valuable states of affairs T, any S has reason to promote T if S is in a causal position to do so.

So how do consequentialists account for our apparent reasons of intimacy? Sidgwick claimed that "the reasons why it is, generally speaking, conducive to the general happiness that each individual should distribute his beneficence in the channels marked out by commonly recognised ties and claims, are tolerably obvious."[14] In other words, he, like many consequentialists who have followed him, thought that it is "tolerably obvious" that we have derivative reasons to promote the good of our intimates before and to a greater extent than we consider promoting the good of those who are strangers to us. After all, our proximity (both emotional and physical) to our intimates and our greater knowledge of their needs makes it more likely that our benevolence will be well directed when we use as our guides to its distribution "commonly recognised ties and claims."

Thus, even though I have reason to care for my intimates that you may not have, my reason to do so is derivative, i.e., it is partially constituted by my reason to promote intrinsic value. Further, my reason to care for my intimates is not agent-relative, but, rather, it is agent-neutral: anyone in as good of a causal position to care for my intimates has a reason of the same kind and strength as my own to do so. It may be true that unless that other person is also intimate with my intimates, she will not be in such a good causal position, and so will not have a reason of equal strength as my own to care for my intimates. But the significance of the intimate relationship lies only in the type of causal powers that a party to it has: it is, at bottom, no different than the relationship to a drowning person of being on the river bank in a position to throw out a life preserver.

As I will argue in Chapter 2, this understanding of reasons of intimacy as derivative from the fundamental agent-neutral reason to promote intrinsic value is not intuitively satisfying. But it is also true that it has powerful motivation. After all, why should the mere fact that I am intimate with someone, in and of itself, provide me with reason to care for her? Shouldn't the mere fact that S is a person with needs and interests that I am in a position to promote be the fundamental feature grounding my reasons to promote S's welfare? If so, then it simply shouldn't matter whether S happens to be my friend, my colleague, my mother, or even my child. The apparent parochialism of fundamental agent-relative reasons of intimacy can exert a powerful pull toward the consequentialist account of our reasons. So, as philosophers, if we are to reject that account in favor of the commonsense one, we need to offer equally compelling reasons for rejecting the consequentialist account.

The Humean Challenge

Another challenge to the commonsense account of reasons of intimacy focuses not on their allegedly being fundamental agent-relative reasons but, rather, on their allegedly being objective, i.e., by their allegedly not being grounded solely by the agent's interests or concerns. The account of reasons traditionally associated with Hume holds that all reasons are subjective agent-relative:

Humean Reason: S's fundamental reason is to satisfy her desires/promote her interests or concerns. Thus, for any action p, S has a derivative reason to do p if and only if S's doing p would be a logical or causal means to the satisfaction of one or more of S's desires or to the promotion of S's interests/concerns.

So, for the Humean, our fundamental reasons are agent-relative. If an agent S has a desire to have w be the case, she then has reason to promote w. According to the Humean account, it does not follow that S*, S* not identical to S, has a reason to promote w even if S* is in a causal position to do so. The mere fact that *I* want something is relevant to what I have reason to do in a way that it is not relevant to what others have reason to do, no matter what their causal positions.

The Humean has a straightforward account of our reasons of intimacy. It seems part of our concept of intimacy that it involves a certain concern for or interest in the well-being of the intimate. (I discuss this issue in Chapter 3.) If that is the case, then insofar as Tracy is Susan's best friend, Susan will have a reason to care for Tracy: insofar as Tracy is Susan's friend, Susan cares about Tracy's well-being and so has reason to do what will promote that well-being. Susan's reason to care for Tracy is not fundamental, because it is partly constituted by her reason to satisfy her desires. But her reason is agent-relative: Q will not have a reason of the same kind to care for Tracy even if she has the means to do so, unless Q also has a desire to care for Tracy.

Whereas consequentialist reasons fail on intuitive grounds to account for reasons of intimacy because they render those latter reasons derivative, Humean reasons, as I argue in Chapter 2, fail because they render reasons of intimacy subjective. On the Humean account, unlike both the consequentialist account and the commonsense account, an agent's reason to care for an intimate is grounded solely on a feature of the agent herself, not on the nature of the intimate or on the nature of the relationship between the agent and the intimate. The Humean, however, has ontological simplicity on her side in this matter, and also ties reasons of intimacy directly to concern, a central feature of intimacy itself. The Humean also has a nice explanation of agent-relativity: reasons based on my desires are quite clearly mine in a very special sort of way. But, on intuitive grounds, as we will see in Chapter 2, the Humean account fares even less well than consequentialism.

Other Fundamental Objective Agent-Relative Reasons?

So my project is to present and defend an account of reasons of intimacy as fundamental objective agent-relative reasons. Once that project is completed, however, another question naturally arises: are there other fundamental objective agent-relative reasons? And, if so, which are they?

I will limit myself to considering a select group of reasons that have been proposed as being akin to reasons of intimacy: political obligations, familial obligations, reasons of promise-keeping, reasons not to kill or to torture the innocent, and reasons of gratitude. I will argue that our reasons to keep our promises are fundamental objective agent-relative, while none of the other reasons mentioned are. While my rejection of, for example, fundamental agent-relative political obligations may not be so controversial, my rejection of fundamental agent-relative reasons to refrain from killing or torturing the innocent will be very controversial. I will suggest that we adopt the voluntarist constraint on the category of fundamental objective agent-relative reasons, thereby limiting that category to voluntarily assumed commitments.

In Chapter 4, I will offer an ontology and epistemology that makes sense of reasons of intimacy as being fundamental objective agent-relative reasons, and of our knowledge of our having such reasons. I will use this philosophical metaethics to bolster my defense of certain fundamental objective agent-relative reasons and my rejection of others. But, while I am sure that many readers will remain unconvinced by my metaethical backstory and by my defense of the voluntarist constraint on the category of fundamental objective agent-relative reasons, I hope that more will agree with my account of reasons of intimacy. Then we can at least have some common ground prepared for the task of relative evaluations of metaethical backstories, and for assessing the range and scope of our fundamental objective agent-relative reasons.

IV. THE GROUNDS OF REASONS

My main project in this book, then, is to defend a picture of reasons of intimacy as fundamental objective agent-relative reasons. In the previous section of this chapter, I briefly sketched two accounts of reasons of intimacy that do not understand them as fundamental objective agent-relative. Chapter 2 will be devoted to a detailed defense of the claim that neither of these two accounts adequately captures our 'commonsense' understanding of reasons of intimacy.

However, while I will argue that reasons of intimacy are neither objective agent-neutral reasons nor subjective agent-relative reasons, I will proceed under the assumption that, in addition to reasons of intimacy, we do have both consequentialist and Humean reasons. Much has been written about both types of reasons, and I fear that my defense of either type would add little to the already existent debate. Nonetheless, in this section, I want to do two things: (i) briefly state my reasons for assuming that we do in fact have both objective agent-neutral (consequentialist) reasons and subjective agent-relative (Humean) reasons, and (ii) sketch a picture of the ontology of reasons that, at least in one important way, unifies all types of reasons—objective and subjective, agent-neutral and agent-relative.[15]

Subjective Agent-Relative Reasons

Why suppose that we have them?

A very simple sort of case can be used to motivate the claim that we have subjective agent-relative reasons:

> Imagine that I am sitting in a cafe with my friend Tracy. We are reading the menu, discussing the available sandwich options. Tracy asks me what I am going to have, and I reply that I am going to order the tuna sandwich on wheat. She then asks me why I am going to order the tuna sandwich, and I reply, "Because I want the tuna more than I want anything else on the menu."

Have I justified my choice of sandwich? It certainly seems as though I have. At the very least, I have offered *prima facie* justification for my ordering the tuna sandwich. If it turns out that the restaurant uses tuna caught in nets that capture and kill dolphins, I have a reason that counters and may outweigh the reason provided by my wanting to have a tuna sandwich. But the fact remains that I have offered Tracy at least one good reason in support of my ordering the tuna on wheat.

This sort of example is, of course, only the starting point for a discussion about subjective agent-relative reasons. There are many objections that have been raised against the claim that our desires ground reasons, but I am going to address only two of the most powerful of those objections here.

> *Objection (1) to Subjective Agent-Relative Reasons:* It is not the desire itself that grounds a reason for action, but, rather, the objective value of the pleasure that will arise from satisfying the desire.

Someone might insist that the same fact that explains my wanting to order the tuna also grounds my reason for ordering the tuna—the fact that having the tuna would give me more pleasure than would having any other available sandwich, and that pleasure is objectively intrinsically valuable. This objection seems to have particular bite in a case such as the one that I described, because it does seem that our food preferences are often a function of which foods we believe will give us greatest pleasure.

But even in the realm of food choices, I think that we can see why we should not suppose that it is really pleasure rather than desire that grounds our reasons. Imagine that Greg goes on the Atkins diet because he wants to lose weight and he believes that the Atkins diet is a good way to lose weight. He loses all of the weight that he wanted to lose, and correctly believes that he could maintain that weight if he were to go off of the Atkins diet. He does not enjoy the food available to him on Atkins—he loves carbohydrates and is not at all fond of meat, for example—but remains on the diet even once he has reached his optimal weight, a weight that he believes he could maintain even if he were to reintroduce carbohydrates into his diet. When a friend asks him why he remains on Atkins, he replies that he has come to want to enforce upon himself the discipline of the diet even though he would very much enjoy a large serving of spaghetti and some Twizzlers. Doesn't it seem that his desire gives him at least some reason to remain on the diet, even if the pleasure that he would get from a good healthy dose of carbs provides a perhaps weightier reason?

One response that a critic will offer at this point is that Greg must get pleasure from enforcing the discipline of the diet. But why must we suppose that this is the case? We often seem to choose to do things that we do not believe will bring us pleasure (diet, run a marathon, do our duty, fight in a war, etc.). If someone were to continue to insist that in so far as an agent wants something, she must believe that it will bring her pleasure (either directly or indirectly by bringing something that will give pleasure), we would be entitled to wonder whether that person were simply using 'pleasure' to mean 'gratification' or 'satisfaction,' where to be gratified or satisfied is simply to have the object of one's desire realized.[16] Or perhaps the critic is understanding pleasure functionally, such that pleasure is just a state that one wants to be in—but then, of course, it is trivial to suppose that satisfying a desire will bring pleasure, because that claim amounts to saying that the achieving of a desired state results in being in a desired state. If the critic, however, insists that she understands pleasure as some *sui generis* mental state, a la Bentham, then it just seems wrong to suppose that that mental state is the only thing desired intrinsically or that desires can give us reason to act only derivatively insofar as they have that mental state as their object.

At this point, the critic will point out that many things besides pleasure can plausibly be taken to have intrinsic value. In particular, she will insist that maintaining the discipline of the diet is an intrinsically valuable activity. I do not deny that exercising powers of planning and restraint can be valuable uses of our capacities (although not to the point that they outweigh the pleasure gained from eating candy and pasta). And I think that if a critic looks hard enough, she will probably be able to locate some consequence of the satisfying of any desire that could plausibly be construed as intrinsically valuable. But after awhile the searching seems strained: there is a common denominator in all cases, namely the fact that the state of affairs is the object of the agent's desire. If we are so determined to find some consideration to support the claim that the agent has reason to satisfy her desire, why not suppose that the simplest answer, namely the fact of the agent's desire, is also the correct one?

I do not want to be taken as denying that we often want pleasure and aim at other things as a means to pleasure, or that we desire intrinsically valuable things, often under that description. But I am denying the claim that the only thing that we ever want for its own sake is pleasure or intrinsic objective value. And I am asserting that even in those cases where the object of our desire is something that will not bring us pleasure or anything else intrinsically valuable, that we still have reason to pursue the object of our desire merely in virtue of its being the object of our desire. We need to understand 'desire' as encompassing a broad range of states that constitute some sort of concern/care or interest. So my claim is that one source of reasons for action is an agent's concerns or interests, not at all an implausible claim. Given that we can take an interest in or care about many things other than pleasure or those things that are objectively good, our reasons range beyond those arising from the value of the pleasure or objective value that we often get from satisfying our desires.

Objection (2) to Subjective Agent-Relative Reasons: Desires themselves are rationally evaluable and so cannot be, in and of themselves, sources of reasons.

This objection takes as its starting point an example of any of the following sorts: a desire to engage in an immoral activity (harming other persons, torturing animals, organizing neo-Nazi rallies); imprudent desires (excessive alcohol consumption, smoking, eating a lot of high-fat foods, spending too much money on designer clothing); and trivial or superficial desires (having plastic surgery to enlarge one's lips, getting Botox injections, collecting celebrity memorabilia, having a better car than one's buddies). Does Snidely have reason to torture puppies merely in virtue of his wanting to do so? Does Peggy have reason to have repeated Botox injections just because she wants a line-free forehead? Snidely and Peggy, it seems, have reason to eliminate their desires. If so, how could Snidely and Peggy have reasons to act grounded in desires that they have reason not to have? How can irrational or immoral desires be reason-giving?

We need immediately to set aside a consideration that might make the cases seem more compelling evidence for the critic than they actually are. Even if we accept that, for example, Peggy has a reason to get repeated Botox injections, we are not committed to viewing that reason as Peggy's all-things-considered reason for action. Thus, even if Peggy has some reason to get Botox injections in virtue of her wanting to erase the lines from her forehead, she may be irrational if she acts on that desire: she may have other competing reasons that outweigh her desire for a smooth forehead. Similarly, it may be that Snidely's reason to torture small animals is swamped by his other reasons, including his objective agent-neutral reason to avoid causing pain and suffering.

But some critics will insist that it is implausible to suppose that Snidely and Peggy have *any* reason at all to torture kittens or to get Botox injections. At some point, of course, we hit rock bottom with respect to competing intuitions. However, consider again the case of my tuna sandwich on wheat. If it seems that the mere fact that I want to eat the tuna provides me with reason to eat it, shouldn't we say that desires always ground reasons, even when the desires have immoral, imprudent, or trivial actions as their objects? It seems ad hoc to suppose that only certain desires ground reasons while others do not. Of course, the critic might say that my desire to have tuna is not sufficient to give me reason to order and eat a tuna sandwich. And again, we will have reached a stalemate of intuitions.

But, again, all that I have hoped to do is to suggest why it seems plausible to suppose that we have subjective agent-relative reasons, not to offer a definitive argument in support of the claim that we have such reasons. I will be working within a framework that assumes those reasons in order to discuss reasons of intimacy, but one could accept my claim about those latter reasons without accepting that we have subjective agent-relative reasons grounded on desires.

What grounds them?

I have been speaking about subjective agent-relative reasons as grounded by desires. However, I need to be more precise at this point and specify exactly what I take to ground subjective agent-relative reasons.

Reasons are always attributable to agents, so it seems that the agent must, in some way, figure as a component or feature of the grounds of her reasons. So as a first attempt, we might say that the grounds of my reason to pursue D, where D is the object of my desire, is the fact of my being in a state that can be characterized as my caring about or taking an interest in, i.e., desiring, D. But now we need to notice that agents can fail to be aware of their own desires, either through a failure of reflection, self-deception, shift of focus (deliberate or otherwise), repression, or any number of other psychological factors. Do we want to say that I have a reason to pursue D even if I am unaware of the fact that I want D?[17]

One way to approach this question is to think about our intuitions in the analogous case with regard to epistemic reasons. Return to a case that I discussed earlier, the case in which my grandfather took pictures of the government loading aliens onto trucks in the desert outside of Roswell, New Mexico, in the 1950s. My grandfather has put these pictures in a file marked "Pictures of Aliens" that are in an unlocked file cabinet easily accessible to me. But I have never looked through my grandfather's file cabinet, and, thus, have never come across the pictures of the aliens. Do I have reason to believe that aliens landed at Roswell in the 1950s?

It seems plausible to me to describe the case as follows: There is a reason available to me to believe that aliens landed at Roswell, but I do not, as of yet, have such reason. I will have reason to believe that the aliens landed only when I become aware of the pictures and of their representational content—i.e., when I realize that they are pictures of aliens.[18] So to say that there is reason available to me is just a way of stating the conditional that if I were to become aware of some fact then I would have reason to believe.

Thus, I think that it makes sense to say that the grounds of my reason to believe is the fact that provides evidence for the belief in conjunction with my being aware of that fact.[19] I now have reason to draw certain conclusions, whether or not I actually do draw those conclusions. (I am assuming that I have certain minimal capacities for intelligent thought. My cat will not have reason to believe in the alien landing even if she is aware of my grandfather's pictures.)

The parallel way of understanding practical reasons is to say that if I desire D but am not aware that I desire D, then there is a reason available to me (assuming I can get at my desire somehow, i.e., it is not irretrievably repressed) to pursue D, but I do not yet have such a reason. To say that a reason is available to me is a way of stating the conditional that if I were to become aware of the fact of my desiring D then I would have reason to pursue D. Thus, the grounds of my subjective agent-relative reason to pursue D is the fact that I desire D in conjunction with the fact that I am aware that I desire D.[20] Of course, I may have reason to become aware of my desires, but I can have that reason without yet having a reason to pursue D, where D is the content of some particular desire.

But now suppose that I am aware of my desire for D, but would not want D if I were fully informed about the nature of D. (D might be anything from climbing Mount Everest to becoming a philosopher to eating at the new restaurant in town.) Is it still plausible to suppose that I have reason to pursue D, given that I might not want D if I had more information? I think that some of these cases will involve very difficult issues. For example, suppose that I tell you that I want to climb Mount Everest, and then you find out that I believe that Mount Everest is a slight hill in Nepal that tourists often climb for a day's outing. Do I really want to climb *Mount Everest*, where to climb Mount Everest is to climb the world's highest mountain, an activity in which people have died? Problems about reference abound here, as we try to figure out exactly what the object of my desire is.

But let's look at a somewhat clearer case that will do as well for getting at the current issue. Suppose that I want to climb Mount Everest knowing full well that it is the highest mountain in the world and that it is a difficult, potentially life-threatening climb. However, suppose also that I do not reflect on the hardships and risks involved in the climb because my attention is focused on how cool it will be to be able to tell people that I climbed Mount Everest. If it is the case that more robust reflection would extinguish my desire, is it still the case that my present desire (in conjunction with my awareness of that desire) grounds a reason for me to climb Mount Everest?

There is no denying that it is highly likely that I have a reason to reflect on my desire, either because I have a second-order desire to act only on reflective desires or because I will suffer by climbing Mount Everest and am, at some level, aware of this fact (see discussion of objective agent-neutral reasons). I may also have epistemic reason for believing that reflection would extinguish my desire. Nonetheless, I am inclined to think that as things are, I have reason to climb Mount Everest. It is true for any number of our desires that, given certain changes in conditions, the desire would be extinguished. If I were to travel to war-torn or famine-stricken regions of the world, I might very well lose any desire to finish this book, write philosophy papers, and go to the APA meetings, seeing all of these activities as pointless indulgences in a world with so much suffering. Does that show that I now have no reason to act on my desires to finish this book, write philosophy papers, and go to the APA meetings? Surely not. We need to ask whether we have reason to do what would extinguish the relevant desire. However, even if we have such reason, until the desire is extinguished, we also have a reason grounded by the desire.

Again, however, I want to stress that there are a lot of issues about language, reference, our grasp of our own concepts, and the relation of our own concepts to those of other persons, that I am simply leaving unaddressed here. Only once we settle these issues will we be able to say what exactly the object of a person's desire is. (Even then, some ambiguity may remain, because it seems that people can want something that is only vaguely characterized.) My claim is that an agent has reason to pursue those things that she is aware that she is concerned about. I leave it to the philosophers of language and of mind to find ways of determining what a given individual actually cares about.

Objective Agent-Neutral Reasons

Why suppose that we have them?

We can return to the simple case of the tuna sandwich on wheat to motivate objective agent-neutral reasons:

> After telling Tracy that I want to order the tuna, she asks the server some questions about the source of the tuna. Tracy then tells me that the company that supplied the tuna is known to use nets that routinely capture and kill dolphins as a by-product of tuna collection. She then urges me not to support a company that has exhibited such callousness toward dolphins.

Do I have at least some reason not to order the tuna, assuming that my action of refraining from eating tuna will play a role in putting an end to the pointless slaughter of dolphins?[21] Many people will say that I do, and they will not be inclined to alter their answer if they find out that I do not have any concern for dolphins, for my reputation among dolphin-lovers, etc. Why do I have reason not to have tuna? Because my ordering the tuna will contribute to the suffering of the dolphins, and that suffering is bad—not only bad, but objectively so, i.e., bad independently of anyone's attitudes toward the suffering. Similarly, my failing to order the tuna will contribute to the pleasure of the dolphins in living their deep ocean lives, and that pleasure is objectively good.

So my account of the basis of our objective agent-neutral reasons appeals to the existence of objective properties of goodness and of badness, and so I will address as worries about objective agent-neutral reasons two of the most often discussed objections to such objective value properties.

> *Objection (1) to Objective Agent-Neutral Reasons:* If there were objective value properties, they would be 'queer' entities that we could gain knowledge of only via some 'queer' faculty of intuition.

This is, of course, John Mackie's well-known argument from queerness.[22] Mackie's argument is driven by his claim that objective value properties would be 'intrinsically prescriptive,' i.e., they would be such that awareness of them would guarantee motivation to pursue or promote them. In other words, Mackie was assuming that any realist about value properties would have to be a motivational internalist.

> *Motivational Internalism:* Necessarily, if S (sincerely or genuinely) makes a value judgment, then S has some motive to act in accordance with that judgment (to promote a state of affairs judged good, to hinder the production of a state of affairs judged bad).

Since Mackie presented his argument, several realists have rejected internalism,[23] and I think that they are right to do so. I will not rehash their arguments here, except to indicate that I think that they are perfectly right to insist on the possibility of amoralism due to any number of psychological factors including depression, extreme trauma, mistaken adoption of cultural relativism in combination with alienation from one's culture, etc. Further, if we regard psychological generalizations as contingent, then no realist ought to assent to motivational internalism, because doing so just gives the game to the noncognitivist: the only psychological states necessarily connected to motivational states are those motivational states themselves. Thus, the contingency of interesting psychological generalizations would force us to equate the making of a value judgment with being moved if we were to continue to accept motivational internalism. Of course, the noncognitivist wants to force that move, but the realist should push the plausibility of amoralism as a way of resisting it.

Leaving aside the issue of motivational internalism, however, we are not yet done with the objection from queerness. The realist about value properties supposedly has two options: be a naturalist about value, or be a nonnaturalist about value. I say 'supposedly,' because determining whether these really are two distinct options depends upon a clear and adequate account of the distinction between natural properties and nonnatural properties.

Some realists have opted for a characterization of natural properties in terms of the methods by which we can come to know about them: natural properties, it is said, are those properties discoverable via the method of the natural and/or social sciences (see Brink, Shafer-Landau). This characterization threatens circularity unless we can specify the methodology of the sciences without any reference to their objects of study.

More importantly, once we include the social sciences in our characterization of natural properties, we open the door to counting as natural any property discoverable by introspection. After all, psychology, for example, depends upon reports of the phenomenology of its subjects; thus, if psychology studies natural properties, then mental properties—whatever their ontological character—are natural properties. If we can directly grasp objective value properties, why, then, are such value properties not natural? We could, of course, limit our understanding of the sciences to the natural sciences, but we would need some explanation for that limitation.

I think that the focus on the natural/nonnatural distinction in discussions of moral realism has been distracting and unhelpful, and has led to some strange characterizations of views. Nicholas Sturgeon has suggested that one can be a naturalist about value properties without being a reductionist, i.e., one need not see value properties as reducible to or identical with purely 'factual' or 'descriptive' properties.[24] On this account, value properties are natural, but nonetheless distinctive: the naturalist, according to Sturgeon, is committed to seeing that the natural realm includes the normative, because normative terms refer to normative facts and are thus descriptive. David Brink also claims to be a naturalist, holding that moral properties supervene on natural properties, where "it is fairly clear that one property can supervene upon another without those two properties being identical" (474):

> Moral properties are not ontologically simple or independent; but then neither are mental states, social facts, biological states, or macroscopic material objects. It is unlikely that moral properties are identical with physical properties; moral properties could have been realized non-materially. But there is every reason to believe that in the actual world moral properties, like other natural properties, are realised materially. (474)

So Brink, like Sturgeon, wants to be a nonreductive naturalist: moral properties are not physical properties, but they are 'realized' by physical properties in this world.

These views sound an awful lot like Russ Shafer-Landau's realism, a realism that he characterizes as nonnaturalist:

> There is nothing to a case of generosity, or viciousness, or dutiful action, other than the natural features that constitute such properties. Something exemplifies a moral property entirely in virtue of its possessing certain natural features. . . . The difference between the non-naturalist

and the reductive naturalist . . . is a modal one. Non-naturalists can, and reductionists can't, allow for the possibility of a moral property's exemplification by means of some natural property other than the one whose instantiation, at a time, has in fact subserved it. (75)

Shafer-Landau correctly points out that it is hard to see how the views of Sturgeon and Brink differ from the type of position usually identified as nonnaturalist. But I have a difficult time seeing how Shafer-Landau's view is really nonnaturalist in any interesting sense. If being a duty, say, is completely exhausted, in this world, by being such and such natural features, then how could it be 'realized' by some different properties in another world? The 'multiple realizability' is mysterious: if x just is y in this world, then it cannot just be some z, z different from y, in another world. In any case, it is difficult to see how Shafer-Landau preserves what he himself identifies as an essential claim of nonnaturalism: "moral properties are *sui generis,* and not identical to any natural properties" (66). It seems that Brink and Sturgeon, the nonreductive naturalists, do better on this score.

Rather than being too busy trying to differentiate between naturalism and nonnaturalism (a project that extends beyond ethics), I think that we should follow Shafer-Landau in seeing the question of whether moral properties are *sui generis* as the central question. With respect to this question, Brink, the naturalist, actually aligns better with Moore, the nonnaturalist, than does Shafer-Landau, the supposed nonnaturalist. Are moral/value properties unique, a special kind of property in the world? Or are they types of other properties such as physical properties or mental properties? We could then say that the nonnaturalist is someone who regards such properties as *sui generis.*

But once we do that, we can see that Mackie's argument is entirely question-begging. Mackie is claiming that if there are moral properties, then they are entirely unlike anything else in the world. But that is not an argument against the nonnaturalist position, as we are now characterizing it; rather, it is just a restatement of the position. (In Chapter 4, I will show that accepting this kind of ontology does not commit us to any strange value detectors, and will offer a more extensive account and defense of an intuitionist epistemology. So I will leave the epistemological discussion until then.) So unless we have some independent argument for a thorough-going empiricism (which Mackie seems to assume is forthcoming any day now), we need not fear *sui generis* value properties.

Objection (2) to Objective Agent-Neutral Reasons: If there were objective value properties, then they would be explanatorily impotent.

I am not going to spend much time on this objection. Although it has been a highly influential, much-discussed objection to realism about value properties, I actually think that it has been given more weight than it deserves. The objection originated with Gilbert Harman, who claims that we ought not posit objective value properties because, even if there were such properties, they would play no causal role in explaining why we have the moral beliefs that we have: we have an equally plausible psychological story to tell about the genesis of those beliefs, a story that does not require adding anything new to our ontologies. Further, Harman claims, it does not seem that value properties are required to explain anything at all. Thus, such properties are superfluous in our ontology.[25]

I have two replies to this argument. First, which properties in the world are such that we have no alternative story to tell about how we might come to believe that there are such properties? We can always supply a story about the agent's psychology that explains her beliefs without any appeal to objective properties in the world. Of course, Harman is going to respond that we have independent reasons to posit, for example, physical properties, but no such reasons to posit value properties. But now we can see that the argument from explanatory impotence can only function to back up some previous argument against the plausibility of value properties.

Second, the appeal to explanatory power, where explanatory power is understood causally, seems to beg the question against objective value properties. To attribute goodness to something is to say that it *ought* to be promoted, not that anyone is now promoting or even will promote it. Value properties are not like chairs that one can bump into, or river currents that can sweep one downstream. One can be moved by one's appreciation of a state of affairs' being good, where it might not be the case that one would have been so moved if the state of affairs had not been good. Now Harman will say that I would have been so moved if I had falsely so believed, but then of course we might ask, why suppose that I would have believed something to be good even when it was not good? Take the case of my being aware of wanting to have a Twix bar and then being moved to go to the vending machine to get a Twix bar as the result of my wanting one, being aware of that desire, and believing that there are Twix bars in the vending machine. It is true that I would have gone to the vending machine even if I had falsely believed that I wanted a Twix bar. But how does that show that in the case where I am really aware of wanting a Twix bar that it is not in part that awareness that moves me? Again, it seems that Harman needs some independent reason for supposing that I am never really aware of objective value properties for his argument to be anything other than question-begging.

What grounds them?

We can offer a parallel account of the grounds of objective agent-neutral reasons to the one that we offered for subjective agent-relative reasons, merely substituting awareness of objective value for awareness of one's desires. Thus, a reason to promote an objectively good state of affairs (or, to hinder an objectively bad state of affairs) is grounded in an agent's awareness of the goodness (or badness) of the state of affairs in conjunction with her being causally positioned to promote (or hinder) that state of affairs.

But suppose that I am in a causal position to promote the pleasure of the feral cat population in my neighborhood (without thereby causing any pain to humans or other animals) and to prevent certain kinds of suffering currently being endured by the cats. Suppose also that I am aware that I am in this causal situation. What I am not aware of, however, is the goodness of the pleasure that I would cause to the cats (or the badness of the pain that I would prevent). It might be objected to the view that I stated in the last paragraph that that view would yield that I do not have reason to help the cats, because I am not aware of the instrumental value of such an action, given my failure to realize that the pleasure of the cats would be intrinsically good. But surely, the critic will say, I do have reason to help the cats simply in virtue of my being in a position to do so.

We can again appeal to the case of epistemic reasons to see why this objection ought to be resisted. Suppose that I believe P (and have good reason to believe P). Suppose also that P entails Q, but that the entailment is extremely complex. Do I, merely in virtue of believing P and P's entailing Q, have reason to believe Q if I have not performed the logical operations that would take me from P to Q? Even if I have the capacity to perform those operations, it does not seem that I have reason to believe Q until I see that P entails Q. Perhaps I have practical reasons that support performing those logical operations, but until I do so I have no epistemic reason for believing Q. We can say that there is a reason for me to believe Q, but what that amounts to is its being the case that if I engage in some logical reasoning, I will then come to have reason to believe Q.

Similarly, then, we can say that there is a reason for me to help the feral cats in my neighborhood, where that amounts to saying that if I were to think about the nature of the pleasure caused to the cats via my help and were thereby to come to see that that pleasure would be good, that I would then have reason to help the cats. I think that some people will be uncomfortable with supposing that I do not yet have a reason because they will think that that implies that I am not subject to criticism. However, it is quite clear that I would be a better person if I were to be attuned to value properties and responsive to them in my deliberations and actions. So it is quite appropriate for other persons to try to bring me to be aware of the value of the cats' pleasure, thereby making me an agent with reason to help the cats. An agent's rationality is a function of the reasons that she has, but it is quite possible for a perfectly rational agent to be a bad person.

It is important to see that although I have made an agent's reasons a function of her cognitive set, I have not thereby committed myself to motivational internalism. Even once I become aware of the goodness of the pleasure that would be given to the cats if I were to help them, I may not be moved at all to help the cats. People can be bad for many different kinds of reasons, among which are an ignorance of value properties and an indifference to value properties. I have made an agent's reasons a function of her awareness of various features of the world, but such awareness does not guarantee motivation.

What Are Reasons?

One question remains unanswered at this point. I have said that we have subjective agent-relative reasons grounded in an agent's awareness of her own desires, objective agent-neutral reasons grounded in an agent's awareness of objective value properties, and objective agent-relative reasons grounded in an agent's awareness of her own commitments. But what is a reason?

My answer: reasons are reasons. Reasons are *sui generis* normative properties that stand in relations of dependence with both nonnormative and other normative properties. I do not want to reduce reasons to their supervenience bases. Given that these supervenience bases vary a great deal from one another, such a reduction would render our concept of a reason equivocal. But reasons seem all to be the same sort of thing: they are what is relevant to deliberation, what justifies our actions, they can be weighed against one another, varying in strength rather than in ontological kind. If we have rebutted objections to understanding value properties as *sui generis*, then it seems that we have also rebutted objections to understanding reasons as *sui generis*. And to charges of ontological extravagance, all that I can say is that it seems to me hardly extravagant to add two properties to our ontology to account for the entire ethical domain, and to do so with little, if any, cost to our commonsense understanding of morality.

So we are now ready, distinctions in hand and background presuppositions made clear, to turn to reasons of intimacy: Why does common sense not fit with either the consequentialist or the Humean account? (Chapter 2.) What is an intimate relationship? (Chapter 3.) Are there other fundamental objective agent-relative reasons, and, if so, how can we understand our knowledge of such reasons? (Chapter 4.)

2   How *Not* to Understand Reasons of Intimacy

Most of us think that we have reasons to care for our intimates. I am using the term 'intimate' to cover, for example, our friends and our family members.[1] Most of us show a much greater degree of concern for those people to whom we stand in some special intimate relationship than we show for those people who are strangers to us. If asked, we would probably insist not only that we are justified in doing so, but also that we would not be justified in failing to show such differential concern to our friends and families. There are few types of people that we judge more harshly in moral terms than those who fail to take care of their parents or children, those who betray or neglect their friends, and those who are not generous with their resources with respect to their intimates. In fact, the latter class of people is usually judged more harshly than those who fail to benefit, through charitable acts or contributions, those people around the world in need of the basic essentials of life.

These reactions and beliefs may be unjustified, parochial attitudes, our having of which can be explained by appeal to biological or sociological facts about human beings. But before we stop trying to justify our beliefs about our reasons to care for intimates and start looking for the best explanation for why we have such beliefs, we should make every attempt to understand the nature of our beliefs and to seek out possible justifications of those beliefs. After all, whatever the original source of our beliefs, they may very well reflect reality. So my project in this chapter is to present what I take to be our commonsense understanding of our reasons of intimacy. I will do this by showing how two accounts, what I will call the Humean account and the objectivist account (where the consequentialist account is one version of the latter type of account), fail to capture that commonsense understanding. In seeing the ways in which these two very different accounts fail, we will thereby see what any adequate account of reasons of intimacy must look like.

I. REASONS OF INTIMACY: SUBJECTIVE AGENT-RELATIVE?

The Humean Account

I will begin by considering the possibility of understanding reasons of intimacy as subjective agent-relative reasons. In order to do this, we need to begin by considering the nature of subjective agent-relative reasons. These reasons are grounded by our desires, where we are to understand a desire as an intentional state which can be understood as in some way caring about or taking an interest in the state of affairs which is its object.[2] We can divide these desires into two types: those that are long-term and those that are short-term.[3] I am going to call the more long-term desires 'projects.' For example, I now have all of the following projects: I want to write this book and get it published, I want to support my favorite charities, I want to be an effective teacher, I want the Cubs to win the World Series,[4] I want justice for all people, etc. In addition to these projects, I also have desires that are short-term: I want to have a glass of wine with my dinner this evening, I want to buy a new gray flannel skirt and black pumps, I want to unload the dishwasher so that I can get the dirty dishes off of my kitchen counter, etc.

Another distinction among desires (including both my projects and my short-term desires) is that between self-involving desires and non-self-involving desires.[5] Consider the difference between my project that I write this book and my project that the Cubs win the World Series. The first project is self-involving: I am an essential component of the object of the desire—what I want is that *I* write this book, not just that this book be written. If I were to die and my mentor, who knows my views and most of my arguments, were to finish the book for me, my desire would not be satisfied. (Although I do regard the state of affairs in which my mentor finishes my book after my death as better than the state of affairs in which my book is never finished after my death. I may have, in addition to my self-involving project that I write this book, a non-self-involving desire that the book be finished.[6]) On the other hand, my project that the Cubs win the World Series is non-self-involving: I am not a component, let alone an essential component, of the object of the desire. What I want is that the Cubs win the Series. Of course, I also have the desire that they do it in my lifetime and that I watch them win the Series. But my desire that they win is itself non-self-involving even if I have other related desires that are self-involving.

Friendship involves many desires, both projects and short-term desires.[7] With respect to my best friend Tracy, I want that she be happy and healthy, that she eat some of the carrot cake that she bought earlier in the day, that we visit Paris together next spring, that we return to Venice on a larger budget than we had last time we went, that I support her in times of crisis and that she do the same for me, etc. Some of these desires are non-self-involving (such as the first two), and others are self-involving (such as the last three). Most importantly, perhaps, I have a very general desire that I care for Tracy, and this desire is more intense and far-reaching than my desire that I do what I can to promote the well-being of human beings in general.

Once we notice this rather obvious fact about friendship, it seems as though the person who acknowledges only subjective agent-relative reasons, whom I will call the Humean about reasons, has a rather easy task in understanding reasons of intimacy. Our reasons are provided by our desires. On any plausible delineation of which intentional states count as desires, our projects involving our friends will count as desires it seems. So we have many reasons to care for our friends in various ways, and we do not have as many or as strong of reasons to care for strangers—what this comes to is just that we have many more strong desires to care for our friends. And, as I have pointed out, having such desires seems to be part of our very understanding of what it is to be friends.

The Humean account of reasons of intimacy bases these reasons on some feature of the agent whose reasons they are, i.e., these reasons are provided by some psychological fact or facts about the agent. So the Humean account differs from, for example, the well-known Aristotelian view of friendship according to which the acts that friends typically perform for one another are justified by reference to the character of the friend. My reason to care for Tracy is provided by my desire that I care for Tracy (but also by my desire that Tracy be cared for, given the fact that I am in a good position to do so). No facts about Tracy need be known in order for the Humean to conclude that I have reason to care for her.[8] Unlike the Aristotelian, I think that this is an attractive implication of the Humean view, that reasons of intimacy are not dependent on the worth of the character or the moral desert of the friend.[9] It does seem that we have reason to care for our friends even if they are morally flawed or less than intellectually gifted. More can be said on this point, but, since the Aristotelian view understands reasons of intimacy as objective agent-neutral, I will leave such discussion for the following section.

So the Humean account provides us mere moral mortals with reasons of intimacy. It subsumes such reasons under an easily understandable and metaphysically untroubling account of reasons. Why not, then, regard reasons of intimacy as a subspecies of our subjective agent-relative reasons?

The Rejection of the Humean Account

In order to see why the Humean account simply will not do as an account of our reasons of intimacy, we need to return to a more general consideration of our desires. Consider my desire to get a new gray skirt. Insofar as I want a gray skirt, I have a reason to shop for and buy one. Of course, I may have other desires that conflict with this one, such as my desire to stop spending so much money on clothing. Nonetheless, I still have a reason, even if only *prima facie,* to get a new gray skirt.

Suppose, however, that I decide, after looking through my closet, that I don't really want a gray skirt but, rather, some gray flannel trousers. Clearly, then, I no longer have any reason to buy a new skirt: I now have, instead, a reason to buy some gray trousers. I would be clearly irrational if I proceeded to buy the skirt rather than the trousers given that I want the latter and no longer want the former.[10] Similarly, if dinner comes around and I no longer want any wine, then I no longer have any reason to order some at the restaurant. Further, in neither case do I have any reason to try to retain my desires for a skirt and for a glass of wine. I can simply let these desires come and go as they please, and my reasons are determined by their comings and goings.

At the very least, it is unattractive to consider our reasons of intimacy to be on a par with our reasons to have wine or to buy skirts rather than trousers. For consider the implications of such a claim. Currently, I have a desire to care for Tracy, just as I have a desire to buy a new skirt. Tomorrow, as I browse through catalogs, I may decide that I prefer to get some wool trousers. Suppose that I also decide that I would prefer to spend time with and care for Emma rather than spending time with and caring for Tracy. So do I now have reason to care for Emma rather than Tracy, in the same way that I have reason to buy trousers rather than a skirt? Are our reasons to care for our friends as easily determined by the comings and goings of our desires? May I discard a friend as I discard an old skirt? It seems that if, through introspection, I come to realize that my desire to care for Tracy is on the wane, that I then have reason to try to bolster it, rather than simply letting it slip away like my desire to have wine with dinner. We do not, it seems, regard our desires to care for our friends as on a par with desires for skirts and wine.

Now, of course, I have begun with examples of desires that, it would seem, are the least likely to provide a model for our desires to care for our friends. My desires to buy a new gray skirt and to have wine with dinner are both short-term desires, not projects.[11] Short-term desires are more likely to be fickle in their comings and goings, and, at least in most genuine friendships, desires to care for friends are more stable and long-term. So the appropriate model for reasons of intimacy, the Humean will claim, are those reasons provided by our projects. My desire to care for Tracy is much more like my desire to be an effective teacher than it is like my desire to have wine with dinner. Both desires are ones that may wax and wane in terms of intensity, but they have been relatively stable for a long period of time. Given the duration and stability of such projects, our reasons of intimacy will also be long-lasting and stable. So we cannot discard friends like old skirts, because desires to care for friends are like desires to be effective in our chosen careers and our careers are certainly not to be treated like old skirts.

The Humean would be quite right to force a consideration of projects rather than short-term desires in any attempt to accommodate reasons of intimacy. But, of course, in appealing to projects, the Humean is simply appealing to another feature of an agent's psychology. It is certainly true that our desires to care for our friends tend to be stable features of our psychology. Perhaps it is true that we would not even use the term 'friendship' to describe a relationship between two persons until they had developed such projects concerning one another. So the having of such projects is plausibly construed as partially constitutive of the friendship relation itself.[12] For the purposes of the argument here, let us just grant to the Humean that desires involved in friendship (or at least desires to care for the other party to the friendship) are projects.

We can then grant to the Humean that our reasons of intimacy will not come and go as do our desires to have wine with our dinners. In many cases, then, persons simply will not decide to change their friends as they change their wardrobes. But suppose that I *did* decide that I would rather be close to Emma than to Tracy; after all, Emma is both wealthy and generous, and I enjoy spending time with people who lavish me with expensive gifts. Even projects are subject to shifts: I may decide that I no longer want to teach or to write a book on reasons of intimacy. Of course, teaching or writing a book may be instrumental to other things that I do want, such as continuing to support myself as a university professor. But if I cease to want to do that, then the rational course of action is to look for a new career, unless the opportunity costs of doing so would be prohibitively high. Analogously, then, if I decide that I would rather be close to Emma than to Tracy, then the rational course of action is to shift my affections and attention, unless the opportunity costs are too high or my friendship with Tracy continues to be instrumentally valuable in some way.

But is that the correct account of the conditions under which I have reason to try to bolster my waning affection or to weather the storm and maintain my friendship with Tracy? Because my friendship might be a means to something else that I want, or because it might just be too costly to change horses in midstream, as it were? I think that most of us are inclined to think that this is just not an adequate account of our reasons to sustain friendships and to care for our friends. If my friendship with Tracy is not a means to anything else that I want and the cultivation of friendship with Emma would go quickly and smoothly, then, on the Humean account, I would be irrational to maintain my relationship with Tracy; rather, I ought to get out of that friendship and into one with Emma as quickly as possible. This, I think, is a highly unattractive implication of the Humean view.

There is one last tack that the Humean can take to try to rescue her account of reasons of intimacy.[13] Again, she will appeal to an apparent psychological truth about friendships, namely that people's desires to care for friends remain in a dispositional form even if, occurrently, they seem to have dissipated or disappeared altogether. When I am angry at a friend, I might overlook my deep-rooted affection for her or my propensity to want to talk to her in times of crisis. It might, momentarily, appear easier to develop a new friendship and let the old one die. Various emotions guide our focus of attention in ways that are often detrimental to rational action.[14] Thus, given the dispositional nature of our desires to care for friends, we must be very cautious about taking our occurrent mental states as decisive evidence about our reasons.

All of this is very true, and a rational agent will not lightly alter her circumstances and opportunity resources until she is reasonably sure that her desires have shifted, and that they have shifted in a less than transitory fashion. But any discussion of the Humean view will repeatedly come back to the claim that all facts about an agent's subjective reasons are contingent facts about her psychological attitudes. If I really no longer have any desire, either occurrent or dispositional, to continue caring for Tracy because I want to cultivate a friendship with rich, generous Emma, then I have no reason to try to maintain my relationship with Tracy or to continue to care for her anymore than for others who are strangers to me. But we do think that some form of criticism of me would be appropriate, perhaps even more appropriate, if I could so easily transfer my affections and concerns. The Humean, however, is simply unable to make any sense of such criticism, because all criticism is rooted in facts about the agent's own psychology.[15]

My argument against the Humean account of reasons of intimacy has been based upon two claims: (i) the Humean appeal to psychology renders reasons of intimacy too much under the control of the agent whose reasons they are,[16] and (ii) we ought not simply exit friendships in the way that we give up on other sorts of short-term desires or even in the way that we abandon or alter other projects. Someone could challenge (i) by saying that human psychology makes it such that the Humean account of reasons of intimacy will, in a very wide range of normal cases, give us the answers we want.[17] A choice, then, must be made as to whether we can accept the Humean account in unusual cases: I am arguing that our understanding of friendship is not congenial to that account. The other line of attack goes at (ii), claiming that I have seemed to rely on the claim that friendships are permanent and inescapable, i.e., that I have covertly drawn on an overly strong requirement on the project of friendship in contrast to other sorts of projects.[18] Surely we do think that it is sometimes appropriate to end friendships, and my argument may appear to deny that obviously true claim about friendships.

I think that, in at least one way, this would be a fair critique of my argument. In assessing whether I ought to abandon Tracy and cultivate a friendship with Emma, we need to know a lot more about the relationship between Tracy and me than what I have provided for the purposes of this discussion. However, my point has simply been that we do, in fact, need to know more: it is not sufficient to know just what I have told the reader about my own psychology. Once the Humean urges that we need to be provided with more facts about the relationship between Tracy and me, I can rest my case. I will expand on this point in the following chapters. In fact, my argument is going to have as its conclusion the claim that our reasons to care for friends are provided by various facts about our relationships, considered in themselves.

But before we get there, we need to see whether reasons of intimacy can be appropriately classed as a type of objective agent-neutral reason.

II. REASONS OF INTIMACY: OBJECTIVE AGENT-NEUTRAL?

The Objectivist Account

Our rejection of the Humean account of reasons of intimacy seems to have led to the following lesson about such reasons: they will not have the stability that we normally attribute to them as long as they are grounded solely in the changeable attitudes of the agent whose reasons they are. The same worry comes into play with respect to reasons of intimacy that motivates a rejection of Humeanism as a general account of our reasons: such reasons cannot, by their very nature, provide the sort of *external standard* that we generally take our reasons of intimacy to have. These reasons, like our reasons to care for people more generally, seem to hold regardless of our idiosyncratic attitudes.[19]

The natural place, then, to look for a source of such reasons is in the intrinsic value of various states of affairs. Objectivist or neutral attempts to ground reasons of intimacy can be more or less inclusive, by which I mean that they can be accounts of reasons within many or most actual friendships or only within a select group of such relationships. An example of a less inclusive neutral or objectivist account would be the Aristotelian account, according to which it is the nature of the other's character that gives reason to her friend to care for her. An example of a more inclusive account would be a consequentialist account according to which friendship (even friendship between those that are less than exemplars of virtue) is either instrumentally valuable or intrinsically valuable (or both).[20] If an agent's reasons of intimacy are provided by the objective value of a given state of affairs, then those reasons are independent of her potentially fickle attitudes.

A Bit of a Digression

I need to add a couple of caveats at this point. If someone offering the consequentialist account of reasons of intimacy claims that *friendship* is valuable, then the Humean might charge that the consequentialist account renders reasons of intimacy as dependent on changeable attitudes as did the account offered by the Humean. After all, it is certainly plausible to claim that mutual attitudes of affection and concern (in the subjective affective sense) are necessary conditions of two persons standing in the friendship relation to one another. So, if the agent's attitudes shift, then there is no longer a friendship, and, thus, the intrinsic or instrumental value of such a relationship is no longer at issue: such a relationship, and reasons to which it might give rise, has ceased to exist.

This is, of course, the wrong way to look at the issue. One of the difficulties that the Humean theory faced is that it left no room to claim that an agent has reason to struggle to maintain a friendship if she notices another attractive candidate for friendship. We often reach points in friendships which are such that, without effort from one or both of the parties, the friendship will simply dwindle away. Affection and concern rarely, if ever, disappear in an instant: these are slow gradual changes in peoples' attitudes. Friendship seems unlike other projects in that we seem to have reason to try to resuscitate it and to keep it on life support for longer than would be rational for other projects. So it might very well be the case that if someone acts irrationally in allowing a friendship to die, then, as a result, she will have no reasons left stemming from that friendship.[21] But that end result does not show that she did not have reasons to sustain the friendship while it was in existence.

Suppose, however, that human affection and concern for other persons did, in fact, change quickly and often. If affection is a necessary constituent of the friendship relation, and if such affection could wax and wane in an instant, then the nature of an agent's reasons would be different. Once we were aware of the possibility of our attitudes changing in an instant, we would have reason to do what was needed in order to try to fend off such alterations in order to maintain the valuable relationships to which we are party. However, if human beings' affections were so fickle and changeable, the nature of intimate relationships would be drastically altered. As it is, affection is an enduring attitude, and the longer that it endures, the more we subjectively value it and regard it as objectively valuable. If we knew that our affections could disappear or be transferred in an instant, we might very well regard our current affections differently than we now do. Affection based on history and knowledge seems more valuable than that which just assaults us in some way. I will address these questions about the nature of friendship more in Chapter 3.

One last point needs to be made before we can return to a consideration of reasons of intimacy as objective agent-neutral reasons. I have been, throughout this chapter, speaking as though people have control over their attitudes toward other persons. So, for example, I have suggested that we have reason to try to sustain and strengthen our affection for our friends if we see it beginning to wane. But can we have reason to control our affections if such affections are not within our control? An agent's reasons, according to the Humean or the objectivist account, are given by her desires or by objectively valuable states of affairs *when it is possible for her to satisfy her desire or to promote the objectively valuable state of affairs.* Even, then, if we admit that a certain friendship of p's is valuable, we can claim that p has reason to sustain it only if p can take means to sustaining the affections that are essential to friendship.

Without making here any commitment to some particular theory of the emotions, I think that it is clear that we have *some* control over our emotions and attitudes.[22] Even if I cannot control a particular emotion (where I mean the having of an emotion, not the expression of an emotion, which is a type of action) on a particular occasion in the way that I can control a particular action on a particular occasion, I can train myself over time to alter or develop various emotions and attitudes. I cannot get myself, right here and now, not to feel hurt by a friend's thoughtless remark, but I can train myself, through focus on my belief that he really cares about me and does not intend his remarks in the way that they come out, to reconstrue his remarks, thereby avoiding the feeling of being hurt. Whether or not judgments are constituents of or identical with emotions, there is undoubtedly a causal link between our judgments and our emotions, so if we can in some way alter our judgments, we can alter our emotions and attitudes. So if I notice that my affection for a friend is at a low point, I cannot revive it on the spot, but I can focus on the good times that we have had, the support that she has given me in the past, the ways that she can make me laugh, etc. These can all be instrumentally efficacious in reviving my affection, given a little time. So I think that we can take the means to sustain or even to develop emotions.

Back to the Objectivist Account

So let us return to a consideration of how reasons of intimacy might be subsumed as instances of objective agent-neutral reasons. As I have said, the objectivist account can be an Aristotelian less inclusive account or a consequentialist more inclusive account. Here I am going to focus on the latter type of account. I will make clear in my next chapter on the nature of intimacy why I reject an Aristotelian account. In summary, I think that any less inclusive view is simply not acceptable. The Aristotelian gives too few persons reasons of intimacy, and it is not at all clear that the Aristotelian will not be committed to altering friendships if new more virtuous candidates come along.[23]

Return, then, to a case in which my affection for Tracy is waning and I am contemplating diverting my attention and other resources to the rich and generous Emma. The objectivist can point out that friendships involving mutual trust, reliance, affection, and concern are intrinsically valuable and ought to be promoted. Friendships of long standing, given their history and complexity, have an added dimension that is also intrinsically valuable. If we know that a friendship has stood various tests of time, then we ought to be very reluctant to let it die, because sustaining and strengthening it is a means to greater intrinsic value, especially if we think that friendship is even more valuable if it has survived trials. Also, friendship is instrumentally valuable, i.e., a means to promoting intrinsic value. Friends have insight into one another's character and, therefore, into what will best promote each other's well-being. Over time, friends acquire good causal and epistemic positions for promoting each other's good. If we make the very plausible assumption that the well-being of any person is intrinsically valuable, then we ought to take advantage of the privileged positions that result from friendship to promote the good of those who are our friends.

The Rejection of the Objectivist Account

It is certainly true that the objectivist account provides an external standard for evaluating the conduct of friends with respect to one another. So it does not fall prey to the objection to the Humean account, i.e., it does not make reasons of intimacy too dependent on the attitudes of the agent. We have objective reasons to cultivate certain attitudes, in particular, with respect to our friends. On the objectivist account, then, one cannot avoid reasons of intimacy by simply altering one's emotional allegiances—one ought not, on this account, quickly or thoughtlessly alter those allegiances. An established friendship is established value. When starting up a new friendship, we run risks of never getting it very far off of the ground, given our ability to misread both other people and our own abilities to interact with and care for those others.

However, if my reasons to care for my friend Tracy are constituted by the intrinsic or instrumental objective value of doing so, then I do have to be aware of the possibility that other, better opportunities for promoting good might come along. The objectivist account is objectionable because it forces us to engage in the type of weighing and balancing of value considerations that seems quite inappropriate in contexts of friendship.[24] The objectivist requires (i) that we weigh the value of our own current, actual friendships against the potential value of possible friendships that we could form with other persons, and (ii) that we weigh the value of our own current, actual friendships against the value or potential value of other persons' actual or possible friendships.

Begin by considering (i).[25] It is true that I should not risk losing the value of my friendship with Tracy by acting hastily in diverting my attention to Emma. But I might be quite confident that a friendship with Emma would be more valuable than my current one with Tracy. If that is the case, then I *ought* to divert my attention and other resources to developing a friendship with Emma even though this means that I will not have the resources to sustain my friendship with Tracy.[26] It might just be that the pleasure that I derive from having Emma spend money on me is sufficiently valuable to throw the balance of reasons in favor of friendship with Emma rather than with Tracy. Or perhaps Emma can help to advance a sufficient number of my other projects, e.g., by being a good connection to people who can advance my career (if we assume that promotion of my career is either instrumentally or intrinsically valuable). Even more worrisome is a case in which Emma can open up a world in which I will meet more potential friends. Then, by trading Tracy for Emma, I might actually be getting more than one friend as a return on my investment. Now the balance of value is clearly on the side of dumping Tracy in favor of Emma.[27]

Now consider (ii): even if my friendship with Tracy is valuable, the resources that I devote to it might be better used to promote the friendships of other persons. There is no reason to suppose that I might not be able to help other people to sustain their friendships, friendships that are even more valuable than my own. Similarly, even if my friendship places me in an excellent position to promote Tracy's good, I must always consider how well positioned I am to benefit other persons who are in far greater need than Tracy is. Utilitarians such as Sidgwick have relied upon the causal claim that following the general rule 'Benefit your friends' is a good utilitarian policy for each of us.[28] But, as with all good utilitarian policies, this one holds only contingently. Further, I am not convinced that Sidgwick's causal claim is so obviously true.[29]

But it is not the outcome of the empirical calculations that is really at issue. The question is whether the objectivist offers us a plausible justification of our greater concern for our friends, and I have been arguing that she simply does not. In fact, to subject our friendships to the type of balancing that objectivism demands is something that we have reason not to do. It seems that I have reason to promote and sustain *my* friendships and to care for *my* friends that are different in kind than the reasons that I have to promote and sustain friendships in general or to care for persons in general. In other words, reasons of intimacy seem to be agent-relative, not agent-neutral.

Recall the definition of an agent-neutral reason:

> *Agent-Neutral Reason:* S's reason to do or to promote p is an agent-neutral reason if and only if, necessarily, for any Q, Q would also have a reason to do or to promote p if Q were in a causal position to do or to promote p. All other reasons are agent-relative.

The objectivist account regards my reason to care for my friend Tracy as a function of the objective value of Tracy's well-being and of my friendship with her in conjunction with the advantageous causal position that I have as a result of our friendship. But, of course, for any agent S, if S had an equally advantageous causal position for some reason, then S would have exactly the same reasons, of exactly the same strength as my reasons, to promote Tracy's well-being and to sustain my friendship with Tracy.

Now, it may be unlikely that any S would ever be so causally positioned, but the truth of the counterfactual about S is revealing with respect to how the objectivist is forced to view the significance of friendship itself. We do not think that my reasons to care for my friends are merely a matter of my being in the appropriate causal position to do so, whereas other persons are not. When those others are in a causal position to care for my friends, it still seems that they do not have the reasons that I do to care for my friends. Even after I have taken into account the objective value of my friendship with Tracy as compared to others' friendships or my own possible friendships, it seems that

I have further reason stemming from the fact that Tracy is *at the present time my* friend. This feature cannot be captured by the objectivist account, if it remains agent-neutral. At bottom, everyone has the same type of reason to care for Tracy and to promote my friendship with her that I have. Similarly, I have the same type of reason to care for other people and to promote other people's friendships that I have to care for Tracy and to promote my friendship with her. Common sense seems to regard friendship itself as having a fundamental significance that it cannot have as long as it is regarded merely as a causal factor allowing for the promotion of objective value.

We seem, then, to have reached an impasse with reasons of intimacy. One option would be to admit that our reasons to care for our friends are just very different from what we took them to be. I will argue, however, that a proper understanding of friendship and of intimacy considered more generally allows us to understand a type of reason that is objective and yet agent-relative. If we can make sense of such a reason, we will avoid the dependence on changeable attitudes of the Humean account (i.e., by avoiding subjectivity) and also the weighing and balancing inherent in an agent-neutral account (i.e., by granting fundamental significance to the friendship relation itself). We need to accord friendship a significance that goes beyond our desires and beyond our causal situation in the world.

Another way of making this point is to say that we need to find an account according to which reasons of intimacy are fundamental, not derivative, reasons, where a fundamental reason, recall, is understood as follows:

> *Fundamental Reason:* S's reason R to do p is a fundamental reason if and only if S's reason to do p is not constituted in whole or in part by some other reason R*, where R is not identical to R*. Any reason that is not a fundamental reason is a derivative reason.

The objectivist account renders my reason to care for my friends derivative, insofar as that reason is constituted by my reason to promote value in conjunction with my special causal position. The Humean account renders my reason to care for my friends derivative, insofar as that reason is constituted by my reason to satisfy my desire that my friends be well-off. Common sense seems to want to understand reasons of intimacy as fundamental, i.e., common sense seems to want to understand friendship as directly generating reasons in the way that the objectivist sees value as directly generating reasons and the Humean sees desires as directly generating reasons. Can we give common sense what it wants?

III. PROMISING AND REASONS OF FIDELITY

If we give common sense what it wants, reasons of intimacy will not be alone in being fundamental reasons that refuse to fit into either the Humean subjective agent-relative or the consequentialist agent-neutral mold. Reasons of fidelity will be keeping company with reasons of intimacy in this respect. As W. D. Ross said:

> When a plain man fulfils a promise because he thinks he ought to do so, it seems clear that he does so with no thought of its total consequences, still less with any opinion that these are likely to be the best possible. He thinks in fact much more of the past than of the future. What makes him think it right to act in a certain way is *the fact that he has promised to do so—that and, usually, nothing more.* That his act will produce the best possible consequences is not his reason for calling it right.[30]

In fact, not only do we think that it is not the consequences that justify the keeping of a promise, but we also think that we would be unjustified, in a wide range of cases, in breaking a promise in order to bring about better consequences. This objection from promise-keeping has been one of the trusted allies in the fight against consequentialism. Notice how we could rewrite the quotation from Ross to capture the commonsense worry about the consequentialist account of reasons of intimacy:

> When a plain man helps a friend because he thinks he ought to do so, it seems clear that he does so with no thought of its total consequences, still less with any opinion that these are likely to be the best possible. He thinks in fact much more of the past than of the future. What makes him think it right to act in a certain way is *the fact that this is his friend who needs help—that and, usually, nothing more.* That his act will produce the best possible consequences is not his reason for calling it right.

Consequentialists have made many attempts to defeat this particular objection. The most important of such attempts have been made via appeal to the general institution of promise-keeping or to the having of the disposition to keep promises.[31] The latter appeal is particularly unconvincing, given that one can be a person generally disposed to keep promises, and yet be willing to break them in a wide range of circumstances; in fact, I myself and most of the people that I know are persons of just this sort.[32] I do not want, however, to get into a general discussion of the consequentialist hopes for accommodating reasons of fidelity. As with any other reasons besides that to promote maximal good, reasons of fidelity for a consequentialist are derivative, not fundamental. Questions about how well the consequentialist account can line up with our pre–theoretical intuitions are purely empirical questions, and ought not be the focus of our attention. The real question for those of us engaged in metaethical inquiry is whether the consequentialist grounding of such reasons is plausible, and I think that Ross's point is then well-taken.

The other option, that of assimilating reasons of fidelity to subjective agent-relative reasons, also looks fairly hopeless. Of course, genuine promises, or promises that generate reasons, must be voluntary, and so, in some sense, an agent desires to keep the promise when she makes the promise.[33] In any case, she must want to make the promise. But how does her wanting to make the promise and even, let us suppose, to keep the promise *now,* create any reasons to keep the promise in the future? After all, her desires and therefore her subjective reasons may change over time. Often, what seems desirable at the time that one promises, looks less and less appealing as the time for fulfillment draws close: consider a promise to help a friend move. If one has both subjective agent-relative and objective agent-neutral reasons, one can of course, at this point, point to the objective value of promise-keeping. But doing so again subjects reasons of fidelity to the sorts of balancing and weighing deliberations that seem to render them far too unstable.

So it seems that reasons of fidelity resist classification as either objective agent-neutral or subjective agent-relative, at least given our commonsense understanding of such reasons. Thus, reasons of fidelity are analogous to reasons of intimacy. In the next chapter, I am going to explore the nature of intimacy in an attempt to show why intimate relationships generate reasons for those party to them. In doing so, I will show how reasons of intimacy are related to, although not identical with, reasons of fidelity. We will return to the analogy in Chapter 4.

3 Friends and Other Relations

In the last chapter, I concluded that our reasons of intimacy simply cannot be understood in line with common sense if we assimilate them to objective agent-neutral reasons or to subjective agent-relative reasons. In order to see whether we ought to try to accommodate our pre-theoretical understanding of these reasons, we need to turn to a consideration of the nature of intimacy. If intimate relationships generate or ground a special class of reasons, then an examination of the nature of such relationships ought to provide some guidance to understanding reasons of intimacy. After all, the difficulty with the agent-neutral and the subjective accounts of reasons of intimacy seemed to be what they took to ground the reasons: for the former, the focus is on the objective value, either instrumental or intrinsic, of the relationship (or of the parties to the relationship), while, for the latter, the focus is the psychology of the agent herself. The difficulty with the agent-neutral account is that whatever value my relationships have, other relationships of the same type that are not my own will have the same sort of value, as will my own possible but not actual relationships. Thus, the fact that *I* am *actually* intimate with Tracy has no special significance in and of itself in my rational deliberations. However, if we take this fact seriously by moving to the subjective account, we are left with making reasons of intimacy highly dependent upon the agent's own internal states, regardless of the past history of the relationship at stake.

So a promising locus for an investigation into reasons of intimacy would appear to be the relationship itself that is taken to ground the reasons. As I pointed out at the end of the last chapter, the difficulty with certain accounts of promising, both consequentialist and deontological, is that they do not seem to take the fact of a promise as having, in and of itself, rational significance. Thus, we ought to conclude that the similar difficulties that we are encountering in our attempt to offer an account of reasons of intimacy arise from a failure to take seriously the fact of an intimate relationship, considered in and of itself. Thus, an investigation of the nature of intimacy is called for.

I. RELATIONSHIPS: THE IDEAL VS. THE REALITY

Before we begin our inquiry proper, we need to clarify what, precisely, we are inquiring into. My project needs to be distinguished from, for example, Aristotle's exploration of friendship.[1] It is true that Aristotle's concept of friendship was the concept of an intimate relationship. However, his concept of friendship is clearly much narrower than the concept of an intimate relationship as such. Consider his classification of 'friendships' into three varieties: friendships for utility, friendships for pleasure, and complete friendships that are the friendships of virtuous persons. Aristotle, of course, claims that only the latter are genuine friendships: the former two are called 'friendships' only because of certain similarities to the latter. So friendships for utility or pleasure are friendships in something like the sense that rubber ducks are ducks. Friendship, for Aristotle, is a normative notion. So any true or genuine friendship will be a valuable relationship between persons of virtuous characters. Anything less, then, is not really a friendship.[2]

Aristotle's classification is a classification according to the ways in which the parties to the friendship regard one another. In a friendship for pleasure (or utility), the friends care about one another as a means to their own pleasure (or as a means to some other benefit to themselves). In complete friendships, the parties care about one another for their own sake (and usually, in addition, as means to pleasure and other benefits).[3] Further, Aristotle's complete friendship

> is that between good men who are alike in excellence or virtue. For these friends wish alike for one another's good *because they are good men,* and they are good *per se.* (1156b5; first italics are mine)

So it is not sufficient for a complete friendship that the parties to the relationship care about one another for their own sakes—they must care about one another for their own sakes *insofar as they are virtuous.* After all, for Aristotle, the only things that are worthy of love are the pleasant, the useful, and the good. So if two people care about each other for their own sake, *period,* their responses are, in an important sense, incomprehensible. They must love one another in virtue of some features that they possess, and, if their love is to be appropriate, it must be directed to features that are worthy of love. A relationship in which two people care about one another for their own sake, without qualification, is, then, not a relationship that Aristotle even discusses.

I do agree with Aristotle that not all friendships or intimate relationships give rise to the same sorts of reasons. If pleasure and certain character traits are objectively good, then, in both friendships for pleasure and complete friendships, the parties have reasons deriving from the fact that they are in good positions to promote certain objectively valuable states of affairs. However, my project in this chapter and the next involves studying the nature of intimate relationships as such, and seeing whether such relationships, simply in virtue of the sorts of relationships that they are, generate a special kind of reason, what I am calling 'reasons of intimacy.' I am not concerned to grade types of intimate relationships from the best to the least good—that sort of investigation belongs in the realm of investigating objective good.

My question, then, is when is it true of two persons that they are intimate with one another? The uses of the term 'intimate' in ordinary language are diverse, and I am not concerned with all of them, as I will make clear. Thus, I am going to offer a conception of what I will call 'genuine intimacy,' taking friendship as my model of a relationship in which such intimacy exists. Like Aristotle, I will understand certain relationships, those that are not genuinely intimate relationships, as friendships only in some degraded sense. However, unlike Aristotle, I am not making a normative claim in saying that genuine friendships involve intimacy. I am simply making a conceptual claim—questions of value and reasons remain further questions. I want to allow that certain friendships can be bad, involving bad people doing bad things. And even if genuine intimacy is intrinsically good, it can, at the same time, be instrumentally bad: people can put intrinsically good states of affairs to evil work, using the good as a means to very bad ends. It is certainly not uncommon for people in intimate relationships to become insulated and isolated, allowing their absorption in one another to blind them to the needs of the wider community.

II. RELATIONSHIPS: REASONS TO ENTER VS. REASONS TO STAY

We need to distinguish several different questions that we could ask concerning intimate relationships such as friendships. *First,* as I have indicated, there is the question as to what constitutes a friendship, or, more generally, what is necessary and sufficient for intimacy to exist between two persons. This is the question of this chapter: as I have said, we need to understand intimacy before we can understand the source of reasons of intimacy. Actually, I am not so ambitious as to attempt to give necessary and sufficient conditions for intimacy, and my lack of ambition derives from more than merely my estimate of my abilities: the phenomena are too complex for such a clean analysis. In fact, the complexity of intimacy makes the epistemology of reasons of intimacy interesting, as we will see in Chapter 5. For now, I want to attempt to capture enough of the commonsense understanding of intimacy so that, in the next chapter, we can make sense of the claim that intimate relationships ground reasons.

Second, there is the question as to why we ought to enter friendships in the first place. Here we can distinguish two different questions: (i) Why ought I to form any friendships at all?, and (ii) Why ought I to form a friendship with this particular person? I am assuming that these questions can be answered adequately in terms of objective agent-neutral and subjective agent-relative reasons. So, for example, if friendships are valuable relationships, then I have objective agent-neutral reasons to create some. And a friendship with this particular person, say, Tracy, may be particularly valuable. If I like Tracy and want to be her friend, then I have subjective agent-relative reasons to enter into a friendship with her. Further, given my subjective attitudes, a friendship with Tracy will be easy and pleasant to maintain, and so I have further objective agent-neutral reasons to start up a friendship with her.

But, *third,* we then arrive at the question as to why, once I have formed a friendship with Tracy, do I have reasons to continue to care for her in ways that go beyond the ways in which I care about persons with whom I am not intimate? If so, what is the nature of these reasons? This third question concerns the nature of reasons of intimacy and is the question of Chapter 4. What I will show is that an answer to the first question about the nature of intimacy will provide an answer to this third question. Once we see what is involved in two people being intimate with one another, we will be in a position to see why, once in such a relationship, they have agent-relative, and yet objective, reasons to care about each other.

III. INTIMACY

In ordinary discourse we often describe two people, not as being intimate with one another, but, rather, as being close or very close to each other.[4] Under what conditions is it appropriate to say, for example, that Tracy and I are close friends rather than simply acquaintances? In English we have an extremely wide range of terms to describe friends, some of which seem to denote someone with whom we have less than a genuinely intimate relationship (buddy, pal, chum, etc.). Many of these terms seem to denote a relationship rather like Aristotle's friendship for pleasure and nothing more, i.e., the parties to the relationship enjoy each other's company and so engage in various activities together. Sometimes, the term 'buddy' is even modified with the term referring to the type of activity that the persons engage in together: there are drinking buddies, golfing buddies, etc.

It is of course true that persons who begin as, say, golfing buddies, can become close to one another, i.e., can become intimate friends. However, it is important that some process must be undergone before the 'friendship' develops out of shared activities. What must that process consist of and what must the outcome be in order for the resultant friendship to be an intimate relationship? I want to consider several different elements that might be thought to be, in one form or another, important constituents of a friendship relation:

(a) The parties to the relationship must have some positive attitude toward one another that could be appropriately described as liking each other, loving each other, being fond of each other, having affection for one another, or caring about one another.

(b) The attitudes mentioned in (a) must be *mutual* attitudes, i.e., their attitudes of love or affection must be reciprocated, and the parties to the relationship must be aware, or, at least, be in a position to become aware,[5] of this mutuality in attitude.

(c) The parties must have a concern for one another that exceeds their concern for any person simply as a person.

(d) The parties must have desires to share time with one another.

(e) The parties must have, or be making a considered effort to achieve, a certain level of knowledge about one another, a level that goes considerably beyond what a stranger or mere acquaintance would have.

(f) The parties must have actually spent some time in one another's company, or have causally interacted in some other relevantly similar manner.

(g) The parties' history with one another must exhibit or evidence concern.

In what follows it is important to keep in mind that I am attempting to give an account of intimate relationships in general, although, for now, I will usually refer to such relationships as friendships. Our concept of friendship tends, I think, to be rather narrower than the sense in which I will be understanding it. So, for example, we do not typically speak of family members as friends; oddly, we rarely use this term for spouses or lovers even. Thus, I am exploring a wider range of relationships than might be suggested by my terminology.

(a) The parties to the relationship must have some positive attitude toward one another that could be appropriately described as liking each other, loving each other, being fond of each other, having affection for one another, or caring about one another.

Typically, friends like one another and would be willing to assert that they like one another. At the very least, we certainly would not count two people as friends if they loath one another or are indifferent to one another. Part of what is involved in liking someone will be covered in the following: the parties are disposed to seek out one another's company (because they find it pleasant, not because they hope to gain, say, financial advantages as a result), and the parties are inclined to do good for one another. In some sense they approve of various qualities that the other has, but liking a person ought not to be reduced to liking certain qualities that happen to be instantiated in the person or to liking the person insofar as she has certain qualities. It is interesting how often we are unable to say very much about why we like a given person. We say, for example, that the person has a good sense of humor, is kind and generous, knows how to cheer us up when we are down, etc. But we could say the very same things about people who, at least in some sense, we do not like. There are ways in which qualities are combined and ways in which particular combinations 'click' with our own peculiar combinations of qualities that we are simply unable to fully articulate. In the end, we like the person *for the person that she is*.

I do not, however, want to limit the sorts of attitudes that are essential to friendship[6] to only those that can properly be described as liking. Our friends can frustrate and irritate us: this is particularly true of our family members. There simply are people whom we care deeply about whom we think could certainly change for the better in many ways. What is important is that in a genuinely intimate relationship, the parties must care about one another in some sense. It is often a result of our deep concern and/or affection for someone that he or she is able to irritate or frustrate us in such profound ways. These people whom we care about but do not, in many ways, like, are those whom we most wish to change, because, despite ourselves, we are drawn to them and want them to be well-off. Why our affections and concerns work in this way is certainly mysterious, but it is simply a fact that they do work in this way.[7]

It is not the case, however, that any type of positive attitude that we might have toward a person is sufficient for the type of intimate relationship that I am describing. For example, respecting, lusting after, finding attractive, being in awe of, etc., are all positive attitudes that we might have toward someone that are not in the general class of attitudes that constitute a type of concern for a person. Insofar as we have any of the above attitudes toward a person, we will thereby have certain subjective agent-relative reasons for certain actions, but we will not be in the sort of relationship that is genuinely intimate (unless, of course, these attitudes are accompanied by one of the attitudes of concern).

Again, it is important to restate the caveat that I am not here doing conceptual analysis. Rather, I am engaged in describing or delineating a particular type of relationship that is complex and will have many or most of a range of components, and will necessarily include some type of concerned attitude on the part of the parties to the relationship (and may also involve respect, lust, attraction, awe, or any combination of these). My claim in the next chapter will be that the type of relationship described generates reasons that are both objective and agent-relative. So here I am simply describing what I hope will be a familiar sort of intimate relationship, the sort of relationship which, I hope, most readers had in mind during my discussion in the last chapter of my friendship with Tracy.

(b) The attitudes mentioned in (a) must be *mutual* attitudes, i.e., their attitudes of love or affection must be reciprocated, and the parties to the relationship must be aware, or, at least, be in a position to become aware, of this mutuality in attitude.

In order for two people to have an intimate relationship, each of the two must regard the other with an attitude of concern, be it liking, fondness, love, or affection. If the relationship is such that I like Tracy but it is not the case that Tracy likes me (Tracy may be indifferent to me, hate me, or not even know who I am), then we do not necessarily even have a relationship. Rather, all that is true of me is that I happen to have certain attitudes toward some other person who is such that she may have attitudes toward me. Of course, such attitudes will constitute subjective agent-relative reasons. If I am obsessed with Harrison Ford, watch *Raiders of the Lost Ark* over and over again, search magazines for information about him, etc., then I probably have reasons to do certain things for Harrison Ford that others do not have. But, given that Harrison Ford does not even know who I am, there is no sense in which we have any sort of relationship. It is clear that he has no agent-relative reasons regarding me.[8]

I will call this constraint on genuinely intimate relationships *the mutuality requirement*. In recent years, philosophers have appealed to intimate relationships, particularly those between friends and those between parents and children, to model political obligations and even all of morality. These projects have gained even the minimal plausibility that they have by selective focus on certain aspects of intimate relationships in conjunction with a complete disregard of other aspects and of the ways in which all of these aspects work together. So, while friendships satisfy the mutuality requirement, it seems quite clear that relations between, for example, compatriots, do not. With respect to intimate relationships such as friendship, I think that it is obvious that, no matter how strongly I feel about Harrison Ford, he and I are not friends—we are not close to one another or intimate in any way.

Of course, for two people to be friends, they need not have precisely the same sorts of attitudes toward one another, and their attitudes need not be of the same strength. It is sufficient if both have attitudes of concern of one sort or another. In many relationships, inequity in strength of attitudes is often destructive of the relationship: this is particularly true in romantic relationships or relationships in which one of the parties feels quite strongly about the other. Nonetheless, if the parties to the relationship can handle the inequity in feelings, they might very well still have an intimate relationship.

In addition to satisfying the mutuality requirement, the parties to the relationship must be aware that their relationship satisfies that requirement. Here we must be cautious with respect to how we understand this awareness of mutuality. I am trying to rule out as intimate those relationships in which persons admire or 'love' one another without either party having any idea that the other returns her feelings. But in many intimate relationships, persons can be insecure about how the other feels about her. I do not want to rule out as intimate any relationship in which the parties to the relationship have any insecurities with respect to how much or whether the other cares about her. However, if someone has a pathological insecurity about her worthiness to be loved, any relationship into which she enters is unlikely to have many of the features below; for example, such pathologically insecure people are unlikely to be willing to allow others to come to know them. They will always be guarded about their own inner lives. But insecurities come in great varieties: some block intimacy, some do not. Again, I am not doing conceptual analysis, but describing a class of real-world relationships that exhibit great variety. The most I can say is that persons are not friends if they lack any awareness of how the other feels about them. In between, there will be cases in which it is simply unclear, to the person herself even, what her beliefs are about her 'friend's' attitudes with respect to her. I simply cannot say *a priori* whether such relationships meet the current condition—we would need to examine them one by one. Also, it is an empirical matter as to the extent that insecurity will lead a person to be unwilling to open up to or to trust another. And a deficiency in one feature of intimacy may be compensated for by depth with respect to some other feature.[9]

In stating condition (b), I said that the parties to the relationship must at least be in a position to become aware of their mutual attitudes. Thus, we can now see how the insecure person may have doubts about her friend's feelings for her, but she is in an epistemic position that allows her access to the facts that would justify her having the belief that her friend does care about her. Also, people may have wholly or partly subconscious attitudes toward others. We are often surprised when we come to realize the depth of our feelings, either of love or of hatred. So the awareness that the parties to the relationship have of both their own attitudes and the attitudes of the other party to the relationship will vary in both kind and degree from one relationship to another. What I want to rule out are cases in which the parties worship one another from afar or become obsessed about one another without either of them actually having any awareness or being in a realistic position for coming to gain such awareness of the other's attitudes. Probably it is the case that other conditions such as (f) will be sufficient to rule out such cases. Here it is sufficient, I hope, to indicate that the requirement of the parties' being aware of each other's mutual attitudes allows for leeway in the nature, depth, or level of such awareness. Again, I think that we could only evaluate a particular case upon seeing more detail regarding this matter and also regarding the other listed conditions.

(c) The parties must have a concern for one another that exceeds their concern for any person simply as a person.

Friends typically are disposed to benefit one another out of proportion to one another's objective need. Friends will use their resources to promote each other's good and, in most cases, are willing to do far more for friends than they are willing to do for other persons. However, I do not want to make it a condition of friendship that friends *actually* benefit one another out of proportion to each other's need or to a greater extent than they benefit other persons. After all, people can find themselves in straitened circumstances and so have no resources with which to benefit another. Here I am not referring simply to material resources, but also to the more precious resources of time, company, sympathy, and aspects of the self such as humor and insight. Just as I may be materially poor, I may be in a situation, perhaps as a result of severe illness, in which I simply cannot give of myself even to those about whom I care.

So what is important for friendship is that the parties to the relationship have not only attitudes of concern with respect to one another (a) but also that their attitudes of concern toward one another are greater in strength than those that they have for most other persons.[10] If someone has an equal love and concern for all members of the human race, it is not true that she is friends with everyone, but, rather, that she is friends with no one. This will be particularly clear when we look at some of the other requirements, as well as (b). It would be very strange, as a matter of empirical fact, for someone to meet all of the other conditions with respect to her relationship to person x and yet not have greater concern for x than she has for most other persons. However, if this were to occur, then x and the agent are not friends, or, do not have a genuinely intimate relationship.[11]

For example, imagine hearing that some person has died of starvation in the Somalian desert. Given that (let us suppose) there is no one that you know in Somalia, you might be upset at the thought of this sort of human suffering and loss, and angry at social forces that result in such apparently needless deaths, but certainly not devastated. Now imagine, on the other hand, that you receive the news that your best friend has died in an automobile accident. Your response will surely be different than your response to the news that some unknown person has died in Somalia. You will not merely be upset and angry about human suffering and death, but will suffer a type of *personal loss*. By the phrase 'personal loss' I do not mean to denote just the loss of benefits to yourself, i.e., this sort of loss is not to be selfishly understood. It is rather that, in this case, the loss of *this particular person* upsets you, not just the loss of human life considered as such. Also, you are affected in ways that most others are not. If I would be equally upset or grief-stricken at the news that any given person has died as I would be at the news that my best 'friend' Tracy has died (or if I would not be particularly upset or grief-stricken in response to any loss), then it simply is not the case that Tracy is my friend, let alone my best friend.[12]

If there were a person who could actually have the depth of feeling that we have for our friends for all persons in the world *and* she could meet all or most of the other conditions on friendship, then I suppose that such a person would actually be friends with every one of the vast number of people in the world. I am presupposing that human psychology does not allow for any such person to exist, and, thus, no actual person will be friends with everyone. Concern in intimate relationships is concern for the other as the particular person she is, and such concern requires responding to particulars of the person, not just to certain general features that are worthy of concern. I simply do not see how such a particularized concern could be had for more than a few people. So the present condition seems difficult to pull apart from conditions (e) and (f) in particular.[13]

I think that our ordinary practice of describing friends as close to one another captures quite well what I am trying to get at here. In spatial terms, it makes no sense to say of a person that, for any given object, she is just as close to it as she is to any other given object. To say that I am close to my computer carries the implication that, for most other things, they are at a greater distance from me than my computer is. Similarly, people are intimate with or close to one another only if it is true that, for most other persons, they are at a greater distance with respect to affection or concern. So friends must have *special* concern for one another.

Concerning conditions (a), (b), and (c):

All three of the conditions that I have discussed so far have involved some sort of constraint on the attitudes of the parties to an intimate relationship: the parties must have mutual attitudes of special concern for one another. But I have not said much about what an attitude is. Most importantly, is an attitude a cognitive state, an affective state, or a complex state with both cognitive and affective components?[14]

I think that if we are to draw an even remotely plausible picture of intimate relationships such as close friendship we need to understand the sort of concern involved as having both affective and cognitive components.[15] Certainly, concern necessarily involves certain desires regarding the object of the concern, desires that she be happy, that one provide support for her, etc. Desires are clearly intentional states, but they also have an affective aspect: there are characteristic feelings associated with wanting, frustration, satisfaction, etc. Of course, we might say that such affective adjuncts are merely standard causal accompaniments to desire and to its frustration or satisfaction, rather than that part of what it is to desire something is to undergo certain affective transformations as a result of the world's either meeting one's desire or failing to do so. Certainly we can say at least this much: to be frustrated or disappointed is to suffer, to be satisfied is to avoid such suffering, and to want is to be capable of suffering under certain specific conditions and to thereby be subject to some form of anxiety. It is difficult to understand these forms of suffering without understanding them as involving certain types of feelings.

Are any beliefs about the object of concern essential to the concern itself? Some immediate suggestions turn out not to work. So, for example, it might be suggested that concern for x requires a belief that x ought to do well or that one ought to promote x's doing well. But concern need not involve any such beliefs about the value of x's happiness or about one's reasons to promote x's happiness. While it would certainly be odd for concern to be sustained under conditions in which the agent comes to believe that x is unworthy of happiness or of her, the agent's, efforts to bring about that happiness, it is certainly *possible* for it to continue in the light of such beliefs. It is difficult to even think of any range of beliefs which are such that an agent must have some beliefs within that range for it to be the case that the agent cares about x.

Given that concern necessarily involves certain desires, the agent who is concerned about person x will have some motivation to behave in certain ways, especially in ways that promote x's good. In terms of beliefs, it is simply not clear whether the agent will necessarily have any regarding x. I think that it is also the case that we cannot understand an agent who is not disposed to feel in certain ways in response to the object of concern's fortunes as really having concern for that person. Just because a person has made it a rule to behave in certain ways with regard to person x does not imply that that person cares about x. There is a distinction between having a policy to promote x's good and having concern for x. If someone were not disposed to suffer at x's misfortune, to undergo certain types of affective changes, I do not think that we could regard that person as being concerned about x.

Here I think that we need to understand the distinction between caring about person x as the person that she is and caring about person x insofar as x satisfies some (contingent) description. We might make it a policy to promote x's good insofar as doing so will indirectly promote our own good (perhaps x is in a position to confer a benefit upon us), and so we will suffer disappointment and frustration if x falters in some way. But our 'concern' in this case will be transferable insofar as we are concerned about x only instrumentally. If someone else who also is in a position to benefit us takes x's place, we will no longer be disposed to have certain feelings in response to x's good or bad fortunes. This will be evidence that it is not x that we are concerned about, but only x insofar as x can do p for us, or only about the person who satisfies a certain description (and x happens to be that person).

So to say that I am concerned about my friend Tracy is to say that I have certain desires regarding her, most importantly desires that she be well-off and not suffer, and that I am disposed to undergo certain affective changes in response to changes in her fortunes. Of course, it is important that I am *disposed* to feel in certain ways, because when, for example, I am depressed or angry, I may not feel anything in regards to Tracy or may feel in quite an unusual way: it is not that unusual for people to take at least a small amount of pleasure in the pain of a close friend with whom they are angry.[16] But the lack of a general disposition to respond in certain ways will undermine the claim that I am concerned about Tracy.

One possible objection to this conception of concern is that it makes it the case that persons who are not subject to certain types of feelings or to changes in their feelings cannot be party to an intimate relationship. We need to notice that such persons can still have relationships that have other features in common with an intimate relationship. But I do not think that it is implausible that people who lack certain feelings can never be close to another person. Purely rational concern, in the sense of making it a policy to do certain things for people, is *not* enough to put one into a special relationship of intimacy with another person. No one will object that it is unfair to exclude from the possibility of intimacy those who lack certain desires, so why worry about excluding those who are not subject to certain feelings? I think it is because of the common idea that we cannot control our feelings. Even if we cannot, and I doubt that we cannot except in a sense in which we cannot control desires or beliefs either, there is no reason to suppose that everyone has equal capacity for intimacy. Certain innate inabilities may be unfortunate insofar as they exclude one from partaking in relationships that are a great source of value.

(d) The parties must have desires to share time with one another.

Although the requirement that parties have a desire to be together in one way or another seems like an obvious requirement on friendship, I want to be careful in the way that I state it as a requirement on intimate relationships in general. We are intimate with a wide range of people, some of whom we would not describe as friends in the more limited sense of 'friend.' Many relatives are people whom we are close to, and yet we certainly do not wish to spend as much time with them as with chosen friends, lovers, spouses, and even other members of our families. Yet we do want to be 'in touch with' them in some way; further, we want not only indirect news of them, but also want to see or speak to them directly. At the very least, we must want to see our intimates or speak with them occasionally. Of course, the stronger the attitude of special concern that the parties have toward one another, the more time that they will want to spend with one another, especially if they like one another or have great affection or fondness for one another. An 'intimacy' with or knowledge of one another (see (e)) that drives the parties from one another is not what I am considering to be genuine intimacy.

Further, the desires to spend time with one another that the parties have must be desires to spend time with the other person as an end in itself, not simply as a means to some other goal that the parties have. Suppose that Sam desires to spend time with Jasmine because he thinks that by spending time with Jasmine he will be able to talk his way into a promotion, or suppose that Jasmine wants to spend time with Sam because she has heard that he is a good lover and she wants to spend a night with him. Neither of these desires to be with the other person are desires to be with that person considered simply as the person that she is: if Sam can get his promotion some other way, then he will cease to desire to be with Jasmine, and if Jasmine meets another man who is reputed to be a better lover than Sam, then she will cease to want to be with Sam. So an intimate relationship is one in which the parties to the relationship desire to spend time with one another as an end in itself not as a means to financial or professional success or sexual pleasure, or any other end extrinsic to the company of the person considered in herself.

But consider the following case: suppose that Rick desires to spend time with Diane because he finds Diane's company pleasant. He thinks that she is witty, charming, and intelligent, and so likes to be around her. As a result of spending time with one another, he develops a special concern and affection for her, and she for him. Rick's desire to be with Diane seems parallel to Sam's desire to be with Jasmine and Jasmine's to be with Sam: Rick wants to spend time with Diane insofar as doing so produces pleasure for him. Of course, the case of Rick and Diane looks different from either of the cases involving Sam and Jasmine insofar as we find only the first of the following to be an acceptable response to the question, "Why do you like her?": "Because she is witty, charming, and intelligent," "Because she can get me a promotion," "Because of the sex."

However, now imagine that Diane is forced to undergo a course of painful medical procedures and treatment that make her irritable and confused, or imagine that she is suffering from severe depression that results in low mood and being withdrawn in company. Will Rick continue to want to be with Diane? It seems not, if he only wants to be with her because of her wit and charm: she is currently displaying neither quality. He might continue to want to be with her now as a means to her company in the future which, hopefully, will then be pleasant again. It does seem, however, that the nature of Rick's desire reveals something unpalatable about his concern for Diane, given that he views his current time with her as instrumental to his own future pleasure rather than as a way of being with Diane or as an opportunity to cheer Diane up for her sake and not for his own.

The problem with Rick's attitude is that he regards his time with Diane rather in the way that he regards time in front of his television set: both are entertaining. It is not just that Rick will have subjective agent-relative reason to transfer his allotment of time from Diane to another person who is even more charming, but he will also have reason to spend far less time with Diane when he gets digital cable or a satellite dish. Diane is a live show that he can call upon at his convenience and schedule around other pleasing activities available to him. Diane will have reason to be insecure in such a relationship: she must continue to put on a good show or be subject to cancellation. Her friendship with Rick depends on what is on pay-per-view, it seems.

Friends do, however, say that they like each other because of each other's charm or wit. Often, friendships dissipate when one friend undergoes drastic personality changes. If we reject the idea that we desire to be with friends for our own pleasure, can we accommodate the ways in which friendships seem, legitimately, to end? Under what sorts of conditions might a desire to be with another for its own sake cease to exist without the agent being blameworthy in any way?

Questions about how or why special concern and desires to be with someone for its own sake cease to exist are difficult questions. If Rick at first desires to be with Diane for his own pleasure, he might very well then develop a special concern for her that generates a desire to be with her not as a means to another goal but as an end in itself. And if Diane ceases to be charming, Rick will cease to find her company enjoyable and, eventually, he may cease to want to be with her even as a goal in itself. This process is complicated and as our desires to be with friends become weak or disappear, we may find ourselves wondering how much we really cared about them in the first place, showing how entangled are the notions of special concern and a noninstrumental desire to spend time with a person. Whatever the causal genesis or cause of the decline of a noninstrumental desire to be with someone, it will typically be present in cases of genuine intimacy. Without such a desire, special concern will not be present, and subjective agent-relative reasons will be sufficient to account for the reasons that parties to the relationship have to care for one another. After all, time is the most precious of resources, and if we are not disposed to share that resource with someone, we must wonder if we have the dispositions to behave (or motives or desires) that are partially constitutive of special concern.

(e) The parties must have, or be making a considered effort to achieve, a certain level of knowledge about one another, a level that goes considerably beyond what a stranger or mere acquaintance would have.

When someone asks me whether I know Tracy, I respond that I do. In this sense of 'know,' all that is meant is that I have met Tracy or I have enough descriptive information about Tracy to distinguish her from any random Jane Doe. This sort of knowledge is not sufficient for the friendship relation. We know our friends in ways that we do not know other persons. Two people are not intimate if they do not have any more knowledge about one another than they do about mere acquaintances. Of course, this knowledge condition is not sufficient for genuine intimacy: Sam's psychiatrist may know more about him than does any other person, but that does not mean that Sam's psychiatrist is a friend of his. Sam and his psychiatrist do not satisfy the other conditions that I am here discussing.

I have qualified this knowledge requirement by saying that it is sufficient for the relevant sort of intimacy that the two parties be working toward acquiring the relevant sort of knowledge about one another. Getting to know a person takes a long time and a great deal of attention and interaction. Certain kinds of knowledge can only be gained after trust is established, i.e., after the parties already have special concern for one another. We come to care about people while we are in the process of acquiring information about their characters.[17] If the relationship already exhibits all of the other conditions, then, as long as the parties are working toward knowledge of one another, they are parties to the requisite type of intimate relationship.

In criticizing what they call the 'secrets view of friendship' which they attribute to Laurence Thomas, Dean Cocking and Jeanette Kennett say that

> it would be unusual if the closest of friends did not share any such private concerns. Further, . . . the sharing of such concerns can serve to deepen and nurture intimacy. But, . . . it is not the private nature of what is disclosed that counts toward intimacy. Rather, it is the value we assign to the hopes and concerns we share with each other (whether we wish them to be kept private or not) and the fact that we choose to talk to each other about what matters to us that contributes to the growth of intimacy between us. Thus, as my friend, you do indeed gain what Thomas calls "a commanding perspective" on my life but access to my secrets need play very little part in this.[18]

I think that Cocking and Kennett are right in that I need not reveal all of myself to a friend for it to be the case that we are intimate. Imagine that Jasmine has sexual fantasies that she is embarrassed about, and so reveals her fantasies to no one except perhaps her therapist. I do not think that Sam's ignorance of the nature of Jasmine's sexual fantasies is any evidence against their intimacy. It may also be the case that, if we care about someone, we will keep certain secrets. For example, if Rick said something nasty about Diane to Greg, it need not be the case that, in order to maintain intimacy, Rick confess this to Diane: such a confession may only hurt Diane's feelings, and she may not understand that Rick was upset and, in addition, had had one too many glasses of beer. Caring about someone involves knowing when to tell them certain things and when to keep certain secrets. Certain friends are people whom we open up to about certain things but not others. This is particularly true, I think, when friendships are between two people who are of the opposite sex (but the relationship is not a sexual one). Two women talk of, for example, their menstrual cycle insofar as this affects their lives and feelings; however, most women are reluctant to even mention menstruation to men, even to those men whom they consider close friends.

It is rather that we acquire certain information about our friends from our interactions with them and also from the fact that we receive firsthand information that others get only indirectly if at all. Perhaps the term 'under-standing' is better than 'knowledge' in this context, for there are ways of having information that do not involve fully grasping it or being able to understand its role within a complete picture of a person's life. It is interesting that our friends come to know certain facts about our characters before we are aware of them—friends help us to understand our own characters. It is not unusual to have an epiphany about ourselves and then, upon sharing it with a friend, have them respond that they had realized that fact about us long ago. This sort of insight or understanding is what is characteristic of intimacy, not mere knowledge of sexual peculiarities, or, to take Cocking and Kennett's example, morning bathroom routines.[19]

This type of insight or understanding can only be gained through a certain amount of interaction (see condition (f)) coupled with effort and time spent in trying to grasp a person's true character. If I have a special concern for Tracy, I will be moved to promote her good, but a necessary condition of my being able to do so is that I know what her good involves and what would be instrumental in producing it. I must understand Tracy's desires, what she cares about, so that I can understand what sorts of subjective agent-relative reasons she has. In certain cases, we must have some crucial information in order to understand a person in this way. Some people may have psychological secrets which are such that, in keeping those secrets, they prevent anyone from getting close to them, because those secrets have such a pervasive impact on the nature of their reasons and on the rest of their character. But this need not be true for all persons: some are open books, and friends differ from strangers only in their insightful grasp of the whole book.

Coming to understand a person is easier in some cases than in others. Evidence suggests that friendships between women become intimate much more quickly than those between men. This is likely because women simply tell each other things that men think it unseemly to talk about. So one needs to work much harder to acquire information about these sorts of men, because enough interaction of the right sort and enough effort can lead to intimacy.[20] Intimacy requires work and a certain amount of openness: those who are unwilling to be open to a certain extent, either to information presented by the other party in one form or another or to allowing the other party access to themselves in some way, will never be able to achieve intimacy.[21]

Friendships can be called into question when one of the parties learns that the other has been keeping certain types of information secret from her. Again, which sorts of secrets will break a friendship depends on the nature of the friendship and of the parties to it. We will tend to be particularly troubled if we think that, by keeping certain secrets, our friends have misled us about their characters. Oddly enough, then, it is probably true that people who are too agreeable or have too strong of a desire to avoid conflict may not be able to achieve intimacy.

Achieving intimacy, as we all know, is a complicated process. In order to reveal ourselves, either through words or action, we must trust the other person to make a serious effort to understand in a caring way. So the relationship must have proceeded along certain dimensions before it can proceed along the knowledge dimension. Much of the time, we simply trust on faith because of our need to be able to achieve intimacy, and we recognize that we must take that first step before we are absolutely sure of the other. Trying to disentangle the actual causal processes here is far beyond my present project.[22]

(f) The parties must have actually spent some time in one another's company, or have causally interacted in some other relevantly similar manner.

Basically, this requirement says that one cannot be friends with someone overnight or on the spur of the moment. Friendship is a relationship that requires a certain amount of time and interaction. How much time and interaction is necessary will vary with the nature of the persons and the nature and intensity of their interactions. So friends must have a history with one another. Typically, this will be a history of time actually spent in one another's company, but it might involve telephone conversations or e-mail, depending on how good the parties are at expressing their real feelings verbally and at reading between the lines, as it were.

This requirement is simultaneously in accord with and in tension with common sense about friendship. While we do think of our friends as people that we have known for some length of time, there is also a tendency to speak about, for example, love at first sight, or to say things such as "I liked her as soon as I met her." I do not think, however, that we can take such claims as evidence that any sort of appropriate attitude can develop virtually at the first sighting of a person. Particularly with respect to sexual 'love' we confuse a physical attraction with a deeper emotion. (This can happen in nonsexual interactions as well: we can find a person's manner charming or attractive in a nonsexual way.) Then, after the relationship develops, we project our current attitudes toward a person back into our original perceptions of them: we are simply unable to think of them without bringing forth our current strong feelings.

Human beings being what they are, it is simply impossible, in a causal sense, for the requisite sorts of knowledge and attitudes to develop in a moment. People cannot be revealed through a single perception of their physical bodies. We have a tendency to read character into physical traits, thus explaining how both phrenology and racial 'science' acquired their widespread acceptance. So it is not causally possible for the knowledge requirement to have been met unless the parties have interacted for a certain length of time.

But, let us imagine a situation in which two people have acquired mutual attitudes of special concern (and are aware of the other's attitude, because their publisher has informed them of it), desire to spend time with one another (in this case, they have a desire, first, to meet each other in person), and have acquired much knowledge about one another as a result of reading each other's memoirs (published by the person who informs them of their mutual concern for one another). Are these people intimate with one another in the sense that I am here trying to describe?

This is one type of intimacy, but it is not the sort that I am trying to describe. It is difficult to specify exactly what sort of causal interaction will suffice for two people to be in an intimate relationship, because of familiar problems with distinguishing between direct causal contact and indirect causal contact. But the important point here is that the parties to the relationship must have acquired the information about and knowledge of one another that they have in a way that does not allow any given person to have precisely the same sort of information. Relationships are not simply matters of having the right sorts of intentional states with the right sorts of objects; rather, relationships involve having certain intentional states with certain objects as a result of another person with relevant intentional states having interacted with one in appropriate ways. The parties to the relationship must be in causal positions that allow them a perspective on another person that is not or at least not entirely mediated by another. In my earlier example, the parties do have each other's memoirs, but these were not written expressly for the other, but, rather, at the time of the writing, neither knew of the other's existence. Whatever causal results there are of their interaction are not direct (they are mediated by the publisher) or are the result of factors which are available in exactly the same form to others.

(g) The parties' history with one another must exhibit or evidence concern.

The interaction between the parties must take a particular form, namely it must be concerned interaction. This condition will almost surely be met if the other conditions are met. If two people have mutual special concern for one another and are aware of these attitudes, it is hard to see how their behavior could be anything other than an exhibition of such concern. How could two people have dispositions to benefit one another, actually be in one another's company and have gained knowledge about the other's concern, if neither has behaved in a concerned manner or if their behavior has been consistently indifferent or nasty?

It is a peculiarity of the sort of project that I am engaged upon in this chapter, what we might call descriptive philosophy, that even though in real-world relationships this condition would be met in all cases in which the previous conditions were met, there are weird counterexamples given that the sort of necessity involved is only causal necessity. If two people find themselves in straitened circumstances, they may be unable to act to benefit one another; in fact, for external reasons, they may be forced to act in downright cruel ways with regard to one another. Nonetheless, they might have become aware, perhaps through pirated e-mail, that they regard one another with mutual special concern. In such a case, these persons do not have a genuinely intimate relationship until their interaction, as described in (f), can itself be characterized as concerned or caring. Again, a friendship or intimate relationship is a relationship with a particular sort of history involving reciprocal interaction between the parties to the relationship. This interaction must be, at least in part, geared at promoting the other's

000002137760

000002137760

books are worth today!
shipping - see what your old
quote. We even pay the
and get an instant price
Go to sellbackyourBook.com

Sell your books at
sellbackyourBook.con

good, trying to understand the character of the other for purposes of promoting her good and offering comfort and support.

Further, the interaction must involve or partly constitute attempts to make the other a part of one's life in a significant way, a way that is consistent with a noninstrumental view of the other person. Thus, to borrow language from the last chapter, the parties to the friendship will have irreducibly self-involving projects that essentially involve the other party to the friendship. Friends do not simply want good for each other whoever is to produce it, and they also do not simply want that they promote the other's good no matter at what distance. Each wants to do good for the other through the type of reciprocal interaction involved in condition (f), and this reciprocal interaction has corresponding effects on the other party to the relationship. A friend's self-involving projects are essentially other-regarding (where by 'other' I mean 'other party to the friendship'). The interaction between the parties must be interaction that reflects these essentially other(friend)-regarding projects.

IV. FRIENDSHIP AND CHARACTER

The picture that I have drawn of an intimate relationship is of a relationship with a certain sort of history of causal interaction between parties with mutual attitudes of special concern. I have put no constraints on the nature of the characters of the parties to the relationship except insofar as certain capacities for trust, openness, and concern are requisite for the earlier described conditions to hold. Importantly, I have left it open as to whether (i) the parties to the relationship are virtuous or even minimally morally decent, and (ii) the parties are similar to one another in some relevant way or ways.

As to (i) I want to leave it open that two bad people or one bad person and one good person could be intimate with one another. Take the case of two bad people. Insofar as concern involves a disposition to promote the objective good of the object of concern, a bad person will most likely end up steering her friend wrong insofar as the bad person has misguided notions of what is good for a person. In involving a friend in her own projects, she will be involving her friend in her own wrongdoing as well. So bad friends are unlikely to reach the goals that are intrinsic to the concern partly constitutive of friendship. But friendship only demands being directed toward the good of a friend, not successfully promoting that goal or having a full or informed conception of what that goal involves.[23]

In many cases, friends will in fact have similar interests, tastes, and characters more generally, but, as my statement of (ii) indicates, I do not think that this is necessary for intimacy, even as a causal matter. For many people, derivation of pleasure from being with another is what causally sustains their noninstrumental concern for another, or plays some role in causally sustaining it (see condition (d)).[24] Friendships often begin with shared activities or commonality in views, but, again, they need not. The most striking cases of lack of similarity of character and interests are in intimate relationships between adult children and their parents. Particularly in societies in which there is fluidity between classes, children can, as a result of education and profession, become quite different from their parents. But mutual respect and appreciation can help to maintain an intimate relationship in which the closeness is sometimes enhanced by the differences. Also, people who share trials together may come to be intimate even if they would never have been so if they had met in more ordinary circumstances. So intimacy can flourish among many types of people in many different circumstances.

In fact, sometimes the hard-won nature of an intimate relationship makes us subjectively value it to an even greater extent than we would have if the intimacy had developed easily out of vast similarities in character. Gaining insights about others who are very different from us can have marvelous effects on our own characters and on our ability to grasp our objective agent-neutral reasons. People who are different from us can provide us with fresh insights into ourselves and can provide counterballast to our own tendency to see ourselves as quite central to the world.[25]

So why suppose that the relationships that I have described give rise to objective agent-relative reasons? That is the question to which I now turn.

4 Intimacy, Fidelity, and Commitments

This chapter, I fear, will be somewhat anticlimactic to some of my readers. I have spent the previous two chapters describing the nature of intimacy and presenting two apparently inadequate accounts of reasons of intimacy. However, what I have said about why those accounts are inadequate should have prepared my reader for the anticlimactic nature of this chapter's account of reasons of intimacy. If common sense demands that reasons of intimacy not be derivative, then it seems that any account that grounds reasons of intimacy in something other than the intimate relationship itself will inevitably fail to meet the demands of common sense. And so the long awaited answer to the question as to why intimate relationships ground reasons is: because they are the sorts of relationships that they are, namely, the intimate kind as described in the last chapter.

Of course, I could end the chapter here, adding only an injunction that my readers reflect carefully on the type of relationship described in Chapter 3 in order to grasp that such a relationship grounds reasons. However, I think that most of my readers would probably like a bit more. So I am going to return now to reasons of fidelity, which, I suggested at the end of Chapter 2, share with reasons of intimacy their apparent character of being both objective and agent-relative. Many attempts have been made to show why promising grounds reasons, and I want to canvass some of the most prominent of such attempts, focusing on those that understand reasons of fidelity as derivative objective reasons. Some of these accounts view reasons of fidelity as agent-relative; others view them as agent-neutral. But they all understand these reasons as derivative, not as grounded merely on the fact of a promise having been made.

If you are like me, you will find yourself far less sure about whatever has been pointed to as the grounds for reasons of fidelity than you were to begin with about the claim that promises ground reasons. Why must we think that an appeal to promises is insufficient? Why do we think that there must be some explanation as to why promises ground reasons? I think, in fact, that this drive for an explanation is one felt by philosophers, but not by "plain men and women." In our lives as moral agents we recognize certain types of human relationships as, by their very nature, grounding reasons for us. Intimacy and promise-making are two such relationships. So all that I can do is to show the inadequacy of familiar accounts of reasons of fidelity, hoping that, in the process, I can convince you of the fundamental nature of reasons of fidelity.

I. PROMISING AND REASONS OF FIDELITY: FOUR ACCOUNTS

The Utilitarian Account

Ross's 'plain man'[1] seems right, i.e., that it is not the consequences of keeping a promise that justify an agent in keeping the promise. Ross seems to be right in pointing out that we do not always consider ourselves justified in breaking a promise simply because the consequences of doing so would be better than the consequences of keeping the promise. Utilitarians try to point out that there are many hidden costs of promise-breaking, i.e., costs stemming from long-term effects on, for example, the stability of the institution of promising and the reliability of the agent's character. The problem with these utilitarian appeals is twofold. First, the plausibility of such empirical claims is highly doubtful. Many of us have broken several promises in our life-times without serious damage to either the institution of promise-making or to our characters. I admit that I myself have broken quite a few promises (although, I hope, not too high of a percentage of the promises that I have made), and yet the institution of promise-keeping is alive and well, my friends still (I believe) trust me, and I am still a person of reliable character, concerned to respect her reasons of fidelity. The most that the empirical evidence seems to warrant is an obligation to keep *most of* one's promises, making the duty to keep promises imperfect,[2] as is the duty to be charitable: one can justify breaking a particular promise by pointing out that one has been particularly reliable of late. The "I gave at the office" form of excuse now is good both in the realm of charity and in the realm of promises.

The second difficulty with the utilitarian account has to do with the structure of its justification of obligations of fidelity. We usually think that the obligation is to a particular person, and that that person has some sort of particular complaint if the promise is not kept. Even if we grant the utilitarian the empirical claims to which she appeals in her account of promise-keeping, the account appears wrongheaded. After all, the adverse consequences of losing the institution of promise-keeping as a result of lack of trust or of reliable characters or both are remote from my single act of promise-breaking. My promisee's complaint is not personal, cannot just be that I did not do what I promised her that I would do: she must tie my act, causally, to a web of consequences that, she must show, undermines a valuable institution.[3] Her complaint is no different than that of anyone else, and I can right the wrong by doing some act to strengthen the institution as a substitute for doing what I promised to do (perhaps I could facilitate the keeping of some other person's promises to someone other than my promisee). But the act of my making a promise to some particular person is given short shrift in this account: it does not seem to have any fundamental rational or moral significance.

Of course, the utilitarian (or consequentialist more generally) might say that, with this second objection, I have really just begged the question against utilitarianism. After all, the utilitarian is defined as one who takes only consequences of acts as relevant to their rightness/wrongness, not their belonging to some other category of act-type. The only fundamentally relevant act-types are those of being optimific relative to alternatives and of being suboptimific relative to alternatives. This is quite right, but, I think, does not show that my second objection is question-begging. If one is trying to argue that a particular account of fundamentally significant right-making or wrong-making features of action is incorrect, all that one can do is to show that certain types of plausibly right-making or wrong-making features are ignored by the theory or that the account that the theory does take of them seems inadequate. The standard Ross-style of objection to utilitarian accounts of promise-making and promise-keeping that I have borrowed is of this form.

What is missing from any consequentialist understanding of reasons of fidelity is, of course, the claim that such reasons are fundamentally agent-relative: my promises seem to be *my* concern in some special way. It is not just that I am in the best position to keep my own promises and thus to promote the value of promise-keeping. Even if that is right (and it *is* plausible as an empirical generalization), it still seems that it does not capture my peculiar concern with my own promises: *even if* I could better promote a system of promise-keeping by ignoring my own promise in order to assist someone else in keeping her promise, it does seem that my reason to keep my own promise has not necessarily been defeated. Our reasons to keep our promises, then, do not seem to be exhausted by reference to the objective value of our doing so: agent-neutral reasons alone, then, will not do as reasons of fidelity.[4]

A Kantian Account[5]

So let us consider one of the most famous of deontological accounts, that of Kant. Kant's view is an extremely unusual account of promising insofar as it is difficult to grasp the precise role of the agent's act in generating her reason of fidelity. Kant's focus is not so much the agent's own act of having made a promise but, rather, the hypothetical consequences of everyone's breaking a promise when he or she has the same motives (maxim) as the agent under consideration. So in Kant's example, I make a promise to repay a loan when I know that I will not be able to do so. My motive is to get some money for some benefit to myself (it is interesting that the nature of this benefit is unspecified, although the reader is certainly given the impression that it is a self-regarding benefit), and so supposedly represents an instance of the maxim: "I will make a promise that I know that I cannot keep whenever doing so is to my benefit, i.e., is rational in the prudential sense." I am then to notice that if everyone were to act on such a general rule, that the effects on trust and thereby on the institution of promising would be disastrous: I would not be able to achieve my own aims in a world where everyone acted on my maxim. Thus, it becomes clear that I am making an exception of myself, that I cannot will my maxim to be universal law. Therefore, making a promise with no intention of keeping it is not morally permissible according to the first formulation of the categorical imperative.[6]

Kant avoids one of the difficulties of the utilitarian account by the fact that his account appeals to *hypothetical* consequences of everyone's acting on my maxim. He need make no assumptions, plausible or otherwise, about the empirical consequences of my own act of failing to keep a promise. But his account has other problems. First, there is, of course, the difficulty in deciding how to formulate an agent's maxim. Can't I adhere to both of the following maxims: I will not break a promise merely for some smallish personal benefit, and, I will break a promise for a serious (such as a lifesaving) benefit to a loved one? The hypothetical consequences of breaking the promise in the latter sort of case are quite different than are the hypothetical consequences of breaking the promise in the former sort of case. After all, most people, I think, probably are actually such that they would make a lying promise to get a lifesaving operation for a child or a parent (if no other options were available), and, as we can see, the institution of promise-making is durable enough to survive.[7] I do not want to deny that the nature of the promise can affect our all-things-considered reason to keep it or not, but that is because the content is relevant to determining what other sorts of reasons counterbalance our reasons of fidelity, not because the content is relevant to the generation of the reason of fidelity itself.

But it might be that Kant (or some ingenious Kant scholar) could offer some plausible explanation of why maxims need to be stated at the level of generality that Kant seems to state them. It still remains the case that my reason of fidelity is somehow the result of the hypothetical consequences of everyone's failing to keep their promises. When Kant considers the hypothetical consequences of everyone's acting on the agent's maxim of breaking a promise to get some desired benefit, he allows himself to make certain, let us grant, plausible, assumptions about human nature and human interactions. But, given that he makes these assumptions, we can notice that if human beings were more gullible or altruistic or less prone to use induction in their dealings with one another, the hypothetical consequences of breaking a promise would be different than Kant supposes, and, thus, one might very well be able to will one's promise-breaking maxim be universal law. It does not, however, seem right to suppose that my reasons of fidelity are dependent on, for example, the prevalence of the use of induction among human beings.

Kant has placed the focus of his account of reasons of fidelity in the wrong place, it seems. His account does not take as central to an agent's reasons of fidelity her particular act and the relationship thereby created to her promisor. As in the utilitarian account, the attention is shifted to some facts about human institutions and interactions considered more generally. The same sort of complaint can be lodged by Ross's 'plain man' against both the utilitarian account of promising and the Kantian account: what will happen and what might happen in some possible world if I or everyone broke promises does not seem relevant as to whether I have at least *prima facie* reason to keep my promises here and now.

The Expectations Account

My discussion of Kant's account of promising suggests that the focus of an adequate account of promising needs to be on the agent, the promisee, or on the relationship between the promisor and the promisee. There seems to be something about my particular act of promising to this particular person that is relevant to my having a reason of fidelity, and it is this and this alone, it seems, upon which my having such a reason depends. One obvious way of placing the emphasis on the promisor clearly will not do: we cannot understand reasons of fidelity as straightforward subjective agent-relative reasons. Our reasons of fidelity outlast our desires, even our dispositional desires, to keep the promises that we make. Further, it is not the case that an agent need have a desire either to do x or to keep the promise to do x, in order for her to have reasons of fidelity arising from her promise to person y to do x. The act of promising needs to be distinguished from the agent's desires and intentions: no matter how much an agent wants or intends to do x, she does not necessarily have reasons of fidelity to do x, and, similarly, even if an agent does not desire or even intend to do x, she might have reasons of fidelity to do x.[8]

All of these facts suggest that reference to the promisee, the one to whom the promise is made, needs to be involved in an adequate account of reasons of fidelity. The most natural account, given such a focus, is a familiar one: when I make a promise, I intentionally raise the expectations of the promisee that I will perform certain acts (which may or may not involve or be directed at the interests of the promisee). When I intentionally raise such expectations, I assume a responsibility to that person insofar as she may then proceed to make plans in accordance with what I have promised to do. Whether or not the breach of promise will actually have the relevant results, i.e., whether or not the promisee's plans will actually be upset, is not relevant to whether the promisor has an obligation to do what she has promised to do. The promisee is now entitled to rely on the performance promised by the promisor; in other words, the balance of claims shifts in light of a promise. The promisee acquires the right to demand performance and the promisor is obligated to perform regardless of the consequences (although, of course, this is a *prima facie* obligation that can be outweighed by the obligation to promote value).[9]

Notice that this account makes reasons of fidelity objective and agent-relative. Consider a case of promising: on Wednesday Sam promises Jasmine that he will help her to move to her new apartment on Saturday. In order for Sam's act to be voluntary, Jasmine must not use coercive means to get Sam to 'consent' to help her to move: if such coercive means are used, then it is not true that Sam has made a promise.[10] Coercive means can be anything from holding a gun to Sam's head to threatening him with refusing to promote him. In this latter case, Jasmine is inappropriately using her power in another context to gain advantage in the bargaining situation. But suppose that Jasmine agrees to go on a date with Sam if and only if he promises to help her to move. If Sam wants to go on a date with Jasmine, he might very well decide that it is worth the price of giving up his Saturday to move heavy furniture. In the latter case, I am inclined to think that Sam has voluntarily bound himself.[11] As a result, according to the expectations account of promising and reasons of fidelity, because Sam has raised Jasmine's expectations, she has a claim against him to perform (and, after he helps her to move her furniture, he has a claim against her that she go out on a date with him). Sam now has a reason to help Jasmine move that no one else necessarily has unless that other person also has made a similar promise, and so Sam's reason of fidelity is clearly agent-relative. The reason is also objective insofar as it remains even if Sam's psychological states change; for example, if Sam no longer desires a date with Jasmine and so no longer desires to help her to move, once he has made the promise, he has agent-relative reason to help her. So the expectations account renders reasons of fidelity objective and agent-relative.

To see why this account will not work in the end, consider Sam's reason for *making* the promise. At least in this case, Sam had a subjective agent-relative reason to make the promise: Sam desired a date with Jasmine, and, as a result, desired to promise her to help her to move insofar as he saw this as a means to what he desired intrinsically (the date with Jasmine). In addition, Sam had an objective agent-neutral reason to make the promise, because helping Jasmine to move and letting her know in advance that he would help her are both means of promoting objective value. Once the promise is made, Sam, in this case, retains both his subjective agent-relative reason (if he continues to desire to go out with Jasmine) and his objective agent-neutral reason (as long as Jasmine's well-being will be promoted by having Sam's assistance, even given the cost of going on a date with him). The latter reason may in fact be strengthened insofar as Jasmine may suffer more from the lack of Sam's assistance in the case where she came to rely upon it than she would suffer in a case where she had no expectation of getting Sam's help.[12]

But surely Sam has some new reason for helping Jasmine to move once he has made the promise to her that he will do so. For consider the case before Sam makes the promise. Let us suppose that Sam does not desire a date with Jasmine and has no intrinsic desire to help her to move. Let us also suppose that Jasmine has plenty of friends who would be willing to assist her in moving, friends who do not mind moving or do hope to exchange their help for something from Jasmine. In this case, Sam has no reason to promise to help Jasmine to move. However, if he does make the promise, then surely he does have a reason to help her, even if Jasmine still has plenty of other friends willing to assist her, and Sam's psychological states have remained the same. The promise, then, generates a reason for Sam independent of his subjective reasons and of his objective agent-neutral reasons.

At this point, the defender of the expectations account of reasons of fidelity will argue that what has changed after the fact of Sam's making the promise is that Jasmine's expectations have been raised, and so she has a right to depend on Sam's performance. So the expectations account focuses on the psychological effects on the promisee of the promisor's act of promising, and seems to do a nice job of accounting for the case as thus far described. But the difficulty for the expectations account also arises from its focus on the psychology of the promisee. Thomas Scanlon, who defends an expectations account of promising within a contractualist framework (see footnote 9), offers his case of the 'Profligate Pal' as a potential counterexample to his own expectations account.[13] If Sam were a profligate pal of Jasmine's, Sam would be the sort of person who has a history of making promises and of then welching on them. So when Sam 'promises' Jasmine that he will help her to move, Jasmine politely thanks Sam for his kind 'promise' of help but has no expectations whatsoever that Sam will actually carry through on his 'promise.' In this case Sam's utterance of the words "I promise . . ." does not have the effect of raising his promisee's expectations. But doesn't Sam have an obligation or reason of fidelity nonetheless? Surely one cannot avoid reasons of fidelity through a history of failing to act on one's obligations.

Scanlon's attempts to deal with this sort of case are unsatisfactory. First, he suggests that such cases are "impure cases" that do not suggest a problem with his account of the central cases of promising. This will not do. Whatever reasons are generated by Sam's promise in my first case (in which Sam is *not* a profligate pal) seem to be of the same sort as those generated in the case in which Sam *is* a profligate pal. Something must be common to all cases of promising if we are to account for the apparent fact that the act of promising itself has rational significance. Second, Scanlon's profligate pal borrows money with a promise to repay, so Scanlon concludes that a profligate pal has an obligation of gratitude to repay. My case of Sam and Jasmine does not involve Sam getting anything from Jasmine until *after* he has fulfilled his promise, so, if he does not do what he has promised to do, then Jasmine gives him nothing and Sam could not have any obligations of gratitude to her. It seems that the expectations account must conclude that Sam has no reason of fidelity to help Jasmine to move.

Scanlon places too much of the power of creating a reason in the hands of the promisee: her psychological states determine the nature of the act done by the agent. If I become jaded and cynical about human beings and lose my sense of trust, then it would seem that, by Scanlon's account, no one can make a promise to me. But surely we are bound to do what we promise to do, even when our promises are made to sceptical, paranoid, or anxious people. So the expectations account seems irreparably flawed.

The difficulties with Scanlon-type expectation accounts of promising suggest one last sort of attempt to ground reasons of fidelity by appeal to some fact about the promisee. When I discussed Kant's account of promissory obligations, I focused on the account that arises from application of the first, or universal law application of the categorical imperative. While that account depends on an appeal to hypothetical consequences of everyone's acting on a promise-breaking maxim, the second, or rational nature as an end-in-itself formulation of the categorical imperative grounds reasons of fidelity on certain facts about the promisee.[14] We are forbidden from treating rational beings (and all promises, by their very nature, are given by rational beings to other rational beings) as merely subjective ends, i.e., means to ends determined by our subjective valuings. Rather, we must always treat rational beings as ends in themselves, i.e., as determinative of reasons for us independently of what we may desire. We must, in our actions, respect their nature as beings capable of conceiving of and following a life plan. When we break a promise to such a being, or make a promise that we have no intention of keeping, we treat their existence as a way for us to get what we want regardless of what they themselves want. Whereas this account clearly has links to Scanlon's expectations account (it is wrong to raise expectations of a separate rational being who has plans and projects independent of our own), it avoids a serious problem of Scanlon's account: for Kant, it is irrelevant whether we actually raise the expectations of our promisee. What matters is that it is wrong for us to perform an action that expresses disrespect for the nature of a rational being, regardless of the causal effects of such an action.

This Kantian theory of the grounds of promissory obligations is preferable, I think, to the account that is yielded by an appeal to the first universal law formulation of the categorical imperative. Unfortunately, it suffers derivatively from the difficulties inherent in understanding the second rational nature as end-in-itself formulation of the categorical imperative. Why does respect for a rational being with her own plans generate a requirement to keep promises? The difficulty, of course, lies in the vagueness of the notion of respect. Why does breaking a promise express disrespect even in cases where I know that my promisee has not had her expectations raised and also that none of her plans will be disrupted by my not keeping my promise? This account of promising, then, can only be assessed within the context of a complete discussion of respect and ends in themselves, which I will pursue in another context in Chapter 6. In any case, the claim that breaking a promise is wrong in virtue of being an instance of a certain type of disrespect for persons is a good place to begin my discussion of what I take to be the correct account of promising.

The Intuitionist Account

For all of their radical dissimilarities, the utilitarian and Kantian accounts (as well as Scanlon's expectations account) of reasons of fidelity have one important structural feature in common: both view our reasons to keep our promises as instances of some more general duty. For the utilitarian, reasons of fidelity are derivative from the principle of utility and, for Kant (and many Kantians), they are derivative from the categorical imperative. On neither account is it promising, *qua* promising, that grounds our reasons of fidelity. It is important to see that the point is not about an analysis of the concept of a promise. The utilitarian, Kantian deontological, or Scanlon-style account, is an account of the justification of keeping a promise, not of what it is to make a promise. All three accounts hold that a claim that we have a reason to keep a promise is derived from other claims (about actual consequences, about hypothetical consequences, or about the expectations of the person to whom the promise is made). For all of these accounts, we have some more fundamental duty, belief in which, coupled perhaps with belief in certain empirical claims, justifies our inference that we have a duty to keep our promises (or some particular promise). It is this claim about the derivative status of beliefs about reasons of fidelity to which I am objecting, not to any claim about the possibility of offering an analysis of the concept of a promise.

So let us consider what I will call, for obvious reasons, the intuitionist account of promising. Consider the following claim:

> (P) If S has made a promise to some other person T that S will do P, then S has a reason to do P.

On the three accounts that I have so far considered, (P) is a derivative truth: for the utilitarian, it is derivative from the principle of utility; for the Kantian, from the categorical imperative; and for Scanlon, from principles about unjustified manipulation and due care that yield that one should meet expectations raised. I suggest that the difficulties with such accounts should motivate us to regard (P) as not derivative from any more basic moral or rational principle about reasons.

Our felt need to support (P) in some way or another suggests that we believe (P) to be true and then search for some principle from which we can derive it. But there is another option available: we could hold that our belief in (P) is justified noninferentially, i.e., we can be justified in believing (P) without deriving (P) from other truths. Of course, in claiming that some beliefs can be noninferentially justified, an intuitionist need not claim "that these beliefs are infallible (that is, cannot be false) or are indubitable (that is, cannot be doubted). Nor need they claim that these beliefs are the object of a special faculty of intuition,"[15] any more than the foundationalist in general epistemology must posit some mysterious faculty by which we come to have, say, justified mathematical beliefs.

How could it be the case that (P) could be known directly, i.e., without inference? For good reason, early twentieth-century intuitionists such as Prichard and Ross were fond of using an analogy with mathematics. Consider the following geometrical truth:

(T) A closed three-sided plane figure has three internal angles.

(T) is a synthetic necessary truth. It is not an analytic truth, since the description that is the subject of the sentence makes no reference, either explicit or implicit, to angles at all. Yet (T), while being synthetic, is nonetheless a necessary truth: the very nature of a three-sided closed plane figure involves having three internal angles. Thus, it is not possible for such a figure to have other than three internal angles.

Given that a three-sided closed plane figure, simply in virtue of the kind of figure that it is, has three internal angles, if one, by reflection, understands what it is to be a three-sided closed plane figure, one can thereby understand that such a figure has—and must have—three internal angles. To put the matter somewhat more rigorously, in being acquainted with the property of being a closed three-sided plane figure and with the property of having three internal angles, one can then become acquainted with the relation of (two-way) necessitation that holds between those properties. If you doubt whether (T) can be justified noninferentially, then consider whether you believe yourself justified in accepting (T). If you do, ask yourself what your argument for (T) is. Most of us lack any such argument and even have a difficult time conceiving of what such an argument would look like. Moreover, any such argument would surely have to appeal to the relation that I am claiming holds between the two properties. But to be justified in appealing to that relation *just is* to be justified in believing (T). Thus, it is highly plausible to suppose that (T) can, and indeed *must,* be justified noninferentially.

Now let us return to the case of promising. My claim is that (P), like (T), can be justifiably believed without inferring it from any more basic moral principle. If one understands what it is to make a promise, one will thereby understand that insofar as one has made a promise, one has—and must have—a reason to do what one has promised to do. Again, to put the matter more rigorously, in being acquainted with the property of having promised and with the property of having a reason, one can then become acquainted with the relation of (one-way) necessitation that holds between those properties. It is not the case that one infers from a claim about x's having made a promise, in conjunction with some more general claim, that x has a reason to keep his or her promise. It is the very nature of a promise that generates the reason to do what one has promised to do.

As my discussion in the earlier parts of this chapter makes clear, many philosophers do not regard (P) as foundational, i.e., as justifiable noninferentially. Rather, they feel compelled to look for some more general and more basic claim from which the reason-giving nature of promise-making can be inferred. To such philosophers, Ross replied:

> To me it seems as self-evident as anything could be, that to make a promise, for instance, is to create a moral claim on us in someone else. Many readers will perhaps say that they do *not* know this to be true. If so, I certainly cannot prove it to them; I can only ask them to reflect again, in the hope that they will ultimately agree that they also know it to be true.[16]

In saying that a claim such as (P) is self-evident, Ross is certainly not saying that it is obvious to anyone who considers it. In fact, one of the best statements of what it is for a belief to be self-evident comes from Richard Price, who has a good claim to being the original intuitionist:

> The *second* ground of belief is INTUITION; by which I mean the mind's survey of its own ideas, and the relations between them, and the notice it takes of what is or is not true and false, consistent and inconsistent, possible and impossible in the natures of things. It is to this, . . . we owe our belief of all self-evident truths.[17]

The "natures of things" are not always obvious to us, and so self-evident truths, those that can be known without inference, will not always be obvious to us. And, as with mathematical truths, those that are obvious to me may not be obvious to you, and vice versa. While I may be better at grasping the nature of prime numbers and of friendship, you may be better at grasping the nature of three-dimensional figures and promises.

But this brings us to one of the primary arguments used against intuitionism: it is often claimed that appeal to self-evident truths is really just a cover for a dogmatic assertion of those beliefs for which one has no argument. Christine Korsgaard claims that "*all* he [the realist] can say is that it is *true* that this is what you ought to do. This is of course especially troublesome when the rightness of the action is supposed to be self-evident and known through intuition, so that there is nothing more to say about it."[18] A particularly stark statement of this objection comes from Alasdair MacIntyre, who describes the goings-on in the circle of intellectuals around Moore:

> And what if two observers disagree? Then, so the answer went, according to Keynes, either the two were focusing on different subject matters, without recognizing this, or one had perceptions superior to

the other. But, of course, as Keynes tells us, what was really happening was something quite other: 'In practice, victory was with those who could speak with the greatest appearance of clear, undoubting conviction and could best use the accents of infallibility' and Keynes goes on to describe the effectiveness of Moore's gasps of incredulity.[19]

But these sorts of objections to intuitionism provide only a caricature of the view. There is more that one can do than just merely assert the truths that one takes to be self-evident. First, one can attempt, as I have done at the beginning of this chapter, to show the difficulties inherent in views that try to derive the claim that is supposedly self-evident. Second, one can then do more to describe the relevant state of affairs that one takes to be reason-giving. If this were a book on reasons of fidelity, I would have a chapter on the nature of promising. But, given that this is a book on reasons of intimacy, I have a chapter on the nature of intimate relationships. If intimate relationships, by their very nature, ground reasons, we need to grasp the nature of intimate relationships in order to grasp that they ground reasons. And intimate relationships are complex, temporally extended states of affairs: grasping their nature is much more difficult than is grasping the nature of a three-sided closed plane figure. (I will show in Chapter 5 that it is very difficult to understand what is involved in grasping a concept or property such as that of intimacy.) Third, one can rebut objections to supposing that some claim such as (P) is self-evident.[20]

So, to follow out this third mode of response, it might be objected to the claim that we ought to regard as basic the claim that R has a reason to keep a promise that R has made, that what constitutes a promise can vary across cultures, so that an action that R performs in one culture will constitute the making of a promise while that same action will not constitute making a promise in some other culture. Given the cultural relativity of the signs or expressions of a promise, how could it be a synthetic necessary truth that making a promise creates a reason?

Actually, I think that the cultural variability in what are taken as the performances necessary and sufficient for the making of a promise helps to support rather than to undermine my thesis. Even if the ways in which people make and signify promises can differ, the point is that they are all ways of making and signifying *promises*. So I am happy to admit that the conventions for promise-making are socially determined and that some such set of conventions is necessary for the making of promises. Consider the case of marriage, for example: today people speak vows and sign paper to signify a marital commitment or promise. In the antebellum southern states, slaves would jump over a broomstick to signify such a commitment or promise. However, the commitment is the same in either case, no matter what the external signs used.

The variability in signs of promises can make it difficult to discern, in other cultures, what practices constitute promise-making practices. In part this is due to the fact that while we can often pick out individual cases of promises (or not), we have difficulty stating exactly what constitutes a promise. (A similar point holds for the concept of friendship.) And so a grasp of the synthetic necessary truth that promises create reasons depends upon a grasp of the nature of a promise. People can fail to grasp the former claim if they misunderstand what a promise is. In the case of reasons of intimacy, I have made an extensive attempt to bring the concept of intimacy before my reader's mind in order to be more sure to achieve assent to my claim that intimacy generates reasons. In order to try to eliminate disagreement in the case of promises, I would have to engage, as I have said, in a similar lengthy analysis of promising. A self-evident truth is always self-evident *for a particular agent R*, i.e., its status as justified noninferentially depends upon the epistemic set of the agent, on whether R fully grasps the concepts involved in the truth. So initial disagreement does nothing to undermine a claim to the effect that p is a basic moral truth. We have to wait until the end of the day, as it were, before we start worrying about persistent disagreement, and that 'day' may last years, given the time that philosophical analysis and exchange takes. Even at the end of that day, we have no way of being sure that all have grasped the relevant concepts.

So the intuitionist has several tools of defense at her disposal: responding to opposing views, detailed examination of the types of states of affairs mentioned in alleged self-evident truths, and rebuttal of objections aimed at a claim of self-evidence. If it is suggested that the intuitionist, despite these resources, is really unable to defend her view, what must be meant is that she cannot derive the alleged self-evident truth from other, more basic truths. But, of course, she would be refuting her own view by any such derivation, so the charge that lack of such derivation is devastating is just to beg the question against the intuitionist. Hopefully, this book constitutes a rebuttal of the claim that there is nothing that an intuitionist can do in order to support an assertion that a certain purported truth is self-evident. So I want to return to reasons of intimacy, and employ more of the tools at my disposal.

II. RELATIONSHIPS AND REASONS OF INTIMACY

I have already engaged in two of the types of defense that I have claimed are available to the intuitionist: in Chapter 2, I showed the inadequacy of two attempts—the Humean and the utilitarian—to derive reasons of intimacy from some more fundamental type of reason, and in Chapter 3, I described in detail the type of relationship that, I am claiming, grounds, by its very nature, reasons. What I want to do now is to use the model of reasons of fidelity to make more plausible the idea that reasons of intimacy are fundamental objective agent-relative reasons. First, I will show that reasons of intimacy are not straightforwardly reducible to reasons of fidelity. Second,

I will show that intimacy is analogous to promising in ways that encourage an analogous account of reasons of intimacy and reasons of fidelity.

Intimacy and Promises

So promising is an act that creates a relationship between promisor and promisee, a relationship upon which the property of being reason-giving supervenes.[21] It is a necessary truth that if a person makes a promise, then she has a reason to do that which she promised to do.[22] Reasons of fidelity are both objective and agent-relative: if Sam makes a promise to Jasmine to help her to move, then *Sam* has a reason in virtue of having made the promise. In general, x has a reason of fidelity to do p if and only if x has made a promise to some y (y not x) to do p. So the act of making a promise creates a reason for the agent who makes the promise, a reason not necessarily shared by others.[23] But this reason, while agent-relative, is not subjective—it is objective. Its existence does not depend upon the agent's desires or valuings. The bindingness of a promise does not depend on the agent's continuing to want or ever having wanted to do what she promised to do or to keep her promise. The object of the awareness upon which the reason supervenes is not a subjective state (or, not only a subjective state) of the agent.

It is perhaps one of the least controversial of ethical theses that a promise creates an obligation. The dispute is usually over why or how a promise creates an obligation, not whether it does. Even consequentialists and rational egoists such as Hobbes are eager, as we have seen, to have some explanation of reasons of fidelity. The difficulty with the accounts is that they are trying to explain something that cannot be explained in the way that they want. In Chapter 2, I showed that we can understand reasons of intimacy as neither agent-neutral nor subjective. We now have a rather unproblematic case of an objective agent-relative reason that we can use as a model for reasons of intimacy, the case of reasons of fidelity. The natural first thing to try, then, is a reduction of reasons of intimacy to reasons of fidelity.

There are several attractions to an account of reasons of intimacy that would understand them as instances of reasons of fidelity. First, we would obviate the need to add yet another type of reason (where the type of a reason is a matter of its grounds) to the many that we already have. Promising would remain the only instance in which an agent has agent-relative reasons not dependent upon her subjective states. For those who regard economy as a hallmark of good theory, any such reduction would be welcome. Second, there is something about promising that makes it a nice, neat model of the acquisition of reasons over and above the objective agent-neutral and the subjective agent-relative. As I have indicated in previous chapters, there is good motivation for both the agent-neutral and the subjective: these two categories seem to capture well our ideas about the externality of certain reasons and the internal motivating drive of others. If we are going to disrupt this nice dichotomy by adding yet another category, we need good (epistemic) reason to do so, and a persuasive understanding of the new type of reason. Promising seems to fit the bill. In fact, promising seems to be an act in which the agent simply steps forward, as it were, and voluntarily assumes an obligation or reason. So our reasons derive from some objective property (goodness), our own internal states (desires), or our acts of assuming reasons. Additional reasons that do not fit into one of the former two categories, then, must, it seems, be an instance of a reason of the third type.

In fact, it is not uncommon to try to explain the residue of reasons in relationships by appealing to some sort of contract or promise, either explicit, or, more plausibly, implicit. The objective goodness of my relationship with my best friend does not explain why my reasons of intimacy are peculiarly mine, while the desires that I have to care for my friend do not explain why we have reasons, in intimate relationships, that extend beyond our desires. Here the notion of a promise seems ready to solve the dilemma. In creating an intimate relationship with someone, we have thereby entered into certain agreements with that person, the force of which extends beyond our own desires. Thus, the reasons that arise in intimate relationships can be assimilated to the reasons that we have to, for example, care for our colleagues in certain ways: we have signed on to do so. In the latter case, the 'signing on' takes a very literal form, i.e., is accomplished via the signing of an employment contract. This sort of more formal 'signing on' is also prevalent in, for example, religious organizations, political parties, sports teams, and clubs of many diverse sorts, including book clubs, gardening clubs, athletic clubs, and support groups. The contractual assumption of obligations occurs in many other relationships in our society, including that between physician and/or therapist and patient, priest and confessor, attorney and client, and tax accountant and client.[24] Our normal understandings of such associations and relationships would have to be jettisoned if we did not admit irreducible reasons of fidelity[25] into our moral ontology: the objective value of the associations and relationships in conjunction with subjective desires of members will not explain the obligations of members any more than similar reasons could explain reasons of intimates to care for one another. So if contractual reasons seem to take up the slack in all of these other associations, then we can hope that they can do so in intimate relationships as well.[26]

It is clear that there is a great difference between intimate relationships and the paradigm instance of a promise or a contract. For example, when I say to a student that I promise to read her paper by Monday, there is a very clear, temporally discrete act that we can point to as the act by which I bound myself to read the paper by Monday. Further, the content of the obligation that I have assumed is also clear—I now have a reason to insure that I read the student's paper by Monday. But this disanalogy is not sufficient to rule out reasons of intimacy as reasons of fidelity. After all, consider other associations or relationships in which it seems clear that obligations or reasons are to be understood as reasons of fidelity, associations such as that of a philosophy department. When I accepted my job, certain terms were quite clearly spelled out to me; for example, it was made clear that I was expected to teach a certain number of courses each year, undertake administrative tasks, and be productive as a researcher. But notice how open-ended and vague this job description really is. Furthermore, there are unspoken expectations that I will be a *good colleague*. What exactly is involved in upholding standards of teaching, philosophical research, and collegiality is never spelled out. As professional philosophers in a certain cultural context, we all know what is expected and can state it in general terms, even if it is not detailed in any written or spoken employment contract. Episodes of crisis arise in departments when different interpretations of standards rise to the surface and cause conflict about what members are committed to doing. This sort of disagreement is a disagreement about what exactly was undertaken when one joined a department, not whether one in fact has any reasons of fidelity to one's colleagues.[27] So reasons of fidelity need not be as clearly delineated with respect to their content as they are in the example with which I opened this paragraph.

This, then, leaves open the possibility that reasons of intimacy are reasons of fidelity that are vaguer and more open ended than in straightforward instances of promising. We might understand friends as promising one another to care about and for one another. Crises in a friendship arise, under this understanding, when disagreements about what such caring requires arise. The fact that no single discrete act in which the words "I promise . . ." occur is also not a good reason to reject a reduction of reasons of intimacy to reasons of fidelity. Temporal extension or dislocation does not necessarily undermine a claim that an individual has voluntarily assumed reasons of fidelity, i.e., has made a promise or entered into a contract.[28] One can make it clear that by performing a series of acts, one thereby assumes an obligation to perform some further act: the nature of our shared understandings regarding which acts are promises or contracts is complex. However, it is also not the case that voluntary assumption is sufficient for the reasons assumed to be considered reasons of fidelity. In Chapter 7 I will show that an important element in a defense of reasons of intimacy involves showing that they meet the requirement of being voluntarily assumed. The further claim that I think that we ought to resist is that any such voluntary assumption makes a reason a reason of fidelity. In order to see why, we need to consider implicit promises, the sort that would have to be appealed to in order to reduce reasons of intimacy to reasons of fidelity.

It seems clear that most friends never explicitly make promises to each other that encompass all that we and they think that they owe one another in virtue of being friends. So they do not explicitly promise, i.e., they do not promise by saying or doing anything. The possibility remains open, however,

that they implicitly promise, i.e., promise by refraining from certain utter-
ances or acts. There are clear-cut situations in which such refraining can be
taken as a sign of a promise; for example, if Jasmine says to Sam, "Tell me if
you do not agree to help me to move," and then Sam remains silent, it seems
that Sam has made a promise to Jasmine to help her to move. As A. John
Simmons points out, what seems relevant in this case is:

1. Sam knows that this is a situation calling forth a promise or consent.
2. Sam knows when he should tell Jasmine if he does not agree to help
   her to move, and he has a reasonable and clearly delineated length of
   time in which to make up his mind and voice his dissent or unwillingness to help.
3. Sam knows what to do in order to indicate dissent.
4. Sam can dissent by performing some reasonable act and the consequences of so dissenting are not unreasonable.[29]

What counts as reasonable or unreasonable in condition 4 can, of course,
be debated, but there will be clear-cut cases: Jasmine cannot require that
Sam, who is 5'2", perform a slam dunk in order to indicate dissent, but she
can require him to say, "I will not help you to move." (I am assuming that
Sam is able to speak English.)

To make the picture of explicit (express) consent/promising vs. implicit
(tacit) consent/promising clearer, consider the classic example, Locke's
understanding of native-born citizens of a country giving tacit consent to
obey the laws of their country. Consider the following passage from Locke's
Second Treatise of Government:

> The difficulty is, what ought to be looked upon as a *tacit consent*,
> and how far it binds, *i.e.* how far any one shall be looked on to have
> consented, and thereby submitted to any government, where he has
> made no expressions of it at all. And to this I say, that every man, that
> hath any possessions, or enjoyment, of any part of the dominions of
> any government, doth thereby give his *tacit consent*, and is as far forth
> obliged to obedience to the laws of that government, during such enjoy-
> ment, as any one under it; . . . and in effect, it reaches as far as the very
> being of any one within the territories of that government.[30]

In effect, Locke is saying that if one fails to leave the territory of a given
government, one has thereby bound oneself to obey the laws of that government. So one's current position is residence—which involves enjoyment of
various benefits provided by the government—and staying in that position,
i.e., refraining from leaving, constitutes agreeing to obey the laws. Thus,
the way to dissent from obedience is to leave the territory. Here, consent
requires merely failing to alter one's situation, while dissent requires taking
some action to alter one's residence.

The case of friendship is more complicated, precisely because there is no clearly delineated 'starting point' of persons before they become friends, because there is no clear point at which they become friends as opposed to acquaintances, mere colleagues, or golfing buddies. Just try to say when a colleague or neighbor actually became your friend—a period of time will come before your mind such that it is clear that you were not friends at t_1, while you were clearly friends at t_{1+n}, but you will be unable to find some t_{1+m}, m less than n, such that t_{1+m} is the first point in time such that you were friends. And this is not merely an epistemic matter—it seems right to suppose that there really is a certain indeterminacy in our concept of friendship (an indeterminacy that will be discussed further in Chapter 5), such that there really is no t_{1+m} that constitutes the first temporal instant of friendship.[31] So there is no point at which we can say to someone, 'either refrain from that specific action or you will be taken to have consented to all of the obligations of caring that friendship entails.' The choice is not as clear-cut as either continuing to reside in the United States—and be obligated to obey the law—or leave the country and avoid obligation to its laws.

These features of friendship do not, however, constitute any sort of decisive objection to understanding reasons of intimacy as instances of reasons of fidelity. All that follows is that persons would have to tread more carefully, as it were, when they are in the realm of actions that could be the beginning of a series of actions/interactions that constitute friendship. We can all be expected to recognize the complexities of friendship, and, thus, we can be expected to know that once we start down a certain path, we may find ourselves in a position such that, before we know it, we are friends with someone. So the advocate of the promising/consent model of reasons of intimacy can acknowledge the epistemic difficulties inherent in friendship without denying that not refraining from doing certain things for another person or not refraining from interacting with her in certain kinds of ways constitutes consenting to care for her.

The more important worry about the promising/consent model of reasons of intimacy is similar to the one that Hume raised for the Lockean consent theory of political obligation: (i) Is the detour through reasons of fidelity really necessary to account for our reasons to obey the law?, and (ii) Is the appeal to reasons of fidelity faithful to our understanding of why we are bound to obey the law? Hume, of course, answered 'no' to both questions.[32] The details of Hume's response to Locke need not be explored here. However, my argument concerning reasons of intimacy will proceed via an exploration of how we understand our reasons of intimacy in order to establish that the detour through reasons of fidelity is unnecessary and misleading. My conclusion will be that we need to recognize a range of types of commitments of which reasons of fidelity are only one form. To attempt to squeeze a commitment such as friendship into the model of promising/contracting/consenting is to oversimplify and distort the phenomena.

Consider a related sort of situation, that of a parent's obligation to care for his or her children. It does seem right that the voluntary bringing into being of a helpless child creates certain obligations over and above those that any persons have to care for the vulnerable: it is certainly not the case that I have no obligations toward other people's children, but it is also certainly the case that I do not have the same range of types of obligations that the parents themselves have. The act of voluntarily bringing into the world a child generates certain objective agent-relative reasons. This is a case in which an agent knows or ought to know that undertaking certain actions binds her in certain ways.[33] How or to what extent she or he is bound can vary from cultural context to cultural context, because it is not 'blood' alone that creates obligations. So, for example, in the Trobriand Islands, men are understood as responsible for sharing the nurturing of the children of the women whose companions they are, even if they are not the fathers: in fact, the Trobriand Islanders reject any notion of men as necessary for the creation of children. In the Trobriand Islands, then, it is a different set of actions that binds men to care for children than in some Western communities.[34] We can, of course, argue about which system has better overall consequences, but, within the context of each existent system, it remains a fact that men acquire obligations through performing different actions.[35]

It could be said, then, that certain actions constitute the making of a promise to care for a child: in the West, this is often understood as being done by not refraining from having a child. Our society can be seen as in a serious crisis right now as a result of confusion or disagreement about who needs to indicate dissent if she or he is not to be bound. For example, does the mere impregnating of a woman bind a man to the child in certain ways? Does the unavailability of abortion indicate that a woman has not voluntarily brought a child into the world? How are we to assess the obligations of those who undertake the risks inherent in sexual intercourse, with or without the use of contraceptives? But, even putting aside the worries raised by these questions, we can see that we are forcing parental obligations into an inappropriate straitjacket by trying to cast them as reasons of fidelity. To whom has a parent made a promise or entered into a contract? Certainly not the child: children are not rational in the sense that is necessary for being a promisee, anymore than are Chihuahuas. Perhaps, then, one has promised 'society' to care for the child. Whether or not this is plausible within our culture, what would we say of parents who, wanting a second child, have one, against the dictates of a society that allows the having of no more than one child? Don't the parents have extra reason to protect the child against state-endorsed infanticide over and above those that anyone has to protect the vulnerable? The conceiving or bearing of a child is not an implicit or an explicit promise to anyone, but, under certain conditions, it is an action that creates certain obligations.

What the example of parental obligations to children shows is that we are forced to revise our understanding of such obligations if we feel compelled to construe them not just as analogous to reasons of fidelity but as mere instances of reasons of fidelity. And I think that it is quite clear that the same is true of reasons of intimacy. The drive to assimilate reasons of intimacy to reasons of fidelity arises, I believe, because of an important similarity between the two cases: both are grounded in voluntary actions of the agent, in the latter case making various conventional expressions (active or passive) and in the former case interacting with another person in friendship-constituting ways over an extended period of time. But instead of assimilating obligations such as those between friends or those of parents to their children to reasons of fidelity, we can instead just recognize that we can commit or bind ourselves in different ways, and promising/contracting is only one of those ways.

What I am suggesting is that we understand giving birth to a child (under certain kinds of circumstances), developing a friendship with someone, and making a promise or entering a contract, as different ways in which one can assume a role that grounds objective agent-relative reasons to act in certain ways. Voluntarily assumed roles that ground reasons, including the role of promise-maker and the role of friend, are all forms of commitment. One can commit or bind oneself by using certain kinds of conventions for promising/contracting, by becoming someone's friend, etc.

There are at least two potential worries about what I have said so far. First, it might be denied that I have made out a case for the claim that 'commitment' is not just another term for 'promise,' and, thus, that I have failed to establish that not all objective agent-relative reasons are or can be reduced to reasons of fidelity. In a way, I agree with this charge, because I think that fully establishing my claim would involve doing far more than I have done to explicate a complete understanding of the nature of promises and contracts. Doing such would be a book unto itself, a book that would involve a full analysis of the notion of voluntary action, something that I cannot claim to be able to undertake at this time. But, perhaps more importantly, I am not sure that a clear and sharp line can be drawn between a promise or contract as such and other sorts of commitments. Commitments occur on a continuum, some among those that are not promises nonetheless being much more similar to promises than are others such as intimate relationships. For now, I will just conclude by saying: there are different sorts of actions that have the common feature of being such that reasons supervene upon their performance. The simplest and least controversial of such reasons are promises or contracts, those that are simply and straightforwardly the assumption of an obligation (either through action or inaction). Other sorts of commitments are actions that entail the assumption of an obligation without themselves actually being such an assumption. Where to draw the line is not always clear.

Second, the reader is probably hoping for a general criterion for distinguishing actions that are commitments. Unfortunately, here the reader is going to be disappointed. I do not want to make the claim that such a criterion could not be offered or that there is no such criterion; however, I can quite confidently assert that *I* cannot offer such a criterion to my reader. I do have my doubts as to whether there are any conditions, both necessary and sufficient, for an action's (or series of actions) constituting a commitment. Of course, one necessary condition on such actions is that they are voluntary and that the agent knows or ought to have known that such actions entail obligations. It is the sufficient conditions for a commitment that I doubt exist. All that we can do is to subject to analysis cases of actions that we think constitute commitments and see if it is really plausible to suppose that such is the case.

III. DEFENDING THE INTUITIONIST COMMITMENT VIEW

In Section I of this chapter, I argued that familiar accounts of promising—namely, the Kantian, utilitarian, and expectations account—are not as intuitively satisfying as the intuitionist account. In Section II I argued that promising provides a good model for reasons of intimacy, although it is misleading and artificial to understand reasons of intimacy as reducible to reasons of fidelity. In light of this, I suggested that we view both friendship and promise-making (and the creation of a child) as types of commitments, i.e., as voluntarily undertaken actions that ground objective agent-relative reasons.

If we continue to take as given objective agent-neutral reasons and subjective agent-relative reasons, then we have three types of reasons once we add on the objective agent-relative. The first type of reason, grounded on an agent's awareness of objective value, captures our concept of a reason that is in some way external to our particular concerns and goals. The second type, grounded on an agent's awareness of her own desires, captures our concept of a reason internally connected to motivation and to our own projects and ends. The third type captures our sense that our choices often carry moral implications, especially when those choices bring us into certain kinds of relations to other people—who we have made ourselves has moral significance over and above what is objectively, impartially valuable, and over and above our ever-changing psychology. Who I am gives me reasons that no one else has.

In recent years several philosophers have argued that who we are is reason-giving, even when the relationships that determine our roles are not voluntarily undertaken. In Chapter 7 I will argue that we need to abandon that part of commonsense morality that would allow commitments to extend to unchosen social roles. But before we broaden the scope of our inquiry beyond friendship, I want to explore some interesting implications for moral theory of the complex nature of friendship.

5 Friendship and Particularism

The intuitionism that I defended in Chapter 4 is a moral epistemology based on the status of certain moral truths as synthetic truths stating the relationship of necessitation between certain states of affairs and the property of being reason-giving. These truths can be known directly, i.e., without inference from other, more basic truths. If one grasps the nature of the relevant state of affairs, one can—but may not—thereby grasp that that state of affairs is reason-giving for some individual.

This was the picture presented by early twentieth-century intuitionists, in particular, G. E. Moore, H. A. Prichard, and W. D. Ross. A major reason why many people have rejected the intuitionist picture is that it seems to imply an oversimplified understanding of the nature of moral reasoning. Moral reasoning, critics say, involves complex capacities of sensitivity to other persons and their needs and goals, and to one's own situation and place in a web of relationships. This is then contrasted with the supposed intuitionist approach to moral reasoning: sitting in one's armchair grasping basic, abstract moral truths and then going out in the world and applying them to situations in the way that one grasps axioms of Euclidean geometry and then uses them in encounters with real-world triangles and trapezoids. Moral reasoning is seen by the critics of intuitionism as much more bottom-up—going from particular instances and then, if at all, abstracting to general truths—than geometrical reasoning, which is top-down from abstract and very general axioms to more particular conclusions. Moral reasoning also seems to involve the use of sympathetic capacities and emotional engagement rather than the purely intellectual or cognitive apprehension involved in a grasp of Moorean nonnatural qualities or Platonic forms.

These kinds of worries about intuitionist moral reasoning can be blamed, at least in part, on Moore, Prichard, and Ross themselves. They relied—as did I in the previous chapter—on the well-worn analogy to mathematics, an analogy that was used by Price over two hundred years ago. But an analogy is just that, an analogy—it suggests similarities between two domains without insisting that they are identical in all respects. Moral reasoning *does* involve capacities beyond those employed in mathematics and geometry, precisely because the subject matter of the former is people and animals capable of states such as pain, pleasure, hope, and fear, rather than numbers and rectangles that have no intentional states or emotions. In order to understand both theoretical and practical moral reasoning, we need to understand the nature of the states of affairs that have moral properties such as being good/bad and being reason-giving. If those states of affairs are complex and graspable only with the help of imaginative and sympathetic capacities, then moral reasoning will require the use of capacities beyond the purely cognitive.

In this chapter I will show how and why moral reasoning on an intuitionist model does not at all match the mathematical or geometrical model of sitting in one's comfy chair and just thinking hard. I will do this by examining the recent debate in moral theory regarding what is known as *particularism*. I will first try to pull apart the various theses that seem to be defended under the guise of particularism, and then, I will return to friendship to show that, on either of two plausible understandings, the nature of our concept of friendship supports certain kinds of particularism. At the end of this chapter, I hope that the reader will have come to see that the intuitionist picture of moral reasoning is much more complex than its critics would allow.

I. THREE TYPES OF PARTICULARISM

Particularists are not united amongst themselves as to the central particularist thesis, or, if they accept more than one particularist thesis, as to what the relationship is between the various theses.[1] So we encounter particularists defending all of the following, in various combinations: there are no general moral truths, there are no codifiable moral rules, there are no necessary connections between normative and nonnormative properties, and, moral agents ought to make (or, actually do make) decisions by paying attention to particulars rather than by attempting to apply general rules or truths. So particularism is not itself a theory, but, rather, a family of theses concerning the nature of moral knowledge, of moral ontology, and of moral practice. Further, the various particularist theses need to be stated as theses about a given normative property, such as goodness/badness, reason-givingness, or rightness/wrongness, thereby creating yet more varieties of particularism. In what follows, I will focus on the property of being reason-giving, not only because that property is the main focus of this book, but also because many particularists themselves focus on that property.[2]

Epistemological Particularism

Jay Garfield defends what he calls 'a particularist moral epistemology,' and claims that the debate between particularists and generalists ought to be located "firmly in the domain of moral epistemology."[3] All particularists seem committed to some epistemological claims, although not all take them as fundamental to particularism, and, I will argue, they ought not to take them as fundamental—doing so leaves their views inadequately motivated.

We can understand epistemological[4] particularism as taking, roughly, four different forms:

- *Linguistic Epistemological Particularism:* We do not have the capacity to linguistically formulate or articulate general truths about the relationship between being reason-giving and other (either normative or nonnormative) features of the world.
- *Representational Epistemological Particularism:* We do not have the capacity to represent, in any form, general truths about the relationship between being reason-giving and other features of the world.
- *Justificatory Epistemological Particularism:* We do not have the capacity to know (or to have justified beliefs about) general truths about the relationship between being reason-giving and other features of the world.
- *Knowledge Acquisition Epistemological Particularism:* We do not come to know (or to have justified beliefs about) particular instances of being reason-giving on the basis of knowing (or having justified beliefs about) general truths about the relationship between being reason-giving and other either normative or nonnormative features of the world.

I have stated the varieties of epistemological particularism in terms of general moral truths, rather than in terms of general rules or principles. McKeever and Ridge (see note 2), in their taxonomy of particularist theses, speak in terms of moral principles, but seem to mean by 'principle' what I mean by 'truth,' given that they understand principles as having a truth value, in fact, as being true. If one is an objectivist and a generalist about morality, then, supposedly, one will think that there are general truths about moral reality, say, about the features of the world that are good, about which actions are right, about how moral agents ought to behave, about what a virtuous character is, etc. For practical purposes, the generalist may think that certain kinds of rules, stated in the form of imperatives, can be derived[5] from those truths in conjunction with various empirical claims. So, for example, a utilitarian will regard the principle of utility as either stating a criterion of or defining right action, but might then insist that we need to formulate what Mill calls "corollaries from the principle of utility" and "secondary" principles that we use to guide our conduct,[6] such as 'Do not kill innocent people and harvest their organs.'[7]

All of the varieties of epistemological particularism are theses about *general* moral truths, so we need to have some understanding of what a *general* truth is. I will take general truths to be truths that relate in some way properties that admit, at least in principle, of multiple instantiations.

So, for example, the claim that Diane is a philosopher is not a general truth even though it could be restated as a universal generalization, i.e., as the claim that for all x, if x has the 'property'[8] of being Diane then x has the property of being a philosopher, because the property of being Diane does not admit of more than one instantiation. Being capable of restatement as a universal generalization is a necessary but not sufficient condition, then, of being a general truth. In the four types of epistemological particularism presented, then, we are to assume that the property of being reason-giving is capable of being instantiated more than once, and the truths with which we are concerned are ones that can be stated as universal generalizations *and* that relate the property of being reason-giving to some other normative or nonnormative properties that allow, at least in principle, of multiple instantiations.

Now, one could simply refer to moral experience in an attempt to support one or more of the epistemological theses. But, as philosophers, we ought not to rest satisfied with one of these theses without exploring various ontological theses. After all, the natural question to ask, once any version of epistemological particularism begins to look plausible for some reason, is "*Why* do we lack the capacity to linguistically formulate/articulate, to represent, or to know (have justified beliefs about) general truths about the relationship between being a reason and other normative or nonnormative properties?" The explanation is obviously not that we cannot know general truths: we do know general truths about numbers, cats, bachelors, etc.[9] So there must be something about the relationship between the property of being a reason and other properties that explains our inability to formulate, to represent, or to know general truths about that relationship.[10]

Ontological Particularism

An ontological particularist thesis will provide us with an explanation of whichever one or more theses of epistemological particularism is being defended. So we can begin with what would be the simplest and most straightforward explanation of an inability to formulate, to represent, or to know general truths about the relationship between the property of being a reason and other normative or nonnormative properties:

* *No Reliable Connections Ontological Particularism:* There are no necessary or universal lawlike connections between other features of the world and the property of being a reason.

According to this first version of ontological particularism, there are no reliable connections of any sort between being a reason and other properties. So the occurrence of the property of being a reason would be a completely random matter, such that we would be unable to predict where or when we would have reasons to act. Obviously, if there were no such necessary or lawlike connections, there would be no general truths describing such connections, and, thus, we would be unable to articulate (Linguistic Epistemological Particularism), represent (Representational Epistemological Particularism), or know (Justificatory Epistemological Particularism) those nonexistent truths.

Sometimes Jonathan Dancy makes claims that certainly suggest something like the no reliable connections ontological thesis:

> The leading thought behind particularism is the thought that the behaviour of a reason (or of a consideration that serves as a reason) in a new case cannot be predicted from its behaviour elsewhere. The way in which the consideration functions *here* either will or at least may be affected by other considerations here present. So there is no ground for the hope that we can find out here how that consideration functions *in general*.[11]

> I maintain that *all* reasons are *capable* of being altered by changes in context—that there are none whose nature as reasons is necessarily immune to changes elsewhere.[12]

Whether we interpret Dancy as accepting the thesis of no reliable connections depends upon whether he thinks that there are necessary (or some sort of lawlike) connections between the property of being a reason and the "other considerations" or "changes in context" that can affect its "behaviour." If there are such connections, then Dancy is really advocating Ontological Holism.

And we should interpret Dancy as holding Ontological Holism rather than the no reliable connections thesis, because to read him as holding the latter would be uncharitable, given the implausibility of the no reliable connections thesis. A more extreme version of the no reliable connections thesis would deny not only necessary and universal lawlike connections, but even accidental lawlike or probabilistic connections. I have not listed such an extreme version because it seems absurd to deny that there are facts about statistical correlations between normative and other properties. The no reliable connections thesis as stated does not deny such accidental correlations, but, nonetheless, does assert that those are the only kinds of correlations that exist between nonnormative and normative features of the world. So we are left to consider each situation in all of its particularity and then see whether or not it happens to be reason-giving here and now. And, if the no reliable connections thesis were true, the nature of a situation would not guarantee its being reason-giving or not—it could go either way. We have no epistemic reason to suppose that the distribution of normative properties is random in this way, and there are more attractive versions of ontological particularism, so we should move on.

- *Too Complex to Formulate Ontological Particularism:* There are necessary or lawlike connections between other features of the world and the property of being reason-giving, but the relationship is too complex to be formulable (or, in *Too Complex to Represent Ontological Particularism*, represented) by human beings.

The too complex to formulate thesis would provide a nice explanation of Linguistic Epistemological Particularism. Human capacities to state or to formulate truths obviously have their limits, so it is possible that the complexity of the normative situation eludes our finite capacities. Similarly, the too complex to represent thesis would provide an explanation of Representational Epistemological Particularism. Also, it certainly does seem that the too complex to represent thesis commits us to Justificatory Epistemological Particularism: it is difficult to see how we could know or even believe that which we are incapable of representing, in any form, to ourselves. Whether the too complex to formulate thesis commits us to Justificatory Epistemological Particularism depends on whether we can know or justifiably believe a truth or claim that we are unable to formulate linguistically. It certainly seems possible that we cannot state or articulate everything that we know: we might be able to grasp certain complex properties for which we have no linguistic terms. In fact, our next version of ontological particularism constitutes an explanation of how this might be the case:

- *No Concepts for Determinate Features Ontological Particularism:* There are necessary or lawlike connections between determinate features of the world and the property of being reason-giving, but we do not have subtle or fine-grained enough terms or concepts to be able to state or to articulate (or, in *No Concepts for Determinate Features**, to represent) the determinate features as opposed to the determinables that ground the property of being reason-giving.

Consider as an analogy our color vocabulary. Some of us, of course, have larger color vocabularies than others, but none of us, I suspect, has a vocabulary sufficient for distinguishing all of the shades of blue in the world or even, probably, all of the shades of blue that we are capable of distinguishing visually. So we may be able to grasp certain distinctions between colors and relationships between colors—for example, whether one shade is brighter than another, whether one shade complements another, which of two shades is closer to a third one—without being able to articulate what we grasp or know. And, given the range of shades of colors, it is plausible to suppose that our finite capacities simply will not allow us to make or to articulate all of the distinctions that there are in the world. Perhaps, then, the base properties upon which being reason-giving supervenes are like color properties: we may not be able to articulate all of the distinctions that we can grasp (Linguistic, but not Justificatory Epistemological Particularism), or we may not be able to grasp all of the distinctions in the world (both Linguistic and Justificatory Epistemological Particularism).

Similarly, we may not be able to represent to ourselves all of the possible shades of blue (Representational Epistemological Particularism) and thus may not be able to grasp truths concerning those shades (Justificatory Epistemological Particularism). In the moral realm, this sort of situation would result in certain kinds of ineliminable gaps in our moral knowledge.

The next ontological option is one that may not be held by any actual particularist:

- *Non-repeatable Particulars Ontological Particularism:* The only necessary connections between nonnormative properties and the property of being reason-giving are between certain non-repeatable particulars in the world and the property of being reason-giving. Thus, the statement of the necessary connection will not be a general truth, because it involves essential reference to a non-repeatable property or irreducibly particular entity.

Consider a certain non-repeatable action, say, Diane's saving a child from drowning at spatial coordinates (x, y, z) and at time t. Suppose that such an action is reason-giving. Even though we could formulate a universal generalization describing such actions as reason-giving—for all x, such that x is an action with the property of being Diane's saving of a child at (x, y, z) at t, x is reason-giving—this universal generalization is not a general truth because the property of being Diane's saving of a child at (x, y, and z) at t is not capable of more than one instantiation. So even if this universal generalization is a necessary truth, it is not a general truth, and so we are committed to all four versions of epistemological particularism: if there are no general truths, we cannot articulate, represent, know, or apply any general truths.

One reason for thinking that some particularists hold the non-repeatable particulars thesis is that it would provide an explanation for certain claims that they explicitly make. For example, Brad Hooker correctly says of some particularists that they "do not deny that moral properties supervene on nonmoral properties. What they do deny . . . is the attempt to determine a moral conclusion about one case by appeal to a conclusion about another case."[13] This seems to be the upshot of Dancy's complaint against what he calls "switching arguments."[14] An explanation of the invalidity of this sort of inference would be that no other action can share the relevant feature of the one currently being described as reason-giving, because the relevant feature is non-repeatable. So we cannot look to see if another case has the relevant feature and then conclude, on that basis, that it also is reason-giving, because no other case can possibly have all of the relevant features upon which the reason-givingness supervenes.

The non-repeatable particulars thesis seems more plausible than the no reliable connections thesis for the simple reason that the former, unlike the latter, at least allows for the possibility of necessary connections between other features of the world and the property of being reason-giving. According to the no reliable connections thesis, it is mere happenstance that any given action or state of affairs is reason-giving: it is equally possible that it not have been so. According to the non-repeatable particulars thesis, insofar as some particular action or state of affairs is reason-giving, it could not have been otherwise. So on the non-repeatable particulars thesis, as opposed to the no reliable connections thesis, we can infer the reason-givingness of an action or a state of affairs from the nature of the action or the state of affairs, and that seems to be an attractive feature of the non-repeatable particulars thesis.

Our fifth version of ontological particularism is *Ontological Holism:*

- *Ontological Holism:* Whether some state of affairs, action, or event, has the property of being reason-giving is, at least in part, a function of features of the world external to that state of affairs, action, or event.

According to Ontological Holism, then, any truth of the form "x is reason-giving" has implicit *ceteris paribus* clauses, and the relevant *ceteris paribus* clauses may be highly complex, thus bringing into play the too complex to formulate (or represent) thesis (and, thus, Linguistic Epistemological Particularism or both Representational and Justificatory Epistemological Particularism). Suppose, for the moment, that we can make sense of the claim that while being reason-giving is a property of x, it is only a property of x if conditions y and z obtain. If we can state conditions y and z, then we can state general truths about the relationship between being reason-giving and other features of the world. These truths will have the form: x is reason-giving whenever both y and z obtain. (Of course, once one realizes this, one should also wonder why it is not the case that the reason supervenes upon the state of affairs involving x, y, and z, and the appropriate relations between them. See my further discussion of Ontological Holism.) And if y and z can be stated, it is unclear why we would be unable to know or to justifiably believe such general moral truths. Thus, I think that an ontological holist such as Dancy, insofar as he accepts Linguistic and/or Representational and Justificatory Epistemological Particularism, should combine his Holism with the too complex to formulate (or represent) thesis.

Although I am primarily concerned with the versions of particularism that are versions of either ontological particularism or epistemological particularism, I think that it is important to discuss a third class of particularist theses, what I call *Practical Particularism.*

Practical Particularism

Much of the motivation for the ontological and epistemological particularist theses derives from putative truths about how people actually go about making moral judgments and engaging in moral debate. So the following practical particularist theses, i.e., theses about the role of general truths in actual moral decision-making, are more likely to be offered in support of one of the epistemological or ontological particularist theses rather than to be offered as the conclusion of an argument. All of these claims require empirical support of one sort or another.

- *Moral Reasoning Practical Particularism:* People do not use general truths about reasons to reach normative conclusions about particular situations or to make decisions about how to act in particular situations.[15]
- *Moral Action Practical Particularism:* People are more likely to act rightly (or rationally) if they do not make decisions on the basis of general truths about reasons, even if such truths can be articulated, represented, and/or known or justifiably believed.
- *Application of Truths Practical Particularism:* Even if we can know or articulate general truths about reasons, such general truths are too difficult and/or complicated to apply, or, at least, to apply in a timely manner.

Of course, if Representational Epistemological Particularism is true, Moral Reasoning Practical Particularism follows: we certainly cannot make appeal to truths that we cannot represent in any way. But Moral Reasoning Practical Particularism does not, however, follow from either Linguistic or Justificatory Epistemological Particularism: we might be able to non-linguistically represent certain truths that we can reliably use to guide our conduct, and we might use general truths to guide our conduct without being justified in accepting or using those truths.

The connection between the various versions of epistemological particularism and Moral Action and Application of Truths Practical Particularism, however, is unclear. We would need to know more about the content of general moral truths, and various facts about the world and human capacities before we could support some claim about our chances of acting rightly or in a timely manner if general truths are appealed to. For example, consider certain claims made by utilitarians (who are generally taken to be epistemological generalists, of the linguistic, representational, and justificatory variety). Utilitarians do seem to think that people use general claims to guide their behavior, but that these claims are greatly simplified derivations from the principle of utility. So, for example, ordinary people use the claim "Killing innocent people is wrong" to guide their behavior. But, according to the utilitarian, this claim is not a truth because, as stated, it is false. However, it is probably the case that people will more often act rightly if they do not appeal directly to the principle of utility, but, instead, use these simplified, strictly speaking, false claims, to guide their behavior (Moral Action Practical Particularism). Further, any general truths about reasons other than the principle of utility itself would have so many *ceteris paribus* clauses attached that such rules would be utterly useless in moral deliberation (Application of Truths Practical Particularism); for example, a general truth would take the form "Killing innocent people is wrong, unless more lives are saved in the long run, those lives collectively are more valuable than the life of the one, etc." Either the truth is too complicated to be useful or it becomes a restatement of the principle of utility: Killing innocent people is wrong unless it promotes greater intrinsic value in the long run than does refraining from killing innocent people.

I think that Moral Reasoning Practical Particularism is probably the most important practical particularist thesis for those who want to defend some version of ontological or epistemological particularism. But notice that the truth of Moral Reasoning Practical Particularism can be used by a paradigm generalist, the utilitarian, as support for her own view. So I think that ontological and epistemological particularism ought to be considered more central to any discussion of the distinction between generalism and particularism; thus, in what follows I will focus on the ontology and epistemology of particularism.

But I think that something like Moral Reasoning Practical Particularism is what critics of intuitionism have in mind when they accuse it of getting moral reasoning wrong. Although I will not directly defend this version of practical particularism, I think that it will become clear, given my discussions of both ontological and epistemological particularism, why the intuitionist who takes friendship seriously should be amenable to it.

II. THE PARTICULARITIES OF FRIENDSHIP

In his discussion of particularism, Dancy takes W. D. Ross as a prime example of a paradigm generalist. Given that the view that I am defending is, in broad outline, the same as that defended by Ross, it would seem that I must reject both epistemological and ontological particularism in all of their forms. But, as I will show in this section, I think that Dancy misconstrues the commitments of intuitionism with respect to particularism. Part of the fault for this misconstrual must be placed at the feet of Moore and Ross, the intuitionists themselves.

Dancy never makes it clear whether particularism in the moral realm is a result of the nature of the property of being a reason, of the nature of the properties that ground (or constitute) being a reason, or of the nature of the relationship between the former and the latter properties. Because he states his particularism as a general thesis about reasons, I am inclined to think that he would say that it is the very nature of being a reason that makes particularism true. In the rest of this chapter, I will argue that, at least in the case of friendship, it is the nature of the subvening base property rather than the nature of the property of being reason-giving that makes certain of the particularist theses true. Moore and Ross never did thorough enough examination of friendship to explore the consequences that such a relationship has for the nature of moral truth and moral knowledge. The complexity of friendship creates corresponding complexity with respect to truth and knowledge.

Friendship and Ontological Particularism: The Complexity of the Base

So let us begin with our ontological particularist theses. Clearly, intuitionists will not accept the no reliable connections thesis, the claim that there are no necessary or lawlike connections between other features of the world and the property of being a reason. Both Moore and Ross held that certain truths, such as 'Friendship is intrinsically valuable' or 'We have *prima facie* obligations to promote the good of our friends,' are synthetic necessary truths. These synthetic necessary truths describe the relation of necessitation that holds between the relationship of friendship and either the property of being intrinsically valuable or the property of being *prima facie* reasongiving. Any relationship that is a friendship will, in virtue of its nature, have the property of being intrinsically valuable or the property of being reasongiving. But, I will argue, the nature of friendship forces us to rethink the nature of claims such as 'Friendship is intrinsically valuable.' It turns out that the question as to whether that claim is a general truth is much more complicated than even the particularists seem to realize. The complexity of that question, however, will not lend support to the no reliable connections thesis, at least not in its current form: we will need to revise our understanding of the content of certain necessary truths, but we will be justified in continuing to believe that there are such general necessary truths.

So let's begin with the too complex to formulate (represent) and the no concepts for determinate features theses, both of which involve the denial of the no reliable connections thesis. Recall those theses:

- *Too Complex to Formulate Ontological Particularism:* There are necessary or lawlike connections between other features of the world and the property of being reason-giving, but the relationship is too complex to be formulable (or represented) by human beings.
- *No Concepts for Determinate Features Ontological Particularism:* There are necessary or lawlike connections between determinate features of the world and the property of being reason-giving, but we do not have subtle or fine-grained enough terms or concepts to be able to state or to articulate (or to represent) the determinate features as opposed to the determinables that ground the property of being reason-giving.

Consider friendship again. Unlike, for example, pleasure, friendship is not a momentary state or experience. Rather, friendships are necessarily temporally extended affairs, involving many different types of interactions between two people. Some friendships involve the sharing of many details of the parties' inner lives, others do not. Some friendships involve the parties wanting to spend (or, actually spending) a great deal of time together, others do not. Some friendships require exclusivity with respect to some one or more features of the relationship, others do not.[16] Some friendships involve very deep attitudes of love and attachment, others do not.

I am not claiming that there are no elements necessary to every friendship. It may well be the case that no relationship in which the two parties loathed one another and wished ill to one another could qualify as a friendship, no matter how much of their inner lives the two share with one another. What I am pointing to is that friendships can vary in degree with respect to any of their features, even with respect to those that are necessary features of any friendship. A serious diminution in, say, affection, may be compensated for by a shared sense of humor or shared revelations about secret fantasies. So it seems to me at least plausible to claim that there are no necessary *and* sufficient conditions of friendship, because, for example, affection can be offset by emotional distance (if two people don't really understand each other, can we really understand them as caring deeply about one another?), love of a charming personality can be offset by revulsion at lack of moral strength, a desire to spend time together can be offset by a reluctance to offer solace and aid in times of need, etc. For all of these reasons, I resisted claiming in Chapter 3 that I was offering necessary and sufficient conditions for a friendship relation, i.e., I resisted claiming that I was doing conceptual analysis.

Complexity and Family Resemblance

If I am right about the way in which friendship is a complex concept, it becomes interesting to explore a couple of novel ways of understanding that concept. Since Wittgenstein we are all familiar with the notion of a family resemblance concept. Consider the example of a sport. We have some paradigm examples such as baseball and tennis. But is synchronized swimming a sport? What about rhythmic gymnastics or ice dancing? Each of the three latter activities has some features in common with our paradigms, but they are also significantly different. For rhythmic gymnastics to be correctly described as a sport, it must bear appropriate relations to baseball and tennis. But convention and agreement will play a role in determining what counts as an appropriate relation. We may be unwilling to extend our concept of a sport to, say, chess, but that is a decision we must make.[17] Of course, we may make decisions that are, in some sense, bad: perhaps our concept becomes less useful insofar as it no longer tracks certain features of the world that we care about and want to set apart, or it no longer tracks features in the world in which we *ought* to be interested or about which we *ought* to care. Perhaps the concept becomes so diffuse so as not to group things together in any way that suits our interests or needs (considered either subjectively or objectively). But in neither case will we have made a mistake with respect to the concept considered as such.

If the concept of friendship is like the concept of a sport, then, in an important sense, there is no determinate complete answer to the question, 'What is a friendship?' It may well be the case that our concept of friendship is such that no relationship that failed to involve, say, affection of some sort between the parties and mutual concern would qualify as a friendship. But there will be relationships that involve affection and concern and yet are not friendships, because the other components of the relationship offset those features. How we are willing to extend beyond our current paradigms is not a matter that we can determinately predict in advance. If friendship is conceived of in this way, then the project of Chapter 3 was to draw out some elements of paradigm cases to give us a baseline of comparison for future relationships in determining whether they are friendships.

If we adopt the family resemblance understanding of friendship, we are not committed to the no reliable connections thesis, but we should be sympathetic to something like the too complex to formulate (represent) thesis. Even though our concept of friendship is a concept that is led by human decision in ways that the concept, say, of color is not, our decisions will be guided by features of the world, beginning with our decisions about the current case's relation to paradigms. Our paradigm cases of friendship are clearly cases of intrinsically valuable or reason-giving relationships. As we extend our concept out from the center, we will be guided by our paradigms, and so we are being guided by relationships that ground value or reasons. Will our concept be able to be stretched to relationships that do not ground value or reasons? This can only be viewed as an open question, because what decisions we will make in the future is a contingent matter.

So what, then, is the status of the claim that friendship is intrinsically valuable or reason-giving? It will not be a necessary truth, given the possibility of the extension of the concept of friendship to include relationships that do not ground either value or reasons. The too complex to formulate (or represent) thesis would follow naturally from this picture of friendship. There may well be combinations of nonnormative features in the world such that whenever those combinations are realized they ground value and/ or reasons. But perhaps we have not latched onto that combination, or are unable to formulate or represent it. Thus, we work with our family resemblance concept, perhaps so far also capturing in our net valuable/reason-giving relationships. It remains an open question the extent to which our concept parallels a possible concept that is a concept that includes in its extension only valuable/reason-giving relationships. But notice that this does not undermine the claim that there are synthetic necessary truths about intimate relationships and reasons. I will be able to grasp that *this* friendship is reason-giving, and the claim that *this* friendship is reason-giving will be a synthetic necessary truth. Also, any relationship that is relevantly similar to this friendship will also be reason-giving, so if I can grasp the relevant similarities between two relationships, I can move from 'this one is reason-giving' to 'that one is reason-giving.'

Notice that the same sorts of considerations that suggest that friendship is a family resemblance concept would support the too complex to represent version of particularism *even if* friendship does in fact have determinate necessary *and sufficient* conditions attached to it. What would motivate an understanding of friendship as a family resemblance concept is the difficulty that we encounter in being able to state friendship's necessary and sufficient conditions, and it may very well be that that difficulty cannot be resolved, at least not with our current linguistic and/or representational capacities. So even if it is necessarily true that friendship is intrinsically valuable, we may not now be able to adequately represent to ourselves what is involved in our own concept of friendship because of the extraordinary complexity of the conditions on friendship. Of course, interesting questions get raised here about what is involved in our having a concept, if it is possible to have a concept and yet be unable to represent what is essential to anything falling under that concept. In the following section, I suggest one picture of what is happening in such a situation.

Complexity and the Distinction Between Determinables and Determinates

The complexity of friendship does not force us to understand it as a family resemblance concept: we might instead adopt the ontological picture of No Concepts for Determinate Features Ontological Particularism. Friendship, like blue, is a determinable: there are determinate types of friendships, just as there are determinate shades of blue. But determinate shades of blue differ from determinate types of friendships in an important way. Any instance of, let us call it powder blue #6, will be exactly like any other instance of powder blue #6, differing only in spatial and/or temporal location. Our difficulties will lie in being able to distinguish powder blue #6 from powder blue #5 or from powder blue #7. We consider all of these determinate shades instances of what is itself a determinable, namely powder blue. We can compare and contrast powder blue with cobalt blue or navy blue, where the latter are, again, both determinate shades of blue, and determinables, given that there are many shades of cobalt blue and of navy blue. (Notice that there are indefinitely many determinables: our concepts carve up the color spectrum in a few of the many, many ways that this could be done.)

But now consider a determinate type of friendship, the romantic type.[18] Romantic relationships clearly differ extraordinarily one from another, some involving sex or the hope or expectation of sex, some not. And, clearly, not all sexual relationships are romantic relationships, as all of my women friends have complained at one time or another. So our concept of romantic friendship, a determinate type of friendship, is itself not a very subtle or fine-grained concept. Each determinate instance of romantic friendship will differ from all others in many ways, and, for any given romantic friendship, it may in many respects resemble various nonromantic friendships more than it resembles some or even any other romantic friendships.

Thus, even if our concepts of friendship and of particular types of friendships such as romantic friendship are not family resemblance concepts, i.e., even if their extensions are not a matter of convention or agreement, it may be the case that we are unable to articulate or to represent the *determinate* features of the world that make it the case that a relationship is a friendship or is some particular type of friendship. If that is the case, we are unable to state or represent the ultimate determinates that ground intrinsic value or reason-givingness. We may not be able to do this because the determinates may be extraordinarily complex. The best analogy here would be to the concept of beauty (assuming we reject a subjectivist account of beauty). Every attempt to state what makes some object beautiful ends in frustration, because, e.g., if we say that the *Mona Lisa* is beautiful in virtue of its perspective, color, composition, etc., we will be able to find something that has all of those qualities and yet is not beautiful, unless our description of the features that make the painting beautiful is really just a complete, exhaustive description of the painting itself, down to the very last detail. (But could we even provide such a description in any medium other than the visual one in which the painting itself exists?) Friendship may be like this: attempt to describe which features of any relationship render it a friendship and one is likely to be frustrated unless one simply offers—if one is able—a complete description of the relationship in its entirety.

If we accept this picture of friendship and of particular types of friendship, we can continue to accept that, for any given relationship, there is an answer to the question whether it is a friendship and whether it is, e.g., a romantic friendship. However, we may not have concepts sufficient for stating or representing what it is in virtue of which the relationship is a friendship or a romantic friendship. According to this view, it may well be a necessary truth that friendship is intrinsically valuable/reason-giving, just as it is a necessary truth that powder blue is lighter than navy blue. In supporting No Concepts for Determinate Features Particularism, we will also have supported Too Complex to Formulate/Represent in certain ways: while we can state that any friendship has the property of being intrinsically good or reason-giving, we cannot state determinate criteria for which relationships count as friendships, we cannot grasp all of the forms that friendship can take, and we cannot give an enumeration of all the determinate features of the world that may be constituents of friendships and, thus, may be constituents of states of affairs that ground the property of intrinsic goodness.

But notice that all of these ontological facts that support the truth of Too Complex to Formulate/Represent and No Concepts for Determinate Features Particularism are facts about the base properties, not facts about the supervening property of either goodness or rightness. So our support of the Too Complex to Formulate/Represent thesis would need to be qualified as follows:

- *Too Complex to Formulate Ontological Particularism**: There are necessary or lawlike connections between other features of the world and the property of being reason-giving, but the relationship will be too complex to be formulable by human beings in cases in which the other features of the world cannot be stated at the level of ultimate determinates, but only at various levels of determinables (or in cases in which the concept of the subvening base is a family resemblance concept).

Similarly, No Concepts for Determinate Features Particularism would have to be restated, indicating that the thesis holds only if certain claims about the base properties are true:

- *No Concepts for Determinate Features Ontological Particularism**: There are necessary or lawlike connections between determinate features of the world and the property of being reason-giving, but, in the case of certain subvening bases, we do not have subtle or fine-grained enough terms or concepts to be able to state or to articulate (or, to represent) the determinate features as opposed to the determinables that ground the property of being reason-giving.

Both of these theses are more theses about friendship and other such base properties than about the property of intrinsic value or of being reason-giving: we could state parallel theses about any properties that supervene upon friendship, not just about normative properties.

I have discussed only two possible ways of understanding the concept of friendship. However, I am fairly confident that other plausible ways of understanding that concept will introduce similar complexities into our picture of the relationship between friendship and various normative properties. But none of these complexities support the no reliable connections thesis, the claim that there are no necessary or lawlike connections between other features of the world and the property of being a reason, although they do show why some might be drawn to that thesis. Our inability—in some cases—to state the determinate features of the world that ground normative properties and our use of concepts that may not completely align with possible concepts of subvening bases of normative properties could easily be viewed as the result of there being no necessary or lawlike connections between nonnormative and normative features of the world. But I hope that I have suggested a more plausible understanding of the situation than that which understands normative properties as being random properties that alight willy-nilly where they will.

Accepting Too Complex to Formulate* and No Concepts for Determinate Features* does not commit us to even a qualified version of the

Non-repeatable Particulars version of Ontological Particularism, although I do think that what I have said so far should lead to a certain cautiousness that might mistakenly suggest that latter version of particularism:

- *Non-repeatable Particulars Ontological Particularism:* The only necessary connections between nonnormative properties and the property of being reason-giving are between certain non-repeatable particulars in the world and the property of being reason-giving. Thus, the statement of the necessary connection will not be a general truth, because it involves essential reference to a non-repeatable property or irreducibly particular entity.

Consider a particular friendship, say, Diane's friendship with Tracy. It is extraordinarily unlikely that any other friendship will ever repeat the exact pattern of this particular one, and no other friendship will ever involve the two particular persons involved in this one.[19] But the intrinsic goodness of this friendship is a function of its having certain relevant features (affection, sympathy, support, enjoyment of one another's company, etc.) to a significant enough degree while having no relevant counterbalancing features, and it is at least possible for those features to be repeated in the same pattern in which they occur in Diane and Tracy's friendship. In a possible world where Dana and Stacy have a friendship indistinguishable from that of Diane and Tracy—Dana and Stacy being indistinguishable from Diane and Tracy—it seems that we are entitled to infer that whatever normative properties the friendship between Diane and Tracy has, Dana and Stacy's friendship also has those properties.

So even though I think that we have no reason to accept Non-repeatable Particulars Particularism with respect to the normative properties that supervene upon friendship, I think that we can see why we should be cautious about those arguments that Dancy refers to as "switching arguments." Recall that switching arguments involve, in Brad Hooker's words, "attempt[ing] to determine a moral conclusion about one case by appeal to a conclusion about another case" (6). And we certainly should be at least hesitant to move too quickly from a claim that some particular friendship is intrinsically valuable to any conclusion about the value of some other relationship. We cannot straightforwardly point to one or two features that the relationships have in common in order to conclude that if one is valuable, then so is the other. Because value supervenes on an extraordinarily complex, temporally extended base that can only be understood in a larger context, we must be very cautious about inferences based on limited analogies. (And if friendship is a family resemblance concept, we may need to leave open the possibility that we will encounter a friendship that is not intrinsically valuable.)

But we ought not let such caution turn into an unwillingness to use those friendships of which we have the best grasp as a baseline or guide for trying to make judgments about other relationships, either our own or those of other people. As long as we are careful not to make hasty or oversimplified analogies, our best and only option is to work outward from paradigm cases. Consider another example of a family resemblance concept, that of a sport: if I am trying to figure out whether synchronized swimming or rhythmic gymnastics is a sport, I have no choice but to begin by comparing and contrasting it with clear examples of sports such as baseball and football, and with clear examples of non-sports such as cleaning out the litter box or writing a chapter on particularism.[20] And if friendship is a family resemblance concept, we may at some point have to make a decision as to whether a relationship can bear sufficient resemblances to paradigms to count as a friendship even if the latter is not intrinsically valuable while all of the paradigms are.

Of course, as we engage in this activity of comparison and contrast, we should keep in mind a perpetual refrain of particularists, that we should not lose sight of the particularities of the relationship that we are considering. But, as I always stress to undergraduates with respect to essay exams, when comparing and contrasting, one must both compare *and* contrast, in other words, you need to notice not only similarities between two relationships, but also differences. And you can only do this by examining the particularities of both relationships involved. So switching arguments do not deflect attention away from particularities, unless we engage in such argumentation in sloppy and superficial ways.

Friendship and Ontological Particularism: Holism

The last ontological particularist thesis that we need to consider is Holism:

- *Ontological Holism:* Whether some state of affairs, action, or event, has the property of being reason-giving is, at least in part, a function of features of the world external to that state of affairs, action, or event.

Like No Reliable Connections Particularism, Holism is a thesis that the nonreductionist will not accept, even in a qualified form. I really think that Holism is a misleading way of stating the truth that the base properties upon which normative properties supervene are often very, very complex, even to the point of being such that we cannot state or maybe even represent them. Thus, if we describe the base properties in some partial or shorthand manner, we will mislead ourselves into thinking that normative properties supervene on those base properties only if certain further conditions hold, when really what is going on is that the base includes those further conditions.

Consider how someone might come to accept the analogous thesis about the property of being a lie:

- *Holism/Lie:* Whether the making of some statement constitutes telling a lie is, at least in part, a function of features of the world external to the making of that statement.

Consider the claim that my making a certain statement, say, 'Aliens abducted me in May 2000,' is a lie. Given that the claim is false, we would initially be inclined to label my making of that statement a lie. But we can imagine circumstances that would make us withdraw that claim: I am playing a role on the television series *The X-Files*, I am suffering from a psychiatric disorder that causes me to suffer delusions, I have no intention of deceiving you because I believe that you will understand me as being ironic, some friends played a very nasty practical joke on me, etc. In light of there being circumstances under which we would say that my claim, although false, was not a lie, we might be inclined to accept Holism/Lie.

But, of course, that would be a mistake. What constitutes the telling of a lie is not just the making of a certain statement, but, rather, the making of that statement under certain conditions. In order for the making of a statement to be a lie, it must be a statement made by a person who has certain beliefs—she must believe her statement to be false—and she must make her statement with certain intentions—she must be intending to deceive her audience. In fact, asserting a true statement can be the telling of a lie if the person making the statement believes the claim to be false and intends to deceive her audience. So a lie is a statement made by a person with certain beliefs and intentions, not just a statement taken in isolation where the statement may or may not be a lie depending upon features of the world external to that statement.

I think that the same should be said in, for example, the case of sadistic pleasures, if one is not inclined to view such pleasures as being intrinsically valuable.[21] Dancy concludes that, given his intuition that sadistic pleasures are not valuable, Holism holds, i.e., that whether some pleasure has the property of being valuable is a function of features external to that pleasure, in particular, its cause. But why not say instead that the property of being intrinsically valuable supervenes not on pleasure, but on a more complex state of affairs, such as pleasure caused by nonmalevolent thoughts, or innocent pleasures? When we say that pleasure is intrinsically valuable, we have described only part of the more complex supervenience base in this case.[22]

Consider another case offered by Dancy in *Moral Reasons*:

> I borrow a book from you, and then discover that you have stolen it from the library. Normally the fact that I have borrowed the book from you would be a reason to return it to you, but in this situation it is not. It isn't that I have some reason to return it to you and more reason to put it back in the library. I have no reason at all to return it to you. (60)

A very similar point can be made about this case as was made about the case of pleasure being intrinsically valuable: the property of being reason-giving supervenes not on the action of returning a borrowed book, but, rather, on the action of returning a borrowed book to which the loaner had certain rights.

But this case also raises another worry about the kinds of examples used by Dancy. For consider the claim that I have reason to return the book that I borrowed. It is hard to see this reason as fundamental, i.e., as not derivative from some more fundamental reason, perhaps a reason to promote value or a reason to respect property rights. But property rights are not at issue here, so I will not fail to respect them if I do not return the book; in fact, in order to respect property rights, I should return the book to the library. Similarly, if returning borrowed items is a rule of thumb aimed at promoting value: such rules will always have exceptions, and cases where the borrowed item was stolen are probably such cases. So Dancy's case, insofar as it involves a derivative reason, is misleading.

Given that Dancy's cases provide no support for Holism, and that Holism, if accepted, would render normative properties very odd, I suggest that we reject Holism.

Friendship and Epistemological Particularism

So what epistemological conclusions does our qualified acceptance of the Too Complex to Formulate/Represent and No Concepts for Determinate Features ontological theses commit us to? Let's proceed by considering our two proposed understandings of the concept of friendship.

Knowledge and Family Resemblance

First, suppose that friendship is a family resemblance concept. As with any such concept, we will acquire our grasp of it via examination of paradigm cases: just as my understanding of a sport will be parasitic upon my understanding of baseball and tennis, so my understanding of friendship will be parasitic upon my understanding of particular paradigm cases of friendship. Our paradigm cases of friendship are instances of valuable and reason-giving relationships. As a result, I may come to accept that friendships are reason-giving. Thus, Knowledge Acquisition Particularism seems correct: our coming to be justified in believing that friendship is reason-giving depends upon our acquaintance with paradigm cases of friendship and our seeing that those paradigms are reason-giving. So knowledge or justification proceeds from the particular to general rules rather than the other way around.

Notice that it is the "open texture" of claims such as 'Friendship is reason-giving' that makes it the case that our knowledge of them must proceed by beginning with paradigm cases, i.e., as Jay Garfield says, the "predicates they employ will evade a precise non-circular specification of satisfaction conditions" (190). Does this open texture lead to an inability to formulate (Linguistic Epistemological Particularism), represent (Representational Epistemological Particularism), or justifiably believe truths about (Justificatory Epistemological Particularism) the relationship between being reason-giving and nonnormative features of the world?

The open texture itself does not have these results. Rather, it all depends on the particular concept at issue, and we may not be able to determine in advance what sort of concept we are dealing with. If it turns out that we will be unwilling to extend our concept of friendship to cover relationships that are not reason-giving, then our belief that friendship is reason-giving is a general truth about the relationship between reasons and nonnormative features of the world that we can linguistically formulate, represent, and justifiably believe. But that will only be determinately true after we make that choice. For now, we can only make predictions based on our knowledge of paradigms and of human psychological tendencies, interests, and needs.

In any case, the claim that friendship is reason-giving will not be a necessary truth, even if there are lawlike connections between being a friendship and being reason-giving. And our knowledge of the general truth will be inductive in nature: I must grasp the concept of friendship based on paradigms, but no one person will be able to have an acquaintance with all of the relationships that are properly subsumed, here and now, under our concept of friendship. So even if our family resemblance concept tracks value in reliable ways, the complexity of the friendship relationship may make it the case that we are unable to represent this fact to ourselves: our own grasp of friendship is not the grasp of some essence or nature but of relations between paradigms and other instances. We can try to infer what is involved in friendship from our paradigms, but, given the role of human choice in these matters, our inferences will not be deductive in nature.

None of this undermines our ability to use general rules to guide our decisions and actions (cf. Garfield). In fact, our own actions and decisions are part of what will constitute the extending of our concept. Such extension is not done explicitly usually—it will evolve out of complex practices and choices of many people over time. Again, then, our knowledge that friendship is reason-giving, if possible, will be the result of knowledge about human practices, conventions, and choices. All of these matters, of course, are contingent.

Knowledge and Determinate Features

Now let's suppose that friendship is not a family resemblance concept, but that No Concepts for Determinate Features Ontological Particularism is relevant where friendship is involved. If this is the case, then Linguistic Epistemological Particularism seems to follow: if we lack concepts for the determinate features that ground value or reasons, then we will be unable to formulate general truths regarding those features. Further, we may be unable to represent those determinate features, thereby supporting Representational Epistemological Particularism. And if we cannot represent the determinate features, then we will be unable to have justified beliefs about those features (Justificatory Epistemological Particularism).

So does No Concepts for Determinate Features Particularism leave us without the possibility of moral knowledge? In order to answer this question, let us return to the analogy with color. Even if we cannot formulate or represent truths about every determinate shade of navy blue or of powder blue, we can know that navy blue is darker than powder blue. At the level of determinables, we can know general truths, even if we cannot grasp every particular instance of those general truths.[23] Nonetheless, we may be able to recognize shade P as a shade of powder blue and shade N as a shade of navy blue and recognize that P is lighter than N and that any shade of powder blue will be lighter than any shade of navy blue.

The case is similar for friendship and reasons. Even if we cannot formulate or represent truths about the ultimate determinates that ground our reasons for action, we can formulate, represent, and justifiably believe the general truth that friendship is reason-giving. And we can identify particular relationships as friendships and, therefore, as reason-giving. So No Concepts for Determinate Features Particularism supports the linguistic, representational, and justificatory versions of epistemological particularism for general truths about ultimate determinates and reasons but not for general truths about determinables and reasons.

What about Knowledge Acquisition Epistemological Particularism? Again, much depends on whether we are talking about general truths about ultimate determinates or about general truths about determinables. With respect to friendship, as a matter of contingent fact, we probably need to have some experience with particular friendships in order to grasp the nature of friendship and to grasp the truth that friendship is reason-giving. But our knowledge of the general truth only takes us so far with respect to identifying particular instances of reason-giving relationships, because of our inability to represent ultimate determinates. So just as we need to see a shade of blue, classify it as powder blue, and then conclude that it is lighter than any shade of navy blue, so we will need to encounter a particular relationship, classify it as a friendship, and then conclude that it is reason-giving. Our general truth, however, cannot do any work here, because it does not identify ultimate determinates that ground reasons.

Thus, whether we accept that friendship is a family resemblance concept or that we cannot articulate or represent concepts for ultimate determinates that ground reasons, the epistemic situation is very complicated. We cannot grasp the moral truth in the way that we grasp mathematical truths and then take that truth into the world as our guide. If friendship is a family resemblance concept, we need to be alert to the boundaries of that concept and the roles that human decision and convention play. If we cannot represent ultimate determinates, then we need to recognize that our general truth does little epistemic work in particular instances. In each instance the difficult task of classification remains, and our general truth only takes us so far.

The complexities of human relationships create corresponding complexities for the acquisition and application of moral knowledge. Whether we understand friendship as a family resemblance concept or as the concept of a determinable such that we cannot state or represent the ultimate determinates, it is clear that we need to have some experience of particular instances of friendship in order to be able to grasp the concept.[24] Thus, knowledge in this area, for the intuitionist, will not be a matter of just sitting and grasping abstract truths: one must have an understanding of a complex and wide range of human relationships. And, given the components of these relationships, such understanding will call forth our imaginative and sympathetic capacities if we are to grasp concern, affection, mutuality, etc.

So the intuitionist picture of moral reasoning is as complicated and messy as the states of affairs that the intuitionist takes to be reason-giving. Coming to understand those relationships that ground reasons is a continuing endeavor: each encounter with a real or hypothetical relationship has the possibility of forcing a revision or extension of the reach of our concepts of reason-giving relationships. Thus, we need to listen to others as they describe their caring relationships, and we need to try to understand our own relationships. Neither task is easy or straightforward, and, thus, neither is moral reasoning, of either the theoretical or the practical sort.

6   Deontological Constraints and Dispute Resolution

Surprisingly, given its obvious inadequacies, the argument from disagreement has been one of the perennial favorite weapons of ethical anti-realists. There are many good reasons not to take the mere fact of disagreement to tell against either the objectivity of ethics or the truth of any particular objectivist theory of ethics.[1] And I think that many ethicists, realist and anti-realist alike, would agree with that claim. However, it does seem that a large contingent of ethicists takes it to be important for an ethical theory to at least show us how, in principle, ethical disputes could be resolved, and to offer some hope that such resolution might actually be forthcoming in the future—I think that this demand is in large part responsible for the popularity of constructivist accounts of morality.[2]

This concern with the resolution of disputes has also motivated a not uncommon worry about intuitionism as defended by Moore, Prichard, and Ross, the worry that the view is really just a cover for dogmatic assertions for which the philosopher offering them chooses not to argue. Alasdair MacIntyre, in a passage previously cited in Chapter 4, indirectly offers such a critique of nonnaturalist intuitionism by referring to Keynes's perceptions of Moore and the latter's followers:

> But, of course, as Keynes tells us, what was really happening [in moral discussion and debate] was something quite other [than rational argument and persuasion]: "In practice, victory was with those who could speak with the greatest appearance of clear, undoubting conviction and could best use the accents of infallibility" and Keynes goes on to describe the effectiveness of Moore's gasps of incredulity and head-shaking.[3]

Of course, one possible response to this kind of worry is that we have no reason to believe that we have the epistemic capacities to come to know the truth and the whole truth about all objective matters of fact, including ethics.[4] But I think that we can still hope for an ethical theory to offer us some procedure that will, at least some of the time, allow rational moral deliberators to get closer to the truth and, thereby, closer to agreement.

My goal in this chapter is to show that intuitionism of the sort presented in Chapter 4 is not subject to the worry that the best that it can do is to offer dogmatic assertions regarding which nonmoral features of the world have some given moral property such as goodness or reason-givingness. I will show that this sort of metaethics not only does not foreclose argument, but actually promotes constructive argument and dialogue. I will show how the nonnaturalist intuitionist can approach the issue of a certain type of deontological constraint, namely the constraint against killing or torturing an innocent person, and can also make surprising and unexpected progress. If I am right in thinking that a desire for progress in dispute resolution is a prime motivating factor in the widespread acceptance of some form of constructivism as opposed to some form of intuitionism, then removing this particular obstacle will be a significant advance in the defense of the latter.

I. CONSTRAINTS

The literature on deontology is littered with discussion of what are known as 'constraints.' Definitions of constraints vary from philosopher to philosopher, although most philosophers do seem quite clearly to have the same types of reasons in mind when they refer to constraints. Rather than canvassing the various formulations in the literature, I will here offer my own characterization of constraints. This particular characterization follows quite naturally from what has been presented in earlier chapters.

We can think of constraints in general as objective agent-relative (and, thus, nonconsequentialist) reasons. So, suppose that S has a constraint reason to do p. Such a constraint reason is agent-relative, i.e., it is *not* necessarily the case that every Q in a causal position to do or to promote p would have reason to do or to promote p. It is also objective, i.e., it is not grounded by the fact that S takes some interest in (or cares about) p or some causal consequence of p. (See Chapter 1 for a more complete discussion of the distinctions between agent-relative and agent-neutral reasons and between subjective and objective reasons.) Thus, both reasons of fidelity and reasons of intimacy are constraints. For example, suppose that Olga has promised Bill that she will cook him dinner on Thursday evening. Her reason to cook Bill dinner on Thursday evening is grounded in the fact that she promised him that she would do so; thus, if Jennie has not promised to cook dinner for Bill, then she, unlike Olga, has no reason to do so. So Olga's reason of fidelity is agent-relative. It is also objective, because even if Olga ceases to want (or, perhaps, never wanted) to cook Bill dinner on Thursday evening, she still has reason to do so: the ground of her reason is her promise, not her subjective state of caring about or taking an interest in cooking dinner for Bill on Thursday.

Importantly, understanding constraints as *objective* agent-relative reasons implies that reasons grounded in an agent's awareness of her own desires are not constraints. The latter sorts of reasons are the paradigmatic *subjective* reasons: they are grounded in facts about what the agent cares about or takes an interest in. The term 'constraint' supposedly is meant to capture the fact that these reasons are objective, i.e., are grounded in facts somehow 'external' to us that bind us in ways that we cannot alter merely by altering our desires. Nonetheless, they are agent-relative—they are 'the agent's own' in a way that reasons grounded in the objective value of a state of affairs are not.

My argument in this chapter is not an argument, then, against constraints as such. The primary project of this book is to defend not only the claim that we have reasons of intimacy, but also to defend a conception of reasons of intimacy as objective agent-relative, i.e., a conception of reasons of intimacy as constraints. I also defended reasons of fidelity, understood as constraints, in Chapter 4. My concern in this chapter is with one particular constraint.

II. THE CONSTRAINT AGAINST KILLING THE INNOCENT

Let's begin with a description of one of the standard cases used to defend the particular constraint that I am concerned with in this chapter:

> *The Transplant Case:* Suppose that Julia is a surgeon in the emergency room of a large urban hospital. One night, the emergency room is extremely crowded as a result of a five-car accident. The drivers of the cars involved each need an organ transplant. Julia has just finished dealing with a patient who needed a refill on his allergy medication, but who is in perfect health otherwise, and who could provide all of the organs needed to save the five drivers. Julia could easily and covertly dispose of the lonely allergy sufferer and use his organs to save the five accident victims.[5]

Should Julia trade in one life for five, assuming that all five have the potential for roughly equally valuable lives? Many, if not most, people think that the correct answer is a resounding "No." The deontologist who thinks that there is a constraint against killing the innocent will agree, given that the value of a net gain of four lives is not sufficient to outweigh the constraint.[6]

In this case, then, we have a clear contrast between the deontologist who defends a constraint against killing the innocent and the consequentialist: if we assume that Julia would maximize intrinsic value by killing the one and saving the five, then, according to the consequentialist, Julia ought to kill the one and distribute his organs to save the five. Notice that the consequentialist is not disagreeing with the deontologist about whether Julia has a *prima facie* reason not to kill the innocent allergy sufferer: the consequentialist will insist that there is such a *prima facie* reason, grounded in the intrinsic value of the life of the allergy sufferer. The deontological constraint against killing the one, then, cannot be differentiated on the basis of its *content,* but, rather, must be differentiated on the basis of its *grounds.* Most importantly, the deontological constraint against killing the innocent is not grounded in the intrinsic value of the consequences of the action of refraining from killing as compared to the intrinsic value of the consequences of killing.

It may be the case that Julia has other agent-relative reasons not to kill the innocent allergy sufferer besides the constraint against killing the innocent. If the allergy sufferer is Julia's mother or spouse, her reasons of intimacy may be sufficient to outweigh the consequentialist reason to promote value. Similarly, if Julia has made a promise, either to the patient himself, to the medical profession, or to the hospital, not to treat patients in certain ways, then her reasons of fidelity may be sufficient to outweigh her consequentialist reason. But, in order to make the case as simple as possible, we need to suppose that Julia has no agent-relative reasons arising from intimate relationships, promises, contracts, etc. The deontologist who claims that Julia has a constraint reason not to kill the innocent holds that she has that reason regardless of what she has done in the past, so the constraint against killing the innocent is not a commitment because it is not acquired via voluntary actions of the agent. This deontologist also holds that Julia has a reason not to kill the innocent regardless of what the innocent has or has not done in the past—this makes the constraint against killing the innocent different from reasons of gratitude or fair play, which will be discussed in the next chapter. Any moral agent has constraint reason not to kill the innocent, regardless of what the agent has done, regardless of what the innocent has done, and regardless of the nature of the relationship between the agent and the innocent. So a crucial question is, what grounds the constraint against killing the innocent?

III. CONSEQUENTIALISM AND CONSTRAINTS

There is a standard argumentative strategy employed by deontologists attempting to defend constraints:[7] first, they argue that consequentialism seems to be out of line with our intuitions about some cases such as the transplant one discussed previously, and, second, they offer some account of a type of constraint that accommodates our intuitions. The first step in the argument is very important. Rhetorically, no one would be much interested in an account of constraints unless they thought that something was wrong with the consequentialist handling of cases such as the transplant one. (The function of Chapter 2 was to show why both the consequentialist and the Humean accounts of reasons of intimacy are unsatisfactory.) Logically, the constraint deontologist needs to show at least the *possibility* that there is a situation in which an agent's all-things-considered reason is not the consequentialist reason to promote the good; after all, if there is a *prima facie* nonconsequentialist reason, it must be at least *possible* for it to win out in the battle with the consequentialist reason.

The fact that the constraint deontologist needs to show only the *possibility* of the consequentialist getting the wrong answer about an agent's all-things-considered reason for action reveals the inadequacy of certain types of consequentialist responses to cases such as Transplant. The consequentialist cannot win the argument by claiming that some case, as described, is far out of the realm of the probable, because the constraint deontologist is attempting to establish that even in cases in the realm of the probable, there is a *prima facie* reason not to kill or torture the innocent. So by pointing to a possible case, no matter how unlikely, in which such a reason is all-things-considered, she can argue that even in cases where it is *not* all-things-considered, it is still present. The constraint deontologist is trying to establish that there is a type of reason that the consequentialist ignores even in those cases in which the latter arrives at the correct answer about all-things-considered reasons.

To be fair to the consequentialist, however, it is important to understand the point in the dialectic at which claims about whether her view gets what seems to be the right answer or not are relevant. It might very well be the case that our intuitions about the all-things-considered right way for Julia the surgeon to behave lead us, *inappropriately,* to conclude that there is a constraint against killing the innocent—after all, an appeal to a constraint provides a quicker and easier route to the conclusion that Julia ought not cut up the allergy sufferer than does any form of consequentialism. So the consequentialist can, at the outset, caution us against taking our immediate reactions concerning the 'answers' in certain cases as evidence that there are constraints. (The same applies to reasons of intimacy, and that is why I spent so much time trying to get the nature of intimacy sorted out, and examining possible alternative accounts of reasons of intimacy.)

Further, the consequentialist can use some of her responses to force us to rethink our intuitions. For example, one standard consequentialist move is to appeal to rules of thumb by which we ought to make our decisions, because, by using these rules of thumb, rather than by judging each case individually on its consequentialist merits, we are more likely to get the right answer, we will not waste precious time in deliberation, we will compensate for personal biases, etc.[8] Of course, the rule of thumb "Do not harvest and redistribute organs on your own initiative," will guide Julia to perform what is in fact, by consequentialist lights, the *wrong* action. But now the consequentialist can explain why we are so convinced that Julia ought not cut up the allergy sufferer: we think that she ought to dispose herself to abide by the rule and not stop to reconsider each and every case on its own merits. In fact, even if Julia performs the right action by cutting up the allergy sufferer, the consequentialist can consistently claim that she is a suitable object of blame and even punishment, given that we have an interest in discouraging such individual initiative with respect to organ harvesting. So our conditioned responses of disapprobation can be explained by the consequentialist, thereby explaining why we appear to have intuitions supporting constraints.[9]

This brings me to one of the points at which I am in thorough agreement with many consequentialists: we need to be cautious about appeal to 'intuitions.' We need to be equipped with some view about why we should take such judgments as authoritative or even as deserving of initial respect. What we are confident about can too easily be plausibly viewed as conditioned responses that do nothing to reveal all of the factors relevant to reaching a decision. One advantage of the metaethical position that I defended in Chapter 4 is that it includes an account of why certain sorts of 'intuitions' have a privileged status—they are synthetic necessary truths that can be justifiably believed without inference. Without such an account, appeal to intuitions may be effective in gaining adherents to the cause, but it is, in the end, philosophically incomplete.

There is a second sort of consequentialist argument against constraints that is too hasty, insofar as it does not really take seriously what the defender of constraints is claiming.[10] One standard sort of deontologist move in grounding the constraint against killing or torturing the innocent is to appeal to some feature of persons such as their dignity or their rationality. The deontologist insists that this feature of persons gives agents a reason not to kill or torture innocent persons even if in so doing the agent could prevent, say, five from being killed or tortured. The too-hasty consequentialist response is: if dignity is so important, we need to notice that the dignity of the five will be violated if the agent does not kill or torture the one. Further, their dignity will be violated in precisely the same way as that of the one.[11] If dignity is significant or important and grounds reasons of nonviolation or of preservation, then why not preserve or prevent as much dignity as possible from being violated? One would do this by killing or torturing the one in order to prevent the five from being killed or tortured by some other agent or agents. This consequentialist argument can be run against any feature of the victim, the agent, or the relationship between the victim and the agent that the deontologist might appeal to as grounding constraints: if feature X is significant or important or valuable, then why not promote or preserve X to the greatest extent possible, even if, in order to do so, one must violate or destroy X to some lesser degree?

Such a consequentialist argument is effective only if we already have some other argument in place against the very possibility of agent-relative reasons. The argument forces us to think of constraints as agent-neutral reasons, such that there is some state of affairs that, necessarily, any agent in a causal position to promote it has a reason to promote it. But, as we have already seen with reasons of intimacy and with reasons of fidelity, agent-relative reasons do not behave in that way: insofar as I have an agent-relative reason to promote p, it does not follow that anyone in a causal position to promote p has reason to do so or even that I have reason to promote any other p-like states. *My* promises provide me with reasons to keep them that are independent of the value of promises being kept, and *my* intimate relationships give me reason to sustain them independent of their value (although, in both cases, I may also have competing reasons stemming from the value of the consequences that will be promoted). So each agent has a type of reason to keep her own promises and to sustain her own intimate relationships that no one else has (even though those others may also have value-based reason to see that she keeps her promises and sustains her intimate relationships). Similarly, then, if there is a constraint against killing the innocent, each agent has a type of reason to refrain from killing the innocent that is independent of the value of her so refraining and is also different in kind from the reasons that others have to prevent her (or anyone else) from killing the innocent.

I am not saying that the deontologist can simply say that we have a non-consequentialist reason to do or to refrain from doing p and then just leave it at that. The defender of constraints needs to point to some feature of persons or of relationships between persons that grounds constraints, and then make plausible the claim that such features really do ground *prima facie* nonconsequentialist reasons. I will argue that nonnaturalist intuitionism gives us a way of evaluating such accounts without succumbing to begging the question in favor of some type of maximizing consequentialism.

IV. KILLING THE INNOCENT

So how are we to understand Julia's constraint reason not to kill the innocent allergy sufferer? The first task facing the nonnaturalist intuitionist is to figure out the status of the following claim: (i) Julia has a *prima facie* nonconsequentialist reason not to kill the innocent allergy sufferer. Supposedly, (i) states that Julia has a reason that is derivative from a more general reason: (ii) Julia has a *prima facie* nonconsequentialist reason not to kill innocent persons.

So what is the status of (ii): is it an inference from some other, more basic claim, or is it such that we are justified in believing it without inference?

One option for the defender of a reason not to kill the innocent is to insist that (ii) is a synthetic necessary truth, because the action type *killing an innocent person* is such that it has the property of being reason-giving.[12] To be more precise, for each action of the type *R's killing an innocent person*, that action has the property of being reason-giving for R. This reason would then have to be weighed against R's other reasons, reasons supervenient upon good states of affairs, promises, intimate relationships, etc., before R can decide what she ought, all things considered, to do.

If the defender of (ii)—and of similar claims—regards such claims as basic, then we have a better idea of how to understand thought experiments: what one wants to do is to bring before one's own and one's readers' minds the property of being the killing of an innocent person, making sure that that property is disentangled from others with which it might usually, as a contingent matter, occur. Only then can one hope to grasp whether the property of being reason-giving for R supervenes upon an action in virtue of its being an action with the property of being R's killing of an innocent person. The best way to do this is to imagine a situation in which other reasons are not present. So consider again the transplant case. We can stipulate that Julia has made no relevant promises, is not intimately related to any of the persons involved, etc. But to make the case even starker, imagine that by killing the innocent person, Julia can save only one other person whose life is equally valuable as that of the innocent allergy sufferer. Does she have a constraint reason not to kill the innocent person?

I myself have a very difficult time answering this question, because I am not sure that in fact I have managed to grasp the act of killing divorced from all of its standard consequences. First, of course, it seems that the act of killing the one has the obvious consequence that someone, namely the allergy sufferer, is now dead. As I pointed out in Section II, even consequentialists will happily grant that there is a *prima facie* reason not to kill, a reason grounded in the negative consequence of the death of the person killed. In order to grasp the property of killing the one divorced from standard consequences, we have to abstract from the disvalue of death and loss of future life. Further, people who kill are often people who become less sensitive, intentional acts of killing set bad precedents, most people are better off acting according to rules of thumb, etc. Also, because the standard response to an overt act of killing, both on the part of the victim and on the part of bystanders, is horror, these responses need to be weighed in the consequentialist balance. There are so many consequences, both subtle and obvious, involved here that it is especially hard to isolate the property of being the killing of an innocent person from the property of having various consequences.

Of course, the situation is even more complicated if we think of the action of killing as involving, by its very nature, the death of the victim. After all, a harvesting of organs is not a killing if some miracle occurs and the victim of the harvesting survives the procedure. If a killing necessarily involves death, then it seems that the very act, not just its causal consequences, is a bad thing. So then we have to try to figure out whether the act has the property of being wrong in virtue of being bad—which would be to concede the field to the consequentialist—or in virtue of its nonnormative properties, the very same properties, perhaps, that make it bad. There is no doubt that this is no easy task.

It is also very difficult to eliminate from the picture all of our subjective reasons, i.e., those reasons supervenient upon our awareness of our own desires. I am aware that I have a desire to avoid being the direct cause of anyone's death, particularly if I would cause that death in such a way that I would be directly confronted by my victim's terror and physical suffering.

My having this desire is probably an instrumentally valuable feature of my character, and so we may have very good consequentialist reasons to raise people to have these sorts of subjective reasons. But such subjective reasons are supervenient upon a person's desires, not upon the action in virtue of its being an act of killing an innocent person.

If the defender of the constraint against killing the innocent insists that (ii) is basic, we can at least understand the function of piling up various counterexamples: we can hope that the more cases that we consider, the closer that we will get to grasping the property of being the killing of an innocent person, and, thus, closer to knowing whether claims such as (ii) are synthetic necessary truths.[13] Most defenders of constraints, however, seem to regard claims such as (ii) as derived from more basic claims. In other words, they seem to think that actions that have the property of being the killing of an innocent person have the property of being *prima facie* wrong in virtue of having some other property (where that property is not the property pointed to by the consequentialist). So in what follows I will consider a couple of views that can be understood as proposals about the claim from which claims such as (ii) are to be derived.

V. PERSONS VS. VALUE

One way in which defenders of constraints have attacked consequentialism is by claiming that they ignore the person or something significant about persons.[14] For example, Elizabeth Anderson claims that the problem with consequentialism is that it requires us "to regard people as merely the extrinsically valuable containers for what is supposedly intrinsically valuable—states of affairs in which welfare exists. The mistake . . . is to lose sight of the fact that what gives the pursuit of or desire for welfare its only point is that *we ought to care about the people who enjoy it*" (27; italics added).[15] So let us consider what a defender of constraints such as Anderson might have in mind.[16]

The consequentialist regards all reasons as supervening upon states of affairs in virtue of the goodness of such states of affairs: if a state of affairs S is intrinsically valuable, then, insofar as R is able to promote S by doing P, S is reason-giving for R—it gives R *prima facie* reason to perform P. So my reasons for performing any given action are the result of that action's being a means to the promotion of some valuable state of affairs. (The action itself may be a component of that valuable state of affairs.) Thus, the consequentialist argument looks like this:

1. State of affairs S is reason-giving for R if and only if S is intrinsically valuable and R is in a position to promote S.
2. States of affairs that involve human welfare (H) are intrinsically valuable.

   3. Therefore, any H is reason-giving for any R in a position to promote that H.

Anderson seems to be claiming that the consequentialist argument ought to be replaced with the following one:

1. We have reason to care about (or to respect) people.
2. One way to care about (or to respect) people is to promote their well-being.
3. Therefore, we have reason to promote people's well-being.

Supposedly, though, as a nonvoluntarist constraint deontologist she would also accept the following argument:

1. We have reason to care about (or to respect) people.
2. One way to care about (or to respect) people is to refrain from killing them.
3. Therefore, we have reason to refrain from killing people.[17]

If I have correctly stated Anderson's complaint, then she seems to take the claims that we have reason to care about (or to respect) people and that we have reason to avoid being uncaring (or disrespectful) of people as basic. So she seems to accept:

(A) Any action A of R's that has the property of being an uncaring or a disrespectful action is such that A is reason-giving for R (R has reason not to perform the action).
(B) Any action A of R's that has the property of being the killing of an innocent person has the property of being an uncaring or a disrespectful action.
(C) Therefore, any action A of R's that has the property of being the killing of an innocent person is such that A is reason-giving for R (R has reason not to perform the action).

Now it is of course true that a consequentialist could accept premise (A); however, the consequentialist would insist that an action with the property of being uncaring or disrespectful is reason-giving *in virtue of* being instrumentally or intrinsically disvaluable. (The consequentialist would probably also understand being uncaring or disrespectful in terms of a lack of responsiveness to or a disposition to hinder the production of intrinsic value.) The nonvoluntarist constraint deontologist is regarding the property of being uncaring or disrespectful as the property in virtue of which such an action is reason-giving.

   In order to assess (A), then, we need to grasp the property of being an uncaring or a disrespectful action. Supposedly, (B) offers us some insight into uncaring or disrespectful actions. But we can understand (B) in one of two ways: (i) as an analytic truth, such that (at least) part of what it is to be the killing of an innocent person is to be uncaring or disrespectful, or (ii) as a synthetic necessary truth, such that it is necessarily the case that if an action has the property of being the killing of an innocent, then it has the property of being uncaring or disrespectful.

Now in order to assess (B), understood either as (i) or as (ii), we must turn to thought experiments. If we can imagine a case in which an action has the property of being the killing of an innocent but does not have the property of being uncaring or disrespectful, then we have reason to deny both that the latter constitutes or partly constitutes the former property and that the former property is always accompanied by the latter (distinct) property. And we do seem to be able to imagine such a case. Consider:

> *The Desert Island Case:* Richard and Greg are stranded on a desert is-land. Greg has been seriously injured and is in excruciating, unremitting pain. Greg's injuries have left him unable to communicate his desires. Richard has no way of alleviating Greg's pain, and he knows that Greg will not live much longer. Richard uses the single remaining bullet in his gun to end Greg's life in order to end his unceasing pain.

Richard's action certainly has the property of being the killing of an (by hypothesis) innocent. But does his action also have the property of being uncaring or disrespectful? I am strongly inclined to say no, and I think that many, if not most, people would agree with me that Richard's action is the only truly caring and respectful option available to him in the circumstances.

The obvious move for the constraint deontologist to make at this point, and many make it, is to deny that there is any constraint against Richard's killing Greg. In fact, Anderson limits constraints to reasons against killing an innocent person *with the intention of preventing others from killing a greater number of innocent persons*. More generally, in order to encompass the transplant case, we can understand the defender of constraints as accepting:

(D) Any action A of R's that has the property of being uncaring or disrespectful of an innocent Q is such that it has the property of giving R a reason not to perform it.

(E) Any action that (i) has the property of being the killing of an innocent Q, and (ii) has either the property of being motivated by a desire to prevent a greater number of innocents from being killed or the property of being motivated by a desire to bring about a greater amount of intrinsic value in the long run for persons other than Q, is such that it has the property of being uncaring or disrespectful of Q.

(F) Therefore, any action of R's that (i) has the property of being the killing of an innocent person Q and (ii) has either the property of being motivated by a desire to prevent a greater number of innocents from being killed or the property of being motivated by a desire to bring about a greater amount of intrinsic value in the long run (taking into account persons other than Q) is such that it has the property of giving R a reason not to perform it.

(E) does not apply to the case of Richard and Greg, so we do not get the implausible result that Richard's killing Greg is uncaring or disrespectful of Greg. But we do get the result that it would be uncaring or disrespectful of Julia to kill the innocent allergy sufferer, because Julia is weighing the lives of the five accident victims against the life of the allergy sufferer. So is (E) plausible?

Once again, we need to ask whether (E) is to be understood as (i) an analytic truth, that is, as at least a partial analysis of the concept of being an uncaring or disrespectful action, or (ii) a synthetic necessary truth asserting that it is necessarily the case that if an action has (E-i) and (E-ii), then it has the *distinct* property of being uncaring or disrespectful of an innocent.

Let us begin with the claim that (E) is to be understood as an analytic truth.[18] So then any action that has the property of being the killing of an innocent for, as I will say from now on, the sake of people other than the innocent herself, has the property of expressing a lack of concern or respect for the person killed, because caring about a person is, in part, to be unwilling to sacrifice her for the good of other persons.[19] In other words, if caring about (or respecting) a person is partly constituted by *not* being willing to kill her for the greater good, then killing someone for the greater good necessarily expresses disrespect or a lack of concern, as a conceptual matter.

Is it true that part of what is involved in caring about or respecting someone is being unwilling to kill her for the greater good? Would it be a *contradiction* to claim *both* that (i) K cares about (respects) Q *and* that (ii) K is willing to sacrifice Q to save a greater number of persons? It certainly is true that if K were able to do so without regret or sorrow, we would have reason to question K's attitude toward Q. But I think that I can conceive of some K caring about or respecting a Q and yet feeling compelled to sacrifice Q—I think that all of the conditions that I discussed in Chapter 3 are compatible with a willingness to sacrifice Q in certain circumstances. In fact, films such as *Sophie's Choice* and *The Third Man* (the latter was discussed in Chapter 1) seem to derive their power from the conflict generated in a person who is forced to sacrifice someone she or he cares deeply about. Sophie loves her daughter and yet sacrifices her to prevent both of her children from being taken to the gas chambers. Holly Martins still cares about Harry Lime in the scene in the sewer in which he shoots him dead—if Holly didn't still care about Harry Lime, the film would not have the tragic impact that it does have.

Why would a constraint deontologist suppose that the conjunction of (i) and (ii) is a contradiction? Why would she suppose that caring about someone is partly constituted by being unwilling to sacrifice that person? The substance of Elizabeth Anderson's motivation seems to be stated in the following comments:

> We need to value people in higher ways than those in which we value lower goods, such as mere use-values. The principles of appropriate treatment for mere use-values are the consequentialist principles of instrumentality, aggregation, indifference to substitution, and so on. To express higher modes of valuation, we must govern ourselves by norms that embody a logic which contrasts with consequentialist logic. . . . If meanings were reformed to wholly coincide with what maximizes our convenience and good fortune, there would be nothing left to contrast with lower modes of valuation, in which things are valued only for what they can do for our independently defined interests. (77–78)

So Anderson might say that caring about Q is compatible with a willingness to sacrifice Q, but that caring about Q in the way *appropriate to persons* is incompatible with a willingness to sacrifice Q. Anderson, it seems, would claim that if K is willing to sacrifice Q, K cares about Q only in the way that K cares about, for example, her favorite pumps or a well-tailored pair of pants.

But surely there are other ways, besides acting on constraints, for an agent to show that she regards people as different from pants or pumps. It is important that Sophie and Holly Martins both (i) are only willing to make their sacrifices given that other people's lives are at stake, and (ii) cannot make their sacrifices without torment, anguish, and regret. People's lives and well-being are uniquely important and valuable, and so ought not to be destroyed carelessly or without regret, because we must always recognize that only in an imperfect world could we be justifiably driven to sacrifice human life or happiness. An overconfidence in our having correctly decided to sacrifice life or well-being reveals a lack of comprehension about what is at stake. (A consequentialist can also point to all of the *prima facie* reasons not to kill innocents discussed in Section II. Given these reasons, any decision to kill an innocent is likely to be a very difficult one.)

So I have serious reservations about (E)'s being understood as an analytic truth. But suppose for a moment that (E) is analytic, and, therefore, a necessary truth knowable *a priori*. In order for the constraint deontologist to move from (E) to her conclusion (F), the claim that there are nonconsequentialist *prima facie* constraint reasons, she needs to establish:

(D) Any action of R's that has the property of being uncaring or disrespectful of Q is such that it has the property of giving R a reason not to perform it.

(D) can be understood as implying that the property of being reason-giving for R supervenes upon any state of affairs that involves an uncaring or disrespectful action of R's in virtue of that state of affairs' involving the uncaring or disrespectful action of R's.

So how are we to assess the truth of (D)? Initially, of course, (D) seems correct—surely we have reasons to avoid what is uncaring or disrespectful. But we need to be very careful at this point, because we need to be sure that we are grasping the property of being uncaring or disrespectful that is now at work in the argument: we cannot let the nonvoluntarist constraint deontologist get away with an equivocation, sliding between one concept of being uncaring or disrespectful in (E) to another in (D). So, for example, all of the following might be taken to be commonsense (full or partial) analyses of being uncaring or disrespectful of Q:

1. indifferent to the well-being of Q
2. not disposed to consider the interests or needs of Q
3. unappreciative of the achievements or good qualities of Q
4. consistently willing to subordinate the needs of Q to self-interest
5. willing to sacrifice Q's interests or needs without reflection or thought
6. takes pleasure in Q's losses or sufferings[20]

We have to put any covert thoughts of properties 1–6 out of our minds. All that is relevant now is being uncaring or disrespectful in the sense of being willing to kill in order to prevent a greater number from being killed or from dying. In fact, in order to make sure that we have not imported any of 1–6 into our conceptualization, we can eliminate reference to being uncaring or disrespectful in the argument:

(D*) Any action of R's that has properties (i) and (ii) (in E*) is such that it has the property of giving R a reason not to perform it.

(E*) Any action that (i) has the property of being the killing of an innocent person Q, and (ii) has either the property of being motivated by a desire to prevent a greater number of innocents from being killed or the property of being motivated by a desire to bring about a greater amount of intrinsic value in the long run is such that it has the property of having properties (i) and (ii).

(F*) Any action of R's that has properties (i) and (ii) is such that it has the property of giving R a reason not to perform it.

Our original argument had the form:

(d) All A's are B.
(e) All C's are A.
(f) Therefore, all C's are B.

Obviously, the argument is valid. And then the constraint deontologist tells us that, in fact, to be A just is to be C, so that we can rewrite our argument as:

(d*) All C's are B.
(e*) All C's are C.
(f*) Therefore, all C's are B.

Now, this would be all well and good if (e) were an interesting and plausible piece of conceptual analysis. But it looks as though (e) is just a stipulative definition of 'uncaring and disrespectful,' given how disconnected it is from the natural partial analyses 1–6. Thus, the use of the notion of uncaring and disrespectful turns out to be a red herring in the argument: the 'argument' is really just a convoluted way of stating that we have reason not to perform actions that have properties (E-i) and (E-ii), i.e., that we have constraint reasons not to kill innocent persons.

Thus, in order to be charitable to the constraint deontologist, we should take (E) to be synthetic, not analytic. I am assuming that the constraint deontologist would not want (E) to be a contingent generalization, so we do best by taking (E) to be a synthetic necessary truth. Premise (E), on this understanding of it, asserts that an action has the property of being disrespectful or uncaring in virtue of having the properties (i) and (ii), where the former property is distinct from properties (i) and (ii). If (E) can be justifiably believed without inference, then insofar as one grasps that an action has properties (i) and (ii), one can grasp that it has the property of being disrespectful or uncaring.

Now we need to try to isolate the properties (i) and (ii) and the property of being uncaring or disrespectful, and see if insofar as an action has the former, it has the latter. I am fairly confident that I grasp (i) and (ii) (putting aside any worries about being able to isolate those properties from standard consequences, as discussed in Section IV), but I am not at all confident that I have grasped the property that the constraint deontologist is referring to by the expression "being uncaring or disrespectful." When I attempt to conceive of someone's being uncaring or disrespectful, I inevitably conceive of some combination of properties 1–6, but none of those properties seem necessarily connected to properties (i) and (ii); for example, it does not seem to be the case that Julia must have one of the properties 1–6 insofar as she performs an action with the properties (i) and (ii).

So we need to get a bead on the property that the constraint deontologist is using "being uncaring or disrespectful" to refer to. As I have said, constraint deontologists such as Anderson make much of treating people in consonance with their natures and distinctive 'higher value.' So people have to be treated as relevantly different than pumps and pants: "We need to value people in higher ways than those in which we value lower goods, such as mere use-values" (77). Consider also the following, similar comments by Francis Kamm:

Individuals whose rights stand as a barrier to action are more potent individuals than they would be otherwise. There being rights and constraints with high thresholds is a mark that the person who has them is a stronger, more valuable type of thing, even if they prevent us from stopping more transgressions. It is true of all those who die because we cannot save them as well as of those who are not violated, that they have these rights. By analogy, a stronger more impressive wall is one that we will not be able to pass through, even to prevent the destruction of comparable walls behind it. One would *expect* that the highest values or rights are intrinsically such that it would be wrong to minimize even a great many violations of them, either for the sake of rights or for the sake of utility, by transgressing them; they would not be so almighty if they could be transgressed. (273)

The fundamental idea here seems to be that persons must be treated *as persons*. To be caring or respectful of someone is to treat her in consonance with her status as a person, and to be uncaring or disrespectful is to treat her in a way only appropriate for entities of a lower status, entities such as "mere use-values."

If this is correct, then (D) seems to be plausible, insofar as it can be restated as:

(D**)   Any action of R's that has the property of treating Q in a way inappropriate to her nature as a person has the property of giving R a reason not to perform it.

In fact, now (D), read as (D**), appears to be an analytic truth, insofar as inappropriate treatment seems to be, at least, treatment that there is reason to avoid, and appropriate action is, at least, action that there is reason to perform.

So it is (E) that we need to assess. (E) can now be restated as:

(E**)   Any action that (i) has the property of being the killing of an innocent person and (ii) has either the property of being motivated by a desire to prevent a greater number of innocents from being killed or the property of being motivated by a desire to bring about a greater amount of intrinsic value in the long run is such that it has the property of treating Q in a way inappropriate to her nature as a person.

What, then, is it to treat a person in accord with her nature?

Both Anderson and Kamm suggest that it is to value them in ways such that our "norms embody a logic which contrasts with consequentialist logic" (Anderson 78), and to behave with respect to them in ways that acknowledge their elevated status as inviolable beings (Kamm 273). So it seems that we are to take the following as an analytic truth:

(G) For R to be willing to govern his conduct in accord with consequentialist norms is for R to fail to treat people in accord with their higher or inviolable status.

But my worry at this point is that the following is also supposed to be analytic:

(H) For R to fail to treat people in accord with their higher or inviolable status is for R to fail to respect deontological constraints.

Unhappily, from (G) and (H), we get the rather unsurprising:

(J) For R to be willing to govern his conduct in accord with consequentialist norms is for R to fail to respect deontological constraints.

But this is to tell us no more than that a consequentialist is, after all, a consequentialist.

I think that it has become apparent that we do not really have any arguments here. The constraint deontologist seems to be revealed as asserting that the following, the apparent conclusion of an argument, is a self-evident synthetic necessary truth:

(F) Any action of R's that (i) has the property of being the killing of an innocent person Q, and (ii) has either the property of being motivated by a desire to prevent a greater number of innocents from being killed or the property of being motivated by a desire to bring about a greater amount of intrinsic value in the long run is such that it has the property of giving R a reason not to perform it.

While it may appear that we have moved in a circle, I think that it is a very instructive circle. We, and the consequentialist, are now entitled to ask whether actions with properties (i) and (ii) have the property of being reason-giving for R in virtue of having properties (i) and (ii) or in virtue of having some other property. The next section will show why, at this point in the dialectic, various familiar consequentialist lines of argument show their real effectiveness.

VI. WHERE THE ARGUMENT STANDS

At this point, of course, the consequentialist is going to return to her claim that there is a *prima facie* reason not to kill the innocent, a reason grounded in the disvalue of death and the value of life. Thus, she will claim, there is a *prima facie* reason not to kill the innocent no matter what one's motivation. So the claim (F) (or some variant thereof) can be viewed by the consequentialist as derivative from a general consequentialist claim plus a plausible, albeit contingently true, claim about the effects of certain kinds of actions:

(K) If an action P of R's is (or would be) instrumentally valuable, e.g., causally productive of intrinsic value (or a causal hindrance to intrinsic badness), then R has a reason to do P.

(L) In standard cases, R's refraining from killing an innocent person is instrumentally valuable.

(M) Therefore, in standard cases, R has a reason to refrain from killing an innocent person.

The consequentialist will reiterate her explanations of our apparently deontological intuitions as explicated in Section III. She will now toss the ball back into the constraint deontologist's court.

I am only going to suggest a couple of ways in which the dialectic between the constraint deontologist and the consequentialist might continue at this point. The deontologist might attempt to defend the claim that (F) is basic by continuing to use counterexamples in order to get us to grasp the relevant properties and the relation of necessitation between them. Or, she might decide to ground constraints in some feature of agency, as many have tried to do. But my objective has been only secondarily to question the arguments for constraints. My primary objective has been to show how the use of the metaethic that I am advocating can clarify and focus debate by forcing us to ask questions about the ontological and epistemological status of the claims that we are making. By seeking to determine which claims are basic, we are forced to clarify the subvenience base of reasons and to press on our uses of ordinary English terms to ensure that we are not using them in misleading or tortured ways. At some point, of course, we will end up 'shaking our heads and gasping in incredulity' at the fact that our opponent does not accept the claims that we regard as basic and in no need of argument. But all argument must end somewhere. The virtue of the approach that I have used in this chapter is that it allows us to see when and why our opponent really has no other response than a gesture of incredulity.

VII. *TU QUOQUE?*

Have I shown reasons of intimacy to be any better off than constraint reasons? After all, I have said explicitly that my discussion of intimate relationships in Chapter 3 was not intended to amount to an analysis of the concept of intimacy. The best that I could do, given what I said about the concepts of intimacy and friendship in Chapter 5, was to elucidate certain features such that all intimate relationships with which we are familiar have a certain number of those features to some degree. The complexity of intimate relationships prevents us, at least for now, from providing any kind of exhaustive statement of the range of relationships that ground reasons of intimacy. So have I failed to specify the relevant subvenience base?

Yes and no. I have argued that the complexity of intimacy and friendship prevent a nice easy statement of the kind of synthetic truth that we would like to have. But we are all familiar with particular intimate relationships, and so I hope that I have gotten in the right neighborhood by my discussion in Chapter 3. The constraint deontologist, on the other hand, is not stymied by the complexity of her subvenience base. Rather, I have argued, she is stymied by an inability to help us to get a bead on the subvenience base to which she is pointing as grounding a constraint not to kill or torture the innocent. The terms that she uses seem not to fix on the relevant properties toward which she is trying to steer us.

I grant that some reader may say the same about my discussion of intimacy, i.e., "I just don't grasp the kind of relationship on which I am supposed to focus as a subvenience base for reasons of intimacy." What is then to be done? Those of us who differ about the content of our constraints can only continue to try to focus one another's attention on the relevant subvenience base. There is no guarantee that everyone will be able to grasp the relevant base. I fully admit that I may not be grasping the base pointed out by those who defend a constraint against killing the innocent. I hope that I have at least shown what they need to do to get people like myself focused on the relevant properties. All that I can do in return is to welcome similar critiques of my account of intimacy and attempt to respond in kind.

7 The Scope of the Objective Agent-Relative

In moral theory a distinction is often made between *natural duties* and *special obligations*. Natural duties are "moral requirements which apply to all men [and women] irrespective of status or of acts performed. . . . These duties are owed by all persons to all others."[1] If we understand one's mere causal position as not constituting part of one's 'status,' then we can understand my category of objective agent-neutral reasons as corresponding to the category of natural duties: these are duties we have regardless of our commitments or our desires. Special obligations, then, are ones that we have only to a limited subset of persons[2] and are a function of our 'status or acts performed.' Special obligations seem to correlate with what I have been calling objective agent-relative reasons.[3]

So far, the types of special obligations or objective agent-relative reasons that I have defended—reasons of intimacy and reasons of fidelity—have both been examples of commitments. As we saw in Chapter 4, we acquire commitments in virtue of voluntary actions that we have performed. But many moral philosophers—and ordinary moral agents—have thought that we have a range of special obligations that are very difficult to construe as commitments: many people think that we owe special consideration to those who have been kind or generous to us in the past, to those who are fellow citizens, and to those who are members of our families. It does not seem that we choose our citizenship,[4] our families, or to have certain people do good for us. So should we deny that we have duties of gratitude, special political obligations, and special familial obligations, or should we resist the restriction of special obligations to voluntarily undertaken commitments?

Those who do restrict special obligations to voluntary commitments are known as voluntarists. In Section I of this chapter, I will explain and motivate the voluntarist requirement on special obligations, and show both how the friendship relation satisfies that requirement and why the requirement poses a challenge for obligations of gratitude, political obligations, and familial obligations. While I am inclined to accept voluntarism, I feel the pull of anti-voluntarist intuitions, particularly in the cases of political obligations and duties of gratitude. However, after examining three anti-voluntarist accounts of special obligations in Section II, I argue that we need to put aside our anti-voluntarist intuitions and opt for understanding our reasons to benefit family members, fellow citizens, and those who have done good for us, in either objective agent-neutral or subjective agent-relative terms.

I. VOLUNTARISM, FRIENDSHIP, AND OTHER RELATIONS

The Voluntarist Requirement

Let us understand obligations to be any objective reasons, either agent-relative or agent-neutral. Our objective agent-neutral reasons—let us call them neutral obligations—are based on the objective value of the state of affairs that we have reason to promote. So, for example, if Emma is drowning in the river, and Kate is in a position to save her, then Kate has a neutral obligation to do so in virtue of the objective value of Emma's life. But, of course, if Sara (or any other moral agent) had been in Kate's causal and epistemic position, then she also would have had a neutral obligation to save Emma's life. Neutral obligations rest upon the intrinsic nature of the state of affairs that we are obligated to promote: when we come within the causal and epistemic orbit of such states of affairs, we all come to have reason to promote them.

How else can we come to have obligations? I have argued that we can acquire additional obligations by voluntarily taking them on, i.e., we can commit ourselves to new, relative obligations. The question remains, however, whether there is any other way to acquire new, relative obligations. The voluntarist claims that there is no other way:

> *The Voluntarist Requirement on Special Obligations:* the *only* way to acquire special obligations—i.e., agent-relative obligations—is through some voluntary action(s) such that we know or ought to know that such action(s) constitutes the assumption of such obligations.

The attraction of the voluntarist requirement is a function of what the apparent options are with respect to the formation of special obligations. Most anti-voluntarists, as we will see in Section II, point to traditions, social institutions, and/or socially defined roles. All of these are human creations, so the question naturally arises as to why we should suppose ourselves bound merely because *other* people have made certain choices or perceive us in certain ways. Of course, if other people choose to undertake valuable projects, as, for example, those who work with Doctors Without Borders or the ASPCA have done, they do effect a change in the reasons that the rest of us have. Such people are responding to human and/or nonhuman animal needs that all of us have a neutral reason to respond to. They set up channels for the rest of us to act in comparatively easy and time-efficient ways to promote well-being, making it rational for us to donate to such organizations and, hopefully, spend our time on more specific, narrowly focused projects. But why suppose that I, *merely* because I happen to be someone's daughter, compatriot, or beneficiary, have reason to respond with differential concern?

In order to be clear as to what the voluntarist is claiming, consider the following criticism of voluntarism, offered by Samuel Scheffler:

> We acquire personal relations and social affiliations of a formative kind before we are able to conceive of them as such or to contemplate altering them. Thus there is obviously no question . . . of our being able to choose all of the relations in which we stand to other people. What the voluntarist can hope to claim is only that the significance of those relations is entirely up to us. However, this claim too is unsustainable. For better or worse, the influence on our personal histories of unchosen social relations—to parents and siblings, families and communities, nations and peoples—is not something that we determine by ourselves. Whether we like it or not, such relations help to define the contours of our lives, and influence the ways that we are seen both by ourselves and by others.[5]

The voluntarist is not committed to saying that the 'significance of those relations is entirely up to us.' There is no doubt that we are each born and socialized into families, communities, and nations, and that the nature of these social groups and of our unchosen places within them have a huge influence on our characters, values, choices, and general outlooks on life. The commitments that each of us ends up making are influenced a great deal by background factors that we have not chosen and may not have had any control over. For example, my decision to become an academic was shaped by my family's great respect for education and intellectual accomplishment, and also by my mother's insistence that her daughter have a meaningful career and be financially independent. But the fact that my choice did not occur in a vacuum does not alter its status as a genuine *choice*—I could have decided to become a landscape architect, an actuary, etc. Similarly, my friendships have resulted from my being placed in circumstances where I met certain people, and also from facts about which people have found me interesting, attractive, funny, or kind. Again, however, none of these facts about the influence on my choice of friends renders my choices something other than genuine choices. (See the following subsection for a discussion of friendship as chosen.)

So we need to be careful to distinguish between truisms about the causal influence of unchosen social facts on the nature of our selves and our lives and on how we perceive those selves and lives, and more controversial claims about whether those unchosen social facts, *taken by themselves,* ground special obligations. I have already allowed that such facts can play a role in determining our obligations to the extent that (i) those facts open up channels for the promotion of objective value (perhaps by being objectively good in and of themselves), or (ii) we commit ourselves to fostering our unchosen roles/relations, or develop intimate relationships with those to whom we stand in, e.g., familial or political relation.[6] But those who reject voluntarism are committed to the further claim that unchosen social roles/relations, *in and of themselves,* ground special obligations. It is this latter claim, not claims about the causal significance of unchosen social roles/relations, that voluntarists reject.

Friendship as a Commitment

I have already defended, in Chapter 4, the idea that friendship can be understood as a commitment, so here I will just reiterate and stress some of the points that I made in that earlier discussion. (It is important to remember that I am using 'friendship' as a way of referring to any intimate relationship.)

It is quite clear that friendships do not satisfy the voluntarist requirement in the straightforward way that other sorts of commitments such as promises and contracts do. There is no discrete act comparable to the uttering of a promise or the signing of a contract that occurs in the normal course of a friendship. When such discrete promises are made, they are usually the result of a breakdown in a friendship as a way of attempting to mend it or set it on new terms. The only times in which it ever makes sense to promise to be someone's friend is if the two persons involved are already friends and reassurance is needed; in other words, such promises merely reaffirm obligations generated by the intimate relationship itself.[7] The words "I promise" in such circumstances are used in a nonstandard way, i.e., not to create new obligations but to assure another that one is aware of the obligations that one already has.[8]

Similarly, the role of friend is not assumed in the way that many other roles are assumed, such as the role of teacher, physician, adoptive parent, or colleague. In each of these cases, we can find discrete events that can appropriately be described as the assumption of the role. One important difference between these sorts of cases and that of friendship is that, at least in a lot of the former cases institutionalization has occurred so that there are formal and conventional modes for assuming the role. Friendship has never been institutionalized in this way, and, because of its nature, cannot be: the nature of friendship is of a relationship that cannot be assumed in some particular discrete event or series or set of events. We cannot know in advance how and even whether intimacy can be achieved between two particular persons.

But the voluntary assumption of a role need not occur in a discrete act or in some predetermined series of acts that is identifiable from one case to another. It is true that in friendship we sometimes have a sudden realization that we are now friends with some person, a fact that appears more like a discovery than a choice.[9] But what is being discovered in such cases is what we have in fact chosen through acts that we have voluntarily chosen to engage in. Whether or not we become intimate with another person is within our control, and the acts that together constitute a friendship are such that persons ought to know that engaging in them will lead to intimacy. Although it may not always be determinate whether two persons are intimate, there is plenty of time before intimacy is determinately achieved for the persons involved to pull back. It may be that they have objective agent-neutral or subjective agent-relative reasons for not pulling back, but acting for reasons, either objective or subjective, certainly does not undermine the voluntary character of what one does.[10] Similarly, although we do not always control the circumstances in which we develop an intimate relationship, we are always in control of whether we actually do become intimate with another person.

Intimacy, as I have characterized it, is a mutual relationship: we can never simply find ourselves in some social structure that assigns to us the role of so-and-so's friend. An institution may use that language, but it cannot, merely by so doing, actually make it the case that persons are friends. Intimacy demands time, insofar as it is a relationship partially constituted by mutual special knowledge acquired through causal interaction. Although it is also partially constituted by certain mutual attitudes, and we do not always have control over our attitudes (at least not at a time), such attitudes are never sufficient for intimacy. While intimacy is a matter of degree, there is always an interval wherein we can disengage ourselves from a relationship before having any significant level of commitment. We can cease to spend time with another, we can refuse to reveal more of ourselves, we can fail to evidence special concern in our interactions with the other, and we can make it clear to the other that we do not want to know anymore than we already do about him or her. Again, we may have objective agent-neutral reasons for not acting in these ways, i.e., we may have objective agent-neutral reasons for forming certain friendships, just as we have objective agent-neutral reasons for making many promises. But, again, this fact certainly does not undermine the voluntary character of actions undertaken for such reasons.

Of course, someone might say, people do not usually proceed in relationships in such a careful way, constantly monitoring and reflecting upon each development in intimacy. Further, it might be said, it is a very good thing that they do not do so: such clear-eyed planning seems antithetical to the spontaneous growth of a friendship, a spontaneity and naturalness that appear to enhance the value of such relationships. Thus, if the objection is right, then only in degraded relationships will the voluntarist requirement actually be met. It certainly would be odd to regard friendship as satisfying the voluntarist requirement if such satisfaction depended upon persons' ability to create a less valuable relationship, even if they do not actually do so.

Worries about over-reflecting on the nature of one's relationships, both considered in themselves and relative to other considerations (in particular, moral considerations), has been what I regard as a worrisome development in contemporary moral theory.[11] Bernard Williams and Susan Wolf have been two of the many who have developed these sorts of worries, and many moral philosophers have responded by showing how reflection need not occur overtly, but need only be reverted to in extraordinary cases when moral constraints are going to be breached.[12] Thus, there seem to be concerted attempts to show that one need not constantly reflect on one's relationships in order to meet the moral demands that come both from within the relationship and from outside of the relationship. The supposedly ideal moral agent is seen as one who acts from her love and other affections, in a spontaneous way, never "one thought too many."[13] The overly reflective agent is one, according to these critics, that no one would want to have as a friend.[14]

As I said, I think that this trend in contemporary ethics is worrisome and needs to be resisted without giving up ground. Individuals need to recognize that the world makes many and diverse claims upon them, in addition to the claims of their own desires. The process of deliberation is always a complex matter, demanding attention to a wide array of facts and persons. More, rather than less reflection is what is needed as we mature and develop more commitments of myriad forms, from simple everyday promises to charitable pledges to professional ties to personal, loving relationships. We need to understand that these commitments generate objective claims upon us, and that we need to monitor how many such commitments we acquire. It is irresponsible to act so that we wake up and discover one day that we have more commitments than we can honor, at least not without stinting on some of them or on our own subjective reasons or our ever-present agent-neutral reasons.

No amount of reflection rules out acting from love for our friends, sympathy and compassion for strangers, respect for colleagues, and concern for students. It is a strange psychology that supposes that calm reflection is incompatible with love. Any love worth its name will be part of a complex intimate relationship. So I am not concerned to show that reflection is compatible with red-hot romantic passion or with all-consuming devotion—these attitudes may be ones that are incompatible with a rational, ethical life. Real love, as part of intimacy, takes time to develop, because it is a response to another person as the person who she is and who she understands herself to be, not any sort of immediate response to the luster of her eyes or the seductiveness of her pose. Both emotional and physical lust are forms of desire upon which subjective reasons supervene, but which generate no objective claims upon us. And these forms of lust are likely to be in conflict with many of our long-term, settled desires—for our own sakes, then, we must control what we do in response to any form of 'love at first sight.' While I am not convinced that spontaneity is all that valuable, whatever value it does have must be weighed against other values and other reasons. This weighing does not happen by itself—it is up to rational agents to do it, perhaps not every minute of the day, but often, and well.

In fact, surely the best forms of intimacy are those in which we reflect, with our intimate or potential intimate, on what is happening between us and on the significance of what is happening. We owe it to others to let them know what our lives are like so that they can understand our already existent commitments and thereby understand what role they can legitimately play in our lives. If a potential friend opposes my concern with objective value and with my personal and professional commitments already in place, then I must recognize that intimacy with such a person is best avoided or kept to a minimum. The best friends are those who can aid us in our deliberations, not those who wish that we could be more simple-mindedly devoted to them. The current trend in ethics is disturbing insofar as it seems to encourage such simplemindedness.

I think that it is probably true that more women than men are adept at the sort of friendship in which aiding one another in deliberation is one of the cornerstones of the relationship. Surely part of the reason for this difference results from the different games that we play as children—while sports develop common deliberation about strategies, playing house and playing with dolls involve make-believe regarding personal situations and thus involve practice for real-life ethical deliberations, especially given that children will often mimic situations that they witness between adults, including situations of conflict.[15] (This is, of course, *a priori* sociology on my part, and so should be taken with some skepticism.) That activity often dreaded by some men, 'talking about feelings,' is an essential part of any responsible engagement in human relationships. No one can rationally afford to avoid it.

Thus, the nature of intimacy itself is fully compatible with the voluntarist requirement, and objections to voluntarism as undermining the worth of close relationships are not compelling, and are, in fact, representative of a very destructive attitude to the rational deliberative life. Before moving on to consider contexts in which the voluntarist requirement might seem to have objectionable consequences for the scope of our objective agent-relative reasons, I want to consider one more potential objection to my voluntarist account of intimacy. This objection is inspired by an account of the justification of special obligations offered by Thomas Hurka in his "The Justification of National Partiality."[16] Hurka claims that we are justified (and, I take it, required) in being specially concerned about those persons with whom we have shared histories either of doing good or of suffering evil. Hurka's account is clearly not a voluntarist account, as seems obvious from the fact that histories of suffering evil together generate special obligations, and rarely do people choose to suffer evil, alone or together. I am not here concerned to show the general inadequacy of Hurka's account, as I have done that elsewhere.[17] What I want to do is to take an example of people suffering together—thrown together in a situation beyond their control—and examine an apparent conflict between intuition and my voluntarist account of intimacy and its resultant obligations.

Suppose that Anne and Edith are Jewish citizens in Germany in 1941. They are both deported to Auschwitz where they are housed in the same barracks and work side by side in the camp. Both Anne and Edith survive the horrors of Auschwitz and eventually emigrate to the United States. In 1950 Anne contacts Edith, asking her for financial help of a serious nature. Does Edith have a special obligation to help Anne in virtue of their having suffered extreme hardship and deprivation together?

This example, I think, is very powerful, insofar as it gets at a very common intuition, similar to the one operative in the case of family members. Whether or not Anne and Edith chose to engage in various actions, surely, it might be said, they owe special obligations to one another in virtue of having suffered together. The difficulty here is that Edith probably has reasons to help Anne that persons who did not suffer with Anne do not have: Edith is in a position to know Anne's needs and how to help her while preserving her self-esteem as much as possible (derivatively relative, but fundamentally neutral reasons), and Edith's own sentiments will provide her with subjective reasons. But this does not imply that Edith has any special obligations to Anne. Edith and Anne were thrust into a horrible situation together; certainly, neither in any way chose to be deported to Auschwitz. In the camp they might have comforted each other and depended upon one another for emotional support: if so, then they might meet the conditions for having developed intimacy. Of course, any such intimacy would have been a good that they were desperately in need of, perhaps to such an extent that only such intimacy would allow them to survive. They might be two people who would never have become emotionally close in less extreme circumstances. However, one's need for a certain form of commitment and one's choosing the best of perhaps a dismal array of available options does not undermine the voluntary nature of what one does. On the other hand, if Anne and Edith developed no such intimacy in the camp, then Edith has no special obligation to Anne. Any person complicit in the horrors of the Holocaust has special obligations to both, in order to make a start toward amends for what has been done to them, their loved ones, and their lives more generally.

So these sorts of cases need to be sorted out: our strong intuitions that the moral situation between Anne and Edith is changed in virtue of their having suffered together are right, but not because Anne and Edith have objective agent-relative obligations to one another. Edith has strong derivatively relative, but fundamentally neutral reasons to help Anne, and probably has strong subjective reasons to do so. In addition, we might think that Edith has objective agent-neutral reason to reach out to Anne and attempt to form an intimate relationship with her. After all, common suffering forms a bridge between two people that can facilitate emotional closeness and mutual comfort and support. We have objective agent-neutral reasons to seize chances to form valuable relationships. But until Edith does so, she has no objective agent-relative obligations to Anne, which is not to say that she may not act irrationally in not aiding her and in not developing such objective agent-relative obligations.

This sort of case is important to keep in mind as we enter the family context. My denial that the mere fact of familial and/or blood connection has any rational significance is not a denial of the claim that family relations usually have significant instrumental impact on the nature of our reasons. To a lesser, but still significant extent, the same is true of our involvement in certain forms of political structures.

Politics, Family, and Benevolence

So the voluntarist can accommodate the intuition that intimate relationships ground special obligations. But the voluntarist is unable to accommodate other special obligations to which common sense is at least as committed; in particular, it seems that the voluntarist is unable to accommodate special obligations to family members, benefactors, and compatriots.

Most people think that they have special obligations to their parents, siblings, grandparents, nieces and nephews, etc.[18] Further, they think that they have special obligations to these people in virtue of their being biologically related in the specified way; for example, the mere fact that Barbara is my mother, or that Olga is my grandmother, is understood to be sufficient to make it the case that I owe differential concern to Barbara, or to Olga. But it is clearly not the case that I have chosen to be Barbara's daughter or to be Olga's granddaughter. Thus, the voluntarist requirement rules out mere biological relation as sufficient for grounding special obligations.

Obviously, the voluntarist in no way denies that I *can* have special obligations to my mother and to my grandmother. If I have developed intimate relationships with them, then I have special obligations to them based on that intimacy. Certain kinds of familial relationships also create excellent conduits for the promotion of objective value, thereby grounding agent-neutral reasons for those party to them to take care of one another. Family members who have spent good portions of their lives with certain people are in excellent causal and epistemic positions for benefitting one another, and aid is often more appreciated and easier to accept when it comes from a beloved family member.[19] So familial relations are often instrumentally valuable insofar as they provide good means for the promotion of intrinsic value. However, the voluntarist is committed to saying that the mere fact of biological relation, taken in itself (i.e., abstracted from intimacy or the promotion of objective value) grounds no special obligations.

The case of parents also illustrates why the voluntarist is committed to denying that we have duties of gratitude, where duties of gratitude are grounded on the mere *receipt* of benefits. When we are young, most of us have parents who do a great deal of good for us: they clothe, nourish, educate, shelter, and love us, dedicating a significant portion of their lives to making sure that we develop into capable, healthy, and happy adults. Our parents provide us with the goods necessary to our being able to take advantage of any other goods that life offers us: without their early nurture and care, our entire future well-being would be seriously jeopardized. But all of this good that our parents do for us is such that we have no ability to refuse it. They begin to care for us before we can care for ourselves, and as small children we are unable to refuse their shelter and nourishment. Until we are sixteen, the law itself coerces us to accept parental benefits. While many people seem to think that we owe special concern to parents in virtue of the good that they have done for us, the voluntarist is committed to denying that we are so obligated: if we cannot refuse the benefits, then our 'acceptance' of such benefits cannot ground special obligations, because such 'acceptance' is not a voluntary action.

The voluntarist can accommodate a type of duty of gratitude, a type grounded not in the *receipt* of benefits, but, rather, in the voluntary *acceptance* of benefits. If I voluntarily take a benefit from some person or group where I had the option of refusing, then we can understand my accepting the benefit as a commitment, i.e., as the voluntary assumption of an obligation to 'repay' in some form the kindness done for me. Again, we need not understand the acceptance of the benefit as constituting the making of a promise or a contract; rather, the acceptance of the benefit is one more way, in addition to promises and contracts, of making a commitment. I am not arguing for the claim that acceptance of benefits constitutes the making of a commitment. But it is important to see that even if a voluntarist accepts that claim, she will not have accommodated the full range of obligations of gratitude that common sense often takes us as having.

The distinction between benefits received and benefits accepted has played a role in discussions about the grounds of special political obligations. Some have in fact tried to understand our obligations to our fellow citizens as obligations of gratitude for what the state has done for us.[20] John Rawls has argued that when we receive benefits within systems of social cooperation that meet various conditions, we then have duties of fair play to do our part in maintaining such social systems.[21] Although a duty of fair play is distinct from a duty of gratitude, the former, like the latter, grounds obligations on the receipt of benefits, whether or not such receipt was voluntary or could be avoided. So the duty of fair play, like the duty of gratitude, is not an option for a voluntarist.

The most famous voluntarist attempt to accommodate political obligations is of course Locke's consent theory. Locke recognized that we rarely give our explicit consent to obey the laws of our countries, i.e., we rarely engage in actions such as taking an oath that constitute the assumption of an obligation of obedience. So Locke decided to appeal to tacit consent, i.e., to actions that we refrained from performing—in particular, leaving the country—such that their performance, and only their performance, would constitute the rejection of an obligation of obedience. Staying in the country, then, constitutes the assumption of an obligation of obedience to the laws.

The literature on consent theory is large, and so I am not going to rehearse the arguments against Locke's appeal to tacit consent. The most effective response to Locke remains, I think, one of the earliest, that offered by Hume in "Of the Original Contract." Hume, with his examples of the poor peasant and of the fellow who wakes up to find himself on a pirate ship in shark-infested waters, stresses the point that consent, as a voluntary undertaking, requires options, and it is just not so clear that we always have many realistic options other than staying put in our countries of birth.

Even if some of us have committed ourselves to our fellow citizens, notice that special political obligations, on the voluntarist account, are not a matter of being obligated merely in virtue of being compatriots with certain persons. Joining the state becomes just like joining a book club or taking a job in a philosophy department. And, just as those who do not join the book club or accept a job in the department have no commitments to those groups, so those who do not join the state have no special political obligations, regardless of their residency and citizenship status.[22]

So the voluntarist does not line up well with common sense with respect to the family, political community, and gratitude. But before we align ourselves with common sense here, we need to examine anti-voluntarist accounts of special obligations, and decide whether the benefits of those accounts are sufficient to outweigh their disadvantages.

II. ANTI-VOLUNTARIST ACCOUNTS OF SPECIAL OBLIGATIONS

In recent years voluntarism has come under attack, particularly in the political context. It is sometimes suggested that we ought not object to special political obligations merely on the basis of the unchosen nature of political connections; after all, it is said, we all think that we have special obligations to family members and connections to family members certainly are not chosen. Of course, no such argument will work once one calls into question the claim that we have special obligations to family members simply in virtue of the familial and/or blood relation.[23] So we need to consider accounts of special obligations that appeal to some unchosen 'feature' of a person or to some unchosen 'relationship' in which she stands to other persons.

The Appeal to Identity and Constitutive Attachments

Perhaps the most influential advocate of an anti-voluntarist conception of special obligations in recent years has been Michael Sandel. His communitarian critique of Rawls and liberal political theory more generally has been widely discussed and cited.[24] I think, however, that Sandel's critique of Rawls is highly confused, although that critique is not relevant to our current discussion. Thus, I am simply going to use some remarks of Sandel's in order to construct an alternative account of special obligations.[25]

Sandel clearly wants to oppose a view according to which special obligations are the result of commitments subject to the voluntarist constraint. He claims that we cannot regard ourselves as *independent* in this way without great cost to those loyalties and convictions whose moral force consists partly in the fact that living by them is inseparable from understanding ourselves as the particular persons we are . . . Allegiances such as these are more than values I happen to have or aims I 'espouse at any given time.' They go beyond the obligations I voluntarily incur and the 'natural duties' I owe to human beings as such. They allow that to some I owe more than justice requires or even permits, *not by reason of agreements I have made but instead in virtue of those more or less enduring attachments and commitments which taken together partly define the person I am.* (179; italics mine)

Sandel is here using the term 'commitment' in a way significantly different than that in which I have used the term, given that he contrasts it with obligations that are 'voluntarily incurred.' Sandel is describing our positions in a "family or community or nation or people," i.e., positions into which we are thrust at birth with no chance to choose or to reject those positions. He calls these positions or relations 'constitutive attachments' insofar as he regards them as partially constitutive of a person's identity. In fact, he thinks, a person without such attachments would be "a person wholly without character, without moral depth. For to have character is to know that I move in a history I neither summon nor command, which carries consequences none the less for my choices and conduct" (179). He thinks that we need to consider these unchosen attachments in any moral deliberation.

Because Sandel's claims are so compressed, it is difficult to know exactly what his view is. On one interpretation, Sandel is a type of metaethical relativist, i.e., he understands the claim that X has a reason to do y as a claim that X belongs to some sort of group that regards X as having a position involving a duty to do y. Because I am not, in this chapter, concerned with such metaethical issues, I will understand Sandel, not as a metaethical relativist, but, rather, within the framework of my own metaphysics. Within that framework, Sandel would be claiming that reasons supervene not only on chosen commitments but also, and more significantly for the agents who have the reasons, on unchosen 'attachments.' Which unchosen attachments generate reasons? It seems that Sandel's answer would be: those that are partially constitutive of our identity.

It is never clear how Sandel (and philosophers who follow or agree with him[26]) want to understand the claim that certain relationships help to constitute our identities. There are (at least) two ways to interpret such a claim: (i) *metaphysically,* such that the person writing this now would not exist if she had not been involved in the various attachments thrust upon her at birth, or (ii) *causally,* such that the person writing this now would be a very different sort of person if she had not been involved in the various attachments thrust upon her at birth. (i) is an implausible claim, but I am not going to evaluate it here, because showing what is problematic about it would take us into issues about personal identity, the mind–body problem, and essentialism. (ii) is an obviously true empirical claim. In what follows, I will also assume the truth of (i) regardless of its implausibility, because I will show that neither (i) nor (ii) can support the sort of normative conclusions that Sandel wants to draw.

So let us suppose that I would not exist or would not be the sort of person that I am if I were not my parents' (biological) daughter, an American, raised in a Catholic family, of German and Danish descent, etc. I do not want to deny that these sorts of facts about me have moral significance, and, in certain cases, *great* moral significance. My derivatively relative, but fundamentally neutral reasons are affected by my placement as a US citizen and as my mother's daughter. I must understand my nature in order to understand how I can promote good and best respond to other persons. My location in a causal web determines what options are available to me. Only a careless deliberator would ignore facts that have had such a great causal influence upon her when she is deciding how to promote value and which commitments to make. Also, we have to pay close attention to our histories and our unchosen communities in order to truly understand our own desires, given that many of them result from the way that we have been educated and raised. That reflection often leads us to revise our desires, once we see that they have been the result of sexist or racist upbringings.[27] Reflection upon our families and communities can also keep us from making hasty rejections of unchosen situations that offer ample and varied opportunities for the promotion of value, both for others and within our own lives.

All of these sorts of claims support Sandel's contention that deliberation for anyone with a substantive character in the world as it is will inevitably involve consideration of features of themselves and their situations that they never chose. But such unchosen 'attachments' do not generate objective agent-relative reasons. In order to see this, consider a constitutive attachment that, more than any other, has a claim to be such that we would not even exist without it, and also plays a large role in determining the types of people that we become: our connections to our biological parents. Our genetic inheritance has a lot to do with who we are. Raymond A. Belliotti argues that "if the acts of the self can create moral requirements (as is universally accepted), then the (other) constituents of self can also. Thus, as my biological parents' genetic [contribution] provides a most enduring aspect of who 'I' am, I owe them certain moral requirements."[28] Belliotti challenges the voluntarist: "if the *acts* of self create moral requirements, why cannot the self *itself* create moral requirements by its very nature" (153).

The simple answer is: because what we become is often a result of the manipulations, deceptions, or downright cruelty of others. If a young woman was seriously abused by her biological parents, and then adopted at the age of ten by a kind couple who nurture and love her, to whom does she owe obligations? Whatever we say about the adoptive parents, it seems absolutely clear to me that she owes nothing to her biological parents. But the fact remains that, given the enormous effect of early childhood experiences, the person that our young woman is, is largely due to her biological parents. In this case, however, it seems that what the parents do generates obligations on their parts to make amends (primarily, by staying out of their child's life), but no obligations on the part of the child.

Playing a role in 'constituting a person's identity' can be done with indifference or with malice and evil intent. In Thailand small girls are sold by their families into prostitution with a high risk of contracting AIDS and dying before the age of thirty. What obligations do these young girls have to their families and to the communities that allow this traffic in human lives? Surely the answer is: absolutely none. We cannot help being born to our parents and into our communities, and we cannot help the nature of our infancy and childhood experiences. But, for many people in the world, this is a tragic fact. All of these facts about themselves are relevant to their deliberations, but not because they owe more to those who have shaped their destiny and their nature through oppression, indifference, neglect, and/or cruelty. Their peculiar positions may generate derivatively relative reasons to offer help to those who are in the same position: so our adopted young woman has good reason to work with abused children, perhaps, and young women who manage to escape Thailand's shameful sexual industry have reasons to campaign to raise awareness about young girls still caught in the trap of that hell.[29]

I want to emphasize that I am not rejecting the Sandel-style view of obligations because it leads to the conclusion that people can sometimes have reasons to do bad things.[30] For example, it seems that constitutive attachments may have made it the case that many Germans had reasons to persecute Jews, even if these reasons were outweighed by their objective agent-neutral reasons. Sandel's view certainly has that implication, but I do not think that that is enough to sink it. After all, I myself am committed to the claim that persons have reasons that supervene on evil desires. Similarly, our intimate relationships might give us reasons to do what is contrary to the promotion of objective value. What is peculiarly unappealing about Sandel-style views is that they allow that *the evil things that others do to us* generate special obligations for us. I hope that the earlier cases make that claim sufficiently implausible.

At this point, someone like Sandel might claim that he is only talking about those constitutive attachments that are crucial to our identity in the sense that we identify with those attachments. Thus, it need not be the case, contra Belliotti, that genetic inheritance counts as a constitutive attachment. Shifting to talk about identification renders the agent in some sense party to the values and ideals of the communities that have shaped her nature. But then how do these constitutive attachments differ from an agent's own commitments or desires? Only if they are attachments from which there is no option of exit, because commitments need not be undertaken and desires create reasons only as long as the agent continues to have them. But then we have gotten back to another implausible claim: if the manipulations or oppression of others are powerful enough to create identification with the ideals and persons of the oppressors, then and only then can our constitutive attachments to these others generate obligations. No doubt oppression has worked in this way, most particularly and for the longest time, in the case of the oppression of women.[31] The success of oppressive structures in getting the oppressed to internalize them, however, does not seem to be sufficient to generate obligations on the part of the oppressed to the oppressors.

So something is wrong in the appeal to mere constitutive attachments, given that such attachments can be the result of oppression and even of conscious malice or indifference. It would be a moral world beyond my ken if the cruel acts of others that have effects on me that I cannot avoid generate special obligations on my part to care for those who have harmed or oppressed me. In response to this sort of worry, some philosophers have tried to state a condition upon unchosen roles which is such that if satisfied, then those roles generate obligations.

Appeals to constitutive attachments, including genetic inheritance, are motivated by a legitimate and serious philosophical concern, i.e., a concern to capture actual lived moral experience. The worry about my voluntarist account of intimacy is that it can cover only part of the territory that many people regard as occupied by the requirements of special obligations. While political obligations may not seem so obvious to us today in light of our recognition of the atrocities that can and have been carried out in the name of commitment to compatriots,[32] people still do feel that their strongest moral ties are those to family. Whereas this term has traditionally been associated with ties between people of either a blood or marital nature, it has been extended in recent years to account for, for example, ties to adoptive or stepparents and ties to lovers or partners even when no legal marital bond exists. While some of these relationships clearly involve mutual contractual commitments, others involve either no contractual commitment or only a one-way commitment, as in the case of adoptive parents. We do not choose our parents, our siblings, or our grandparents. We are simply born into these relationships, and so voluntarism seems to be undermined given that most people will regard their intuitions about familial obligations as stronger than any that they might have about voluntarism. Family and friends seem to be the two paradigmatic groups of persons to whom we have associative obligations, and, if we accept voluntarism, it seems, only the latter remains. Thus, many will think, voluntarism has to go.

In this section, I have rejected the attempt to accommodate familial obligations via an appeal to constitutive or 'identity-constituting' attachments or relations. What we seem to need at this point, in order to make any non-voluntarist view palatable, is a condition upon unchosen roles or positions within a group or community that offers us a principled way to avoid regarding obligations as being created by the cruel or malevolent actions of others. In the following sections, I will examine two attempts to offer such a condition or conditions, attempts offered by Michael Hardimon and Samuel Scheffler. Both views are meant to cover the entire territory of special obligations from the family to the political. Because those two spheres are my primary concern here, I will use examples from both realms in order to show why neither of the views is adequate. I will also show that my view can accommodate a wide range of familial obligations, the range that *reflective* intuition would accept. Political obligations, on the other hand, can no longer be considered within the boundaries of special obligations.

Roles and Reflective Acceptability

So we are pulled in two directions with respect to special obligations: we feel that our range of special obligations is wider than voluntarism seems to allow, and yet the unchosen character of certain roles makes us cautious about their ability to generate obligations when the roles are part of abusive, destructive, or stultifying practices. The most common sort of response to this sort of tension is to place certain conditions upon the nature of the roles and practices such that only roles and practices that meet those conditions generate associative obligations. This is precisely the sort of response offered by Michael Hardimon in his "Role Obligations."[33]

Hardimon offers an account of obligations attached to certain institutionally defined roles, including political and familial roles, where a role is a "[constellation] of institutionally specified rights and duties organized around an institutionally specified social function" (334). He defines a role obligation as "a moral requirement, which attaches to an institutional role, whose content is fixed by the function of the role, and whose normative force flows from the role" (334). Both familial and political obligations are what Hardimon calls noncontractual role obligations, and, as such, are

> in stark opposition to the familiar idea that the only way in which we can acquire role obligations—or, in any case, role obligations with genuine moral force—is by signing on for the roles to which they are attached. (343)

Thus, noncontractual role obligations do not satisfy the voluntarist requirement (what Hardimon calls the volunteer principle).

Hardimon seems to think that the voluntarist requirement gains at least some of its plausibility from an implicit conflation of a person's being born into a role and a person's being coerced into a role or being forced to occupy the role against her will. He says that defenders of the voluntarist requirement assume that roles are either assumed by an explicit act of choice, as when one signs an employment contract, or the result of impressment, as British men used to be captured and forced to serve on naval vessels. For certain social roles, Hardimon insists, there is another option: I did not choose to be my mother's daughter, but it need not be the case that I occupy the role of daughter against my will. What we need, then, is some way of differentiating roles into which we are impressed against our will from roles which we do not choose but, nonetheless, do not occupy against our will.

Hardimon argues that the social roles that generate genuine special obligations are those that are *reflectively acceptable*:

> To say that a social role is *reflectively acceptable* is to say that one would accept it upon reflection. Determining whether a given social role is reflectively acceptable involves stepping back from that role in thought and asking whether it is a role people ought to occupy and play. Determining that a given social role is reflectively acceptable involves judging that it is (in some sense) meaningful, rational, or good. (348)

Social roles need not actually be judged to be acceptable in order to be reflectively acceptable: "in contrast to the volunteer principle [the voluntarist requirement], which calls for a form of *choice* that is actual, the ideal of reflective acceptability calls for a form of acceptance that is *hypothetical*" (348). Thus, Hardimon concludes that "noncontractual role obligations are not morally binding unless the roles to which they attach are reflectively acceptable" (350).

I have elsewhere offered criticisms of the notion of an institution upon which Hardimon's account depends.[34] I will not reiterate those criticisms here, but, rather, focus on some others that, I think, show the problems with his type of view in general. It has become quite popular in moral philosophy to appeal to counterfactuals in order to avoid difficulties with certain types of views.[35] The general trend toward 'naturalizing' in contemporary philosophy lends itself to this sort of appeal. If one is dissatisfied with, say, a straightforward subjectivist account of reasons, one can try to avoid these problems by an appeal to what a person would desire if . . . (here one fills in one's favorite conditions, epistemic, metaphysical, normative, etc.). The philosopher who does so gives the illusion of capturing the intuitions that have driven others to objective realism without 'going metaphysical,' i.e., while still remaining 'naturalistic.' Of course, the illusion is just that—an illusion. Without some account of the truth-makers of counterfactual assertions, it is not at all clear that one has not gone 'metaphysical.'

More importantly, Hardimon never gives a very good idea of what it is for something to be 'reflectively acceptable.' He does tell us that to judge a social role as reflectively acceptable is to judge "that it is (*in some sense*) meaningful, rational, or good" (my italics). But the addition of that phrase 'in some sense' creates distinct problems for this account. There is also a difficulty of understanding what is meant by the notion of a judgment here. We can distinguish several different interpretations, then, of Hardimon's view:

1. To say that a role is reflectively acceptable *for a given individual x* is to say that x would make the judgment that the role is meaningful,

rational, or good if she were to consider, with all of her present attitudes and beliefs, the question as to whether the role is meaningful, etc.

2. To say that a role is reflectively acceptable *for a given individual x* is to say that x would make the judgment that the role is meaningful, etc., if she were to consider, under certain *idealized* circumstances, the question as to whether the role is meaningful, etc.

3. To say that a role is reflectively acceptable *for a given individual x* is to say that x would make the *true* judgment that the role is meaningful, etc., if she were to consider, under either actual or ideal conditions, the question whether the role is meaningful, etc.

Let us call 1 the idiosyncratic understanding of reflective acceptability. This understanding is clearly inadequate to Hardimon's purposes. After all, if social institutions are coercive and oppressive, persons born into them will often develop beliefs and attitudes as a result of oppression. These beliefs and attitudes then lead to confirming the validity of traditional roles merely as a result of their deep embedment in the culture. So the idiosyncratic understanding of reflective acceptability leads us back to all of the difficulties that we faced with the Sandel-style account.

Hardimon probably has something more like 2 in mind. On the idealized understanding, whether or not we need to refer to the agent whom we are considering depends upon what count as idealized circumstances: are we to evaluate the acceptability of the role relative to the agent's epistemic position, i.e., understanding rationality as dependent upon evidence available to her, etc.? If so, then we will still face similar problems as those we faced in the case of the idiosyncratic account: in oppressive societies, it might well be rational for individuals to have various false beliefs, either false causal beliefs about what promotes value, or false normative beliefs about what is in fact valuable. As in the case of the idiosyncratic account, we are left to wonder why oppressive institutions generate reasons if they are oppressive enough to affect people's beliefs or what it is rational for those persons to believe.

So if Hardimon is to avoid these problems, he should understand 2 as an appeal to some agent in ideal epistemic conditions. Thus, we can understand 2 as a universalistic account of rational acceptability: any agent under the ideal conditions will reach the same judgment about the meaningfulness, etc., of the role in question. But why should the fact that some idealized person would find the role to be meaningful, etc., make it the case that we should find unobjectionable the fact that we have no choice in accepting these roles? The only answer that I can think of reduces 2 to 3: the judgment about the meaningfulness of the role is in fact a *true* judgment. (Given that true judgments can be made in less than ideal conditions, I have put 3 in such a way that we allow for a given individual making the true judgment under actual circumstances. After all, even in oppressive conditions—which I take to be less than ideal for making moral judgments—people can come to true moral conclusions.)

But then, of course, why not avoid any appeal to 3 and just say that roles are reflectively acceptable when they *are* meaningful, rational, or good? I agree with Hardimon that we have reasons to fill roles that contribute to overall good—these are objective agent-neutral reasons. However, in looking for special obligations, we are looking for nonderivative, objective agent-relative reasons. In Chapter 2, I argued that reasons of intimacy cannot be accommodated by an appeal solely to objective agent-neutral reasons (or by an appeal to those reasons in combination with subjective agent-relative reasons). Hardimon's account, on the other hand, has been reduced to a claim about obligations of role that depends on a claim about their value. Why, then, according to Hardimon, do we need to add objective agent-relative reasons to our moral ontology?

I think that Hardimon's account gains plausibility in relation to his voluntarist opposition because of his simplistic dichotomy between impressment or coercion and choice, and also because of an ambiguity in what counts as a 'social role.' In the account of intimacy and commitment that I have offered in earlier chapters, I have understood choice as a very complex phenomenon. What we are choosing when we choose an intimate relationship is such that it cannot be chosen at a time in the way that one chooses a meal off of a menu or a dress out of a catalog. Relationships are temporally extended and are partially constituted by a history of certain types of interaction. So if we understand voluntarism as limiting special obligations to contexts in which the choice of the role or commitment takes place in the way that ordering pasta primavera off of a menu takes place, then it is quite clear that voluntarism fails to do justice to the phenomenology concerning our special obligations. But once we understand choice in the complex way that I have suggested, we can see that a voluntarist account can capture a far wider range of special obligations.

Secondly, the notion of a social role is not clearly spelled out in Hardimon's account. Consider the role of daughter. There is the biological understanding of what it is for Diane to be Ron's daughter. But there is another sense of that role: if Diane never knew her biological father and was raised and became emotionally intimate with Ron, then we still understand Diane as Ron's daughter. The notion of a daughter is one that we amend as we reach new moral understandings: it used to be more common for people to remain in monogamous heterosexual relationships, and so roles tracked biology more closely.[36] In today's world, divorce and remarriage have forced us to reconsider our moral understandings, and, as we do so, we find ourselves changing our usage of terms associated with the formerly heterosexual nuclear family. This suggests that our understanding of the roles as 'socially defined' does not precede or ground our moral judgments about what people in those roles owe one another. Rather, it is the other way around: we make our language of roles track changing moral understandings. Because people move at different moral rates within society, there is often confusion and misunderstanding. So appeal to institutional roles as basic in this context is wrongheaded: what we hope is to get our institutions to track our value and other moral judgments. So the notion of some social role does not seem to be basic in generating reasons in the way that intimacy does seem basic.

My argument against Hardimon, then, comes to the worry that he has given us no grounds for supposing that valuable, unchosen roles generate anything other than objective agent-neutral reasons. We can imagine a society in which persons born to sailor parents on board ship are thereby born into the role not only of son/daughter of sailors but into the very role of sailor itself. I grant that this is a conceivably valuable social arrangement and that people born to sailor parents on board ship ought, all things considered, fulfill what are understood to be the duties of a sailor. In such a case would these born sailors have special agent-relative reasons of a nonderivative sort? If they found that it would be equally valuable to switch roles, perhaps to that of helicopter pilot, would it be morally objectionable to do so, in the way that it does seem morally objectionable to switch from one friend to another (or from friendship to another valuable project) when value is on the side of switching? (See my argument in Chapter 2 about our intuitions regarding friendship.)

Value and Special Obligations

Samuel Scheffler, like Hardimon, attempts to defend an anti-voluntarist account of special obligations.[37] For Scheffler, special obligations are grounded by "socially salient connections between persons" (198). What counts as such a "social tie" between persons will vary over time and between cultures. For example (mine, not Scheffler's), on the Earth as depicted in the film *Planet of the Apes,* our common humanity would most likely be a socially salient connection, although it is not here on Earth in the real world. In the actual world, all of the following are socially salient connections: being siblings, being compatriots, being comembers of the American Philosophical Association, being Catholic, etc.

Scheffler begins with the uncontroversial claim that people often value (where I take it that he means by 'value,' 'subjectively value,' not 'judge to be objectively valuable') such relationships. But then Scheffler makes the more controversial claim that valuing such relationships involves seeing such relationships as generating special obligations. He claims that insofar as I value my relationship with another person, I will view that other person as "providing . . . [me] with presumptively decisive reasons for action, reasons that . . . [I] would not have had in the absence of the relationship"; in fact, "I cannot value my relationships (noninstrumentally) without seeing them as sources of special responsibilities" (196). Persons will regard themselves as having certain special obligations, and their so regarding themselves reveals what relationships they value.

As I noted earlier in my discussions of Hardimon and Sandel, oppressive social structures have a great impact on what people actually subjectively value. In order to avoid letting such social structures provide people with special obligations generated by their oppression in others' self-interest, Scheffler claims that X's subjectively valuing a relationship is necessary but not sufficient for X's having special obligations arising from the relationship: the other necessary condition of X's having such obligations is that X have an independent, objective reason to value the relationship (197). If, for example, Jasmine values her relationship with her abusive husband, she does not thereby have special obligations to him, because she has reasons against valuing the relationship that outweigh any reasons that she has for valuing it. So, to summarize Scheffler's view: relationships give rise to special obligations only when persons have an all-things-considered reason to value intrinsically the relationship.[38]

Scheffler's argument is as follows:

1. We have good reason to value (noninstrumentally) certain relationships with other persons.
2. To value (noninstrumentally) certain relationships is, in part, to see those relationships as a source of reasons, i.e., as a source of special obligations.
3. Therefore, we have good reason to see ourselves as having special obligations (200).

So it seems that persons have reason to subjectively value certain relationships, i.e., have reason to acquire special obligations (or, at least, to conceive of themselves as having such obligations). Scheffler concludes that "skepticism about such [special] responsibilities will be justified only if we are prepared to deny that we have good reasons to value our relationships" (200–201).

There are serious worries about the form of argument that Scheffler is using; for example, can we really infer the existence of actual obligations from its being valuable that people conceive of themselves as having those obligations? Surely that is a questionable inference at best. However, rather than focusing on that move in Scheffler's argument, I want to look at his notion of a 'socially salient connection' or 'social tie' and ask whether it is plausible to take such 'connections' or 'ties' between people as the grounds of special obligations.

First, notice how broad Scheffler's notion of a relationship is. Let us return to an example that I adapted from Hardimon, that of persons born into the role of naval sailor. Persons might well value their occupation of the role of sailor, and, as I suggested, under at least certain conditions, they would have reason to value it (where I understand that to mean that their filling of that role is, all things considered, a valuable course of action). Suppose that in our imaginary navy, there are hundreds of thousands of born sailors. Each of these persons came to occupy her role via being born to sailor parents on board of a naval vessel. According to Scheffler, such persons all have special obligations to all other born sailors, because they stand in the relationship of 'com-sailor' to one another.

But, if I am a born sailor, my 'relationship' to any other given sailor involves each of us satisfying a particular description, i.e., born to sailor parents on a naval vessel. In other words, the use of the term 'relationship' here is somewhat misleading. Normally, when we say that, for example, Sam and Jasmine have a relationship with one another, we think that something is true of each of them that could not have been true if the other had not existed. Such is obviously the case if Sam and Jasmine are friends. But the only thing that is true of me as a born sailor that could not have been true of me if my com-sailor Jane had not existed is that I am a com-sailor of Jane, i.e., that I am a sailor simultaneously with Jane being a sailor. But this seems to be better described as a situation in which Jane and I share some property, rather than as a situation in which Jane and I stand in some relationship with one another. In the case of friends, the relationship between Sam and Jasmine necessarily involves each of them having certain relational properties that neither could have if the other did not exist. However, in the case of com-sailors, the 'relationship' is such that it involves Jane and I having properties all of which are such that either of us could still have those properties even if the other did not exist.

Jane and I, however, might share many valuable properties that each of us does in fact subjectively value: suppose that both of us are philosophically minded, generous, compassionate, witty, and pleasant to be in the company of. Given Scheffler's understanding of a relationship, it seems that any one of these features that Jane and I share would generate special obligations. Scheffler would have to admit that such an account of special obligations gains far too much ground for those obligations. However, he would probably insist that his requirement that relationships must be socially salient in order to generate obligations rules out many of the 'relationships' to which I have been pointing.

But what, exactly, is 'social salience'? Further, why should such 'salience' make it the case that shared properties suddenly become obligation-generating 'relationships'? As with the views of Sandel and Hardimon, Scheffler, in his bid to reject the voluntarist requirement, finds himself forced to appeal to some societal criterion in order to narrow the field of special relationships. What his view seems to come to is that if X values her exemplification of property p, X has reason to value her exemplification of p, *and society values the exemplification of p by its members,* then X has special obligations to other persons who exemplify p (even if she is unaware of who those others are). But it now becomes difficult to see any appeal to the view, except that, at least in our society, as a matter of contingent fact, it will turn out that most people have special political obligations and special familial obligations.[39]

While it is true that in ethics, as in philosophy more generally, we simply cannot proceed without taking intuitions as a starting point and then using them as tests of plausibility all along the course of our theory building, we certainly cannot take them at face value. While commonsense intuitions may play a particularly large role in ethics as compared to other areas of philosophy,[40] we need to be especially wary of them in ethics, given the role of self-interest in the determination of what we ought to do. Further, as I have often emphasized in this chapter, social structures have often used views about duty and obligation to reinforce oppression and to promote the interests of some small group of powerful persons. In *The Subjection of Women,* Mill constantly reiterates that views held by both men and women concerning the duties of the latter must be suspect, given the interests of the former in reinforcing those views and their power to do just that. So we must also be wary of views that claim that we have obligations arising not from anything that we ourselves voluntarily do, be it obligations arising from political membership or genetic connection. These views are especially troublesome if it turns out that, according to them, we have special obligations to persons of whom we are unaware and with whom we have never interacted. Such views, as we have seen, inevitably seem to point to some societal determination of which persons are picked out by a 'morally' relevant description. While I do not deny that there may be consequentialist reasons for encouraging people to believe that they do in fact have such obligations, I am highly reluctant to admit that they actually do have those obligations.

Conclusion
Reasons and Relationships

Our reasons are a function of the nature of the world, our natures, and our place in the world. If we were purely cognitive creatures, without affective or conative states of any kind, then we would not have subjective agent-relative reasons. If we never made commitments of any kind, then we would not have objective agent-relative reasons. If we could not come to be aware of intrinsic value in the world, then we would not have objective agent-neutral reasons. As it is, however, we live lives awash in reasons with various grounds, all placing demands on us, and, often, not all of these demands can be met.

While this fact makes our lives rich and deep, it also makes living rationally a complicated, often frustrating affair. The perspective of a rational person is not purely subjective, nor purely objective—but nor are there two distinct perspectives between which we must constantly shift, as Thomas Nagel would have us think.[1] Our task is to live coherently in a single, egocentric perspective, acknowledging various types of states of affairs as grounding reasons for us. Somehow we must do our best to weigh and balance all of our reasons. Moral theory cannot reduce the tensions and regrets that we all must face—all that it can do is show the source of the tension and help us live with the regrets that are unavoidable.

Should we bemoan the fact that we have desires that are not always in line with objective value? After all, if we did not have such desires, then some of the tension and conflict would disappear. But it is often just those desires that do not match up with objective value that make our lives peculiarly rich, satisfying, and, in the end, objectively valuable. If I never cared more for certain persons than I do for others, then I would miss the great (objective) good of personal affection and fondness. If I did not have desires for my cat's well-being beyond the value of my cat's life, then I would miss the great (objective) good of bonding with a creature so different from myself. If I did not have personal projects, then I would miss the great (objective) good of developing my capacities. Similarly, if we were not creatures who made commitments, the world would be without the value of friendship, love, community, and family. To get all of these objective values, we must simultaneously create relationships that generate reasons that compete with those generated by objective value. The truth about the normative world is not without its ironies.

Given the range of reasons that we have, it is also the case that what we standardly think of as moral virtue can come apart from rationality. An individual's desires and commitments can be in such extreme conflict with the demands of objective value, that the rational life for such a person may be one that involves the destruction of goodness and the promotion of badness. Because goodness is only one source of reasons, rationality will not always come down on the side of goodness. The existence of such a person is tragic—our aim as educators and parents should be to raise agents whose rationality supports the promotion of value in their own lives and in the lives of others. Also, hopefully both myself and my readers are the kinds of people for whom it is rational to punish, restrain, and attempt to change those for whom reasons and value become so divorced from making the world a good place.

Also, because I have made some reasons supervene upon an agent's awareness of the objective value of a state of affairs, agents who, for one reason or another, are unable (or, perhaps, unwilling) to recognize objective value in the world, will not have objective agent-neutral reasons. Cats, dogs, small children, and psychopaths all probably lack such reasons. But, again, those of us who are able to recognize objective value have reasons to promote it, and these reasons help to determine how we are to respond to the John Wayne Gacys and Jeffrey Dahmers amongst us: it may be entirely rational for us to punish an individual who acted in an entirely rational way.

Some may think that my view does not give the so-called 'moral' the appropriate priority in our lives. Supposedly the moral reasons are at least the objective agent-neutral and probably also the objective agent-relative. Should we suppose that these reasons always override the subjective agent-relative? I cannot think of why we should suppose that to be the case: after all, all reasons are of the same ontological type, and so they can be weighed against one another. Surely there are cases where my wanting something provides me with a reason to pursue it that is stronger than some one of my 'moral' reasons: if I really, *really* want that little black dress that I saw in the window, isn't it rational for me to purchase it, even if I could instead provide my closest friend with the boots for which she has been yearning? The obvious answer seems 'yes.' All of my reasons are reasons *for me*—I am not an impartial spectator and what is rational for me will inevitably reflect my subjective states.

The picture that I have presented, then, is not neat and unitary, but, I think, that is as it should be: we all know that life is not neat and that our deliberations reveal to us forces pulling in opposing directions. Value and reasons supervene on messy, complicated, and not always cooperative (either with us or with one another) natural facts—in that sense, value and reasons are at the mercy of natural and biological forces. The normative occupies an unusual space, sharing as it does features with the mathematical realm, and yet so much more at the mercy of the empirical insofar as it relates to human beings with all of their empirical and contingent flaws, hopes, loves, commitments, and needs.

Notes

NOTES TO THE INTRODUCTION

1. Ethicists carve up the territory into the normative and metaethical in various ways. What I am pointing to is one standard way of making the division.

NOTES TO CHAPTER 1

1. There are other sorts of explanations of the movements of a person's body or of changes in her psychological states such as "He pushed me," or "The morphine made me feel nauseous," that are not relevant here. So not all causal explanations of either psychological or physical changes in an individual are in terms of explanatory reasons, as I am understanding those reasons here. Much more could be said here, but doing so would take us too far afield into discussions of the nature of voluntary or autonomous action. I am concerned only to distinguish *one kind of explanation* of human conduct from *justifications* of human conduct.
2. Of course, a full explanation of my conduct would involve reference to, e.g., the presence of a pizza and the movement of my arms that transported the pizza to my mouth. I am limiting the notion of an explanatory reason to only those causes that are internal psychological states of the agent, but I intend this not to constitute analysis but, rather, stipulation.
3. See *A Treatise of Human Nature,* Book II—Of the Passions, Part III, Sect. III. Also, for the alleged moral significance of this psychological thesis, see Book III—Of Morals, Part I, Sect. I. Hume, does, however, in other passages in Book III, Part I, Sect. I, seem to retract this claim. For a contemporary defense of the Humean motivational thesis, see Michael Smith, *The Moral Problem* (Oxford, UK: Blackwell Publishers, Ltd., 1994), Chapter 4.
4. It seems that many such theses about motivation end up being trivial, i.e., they simply define desire as any state that is or can be an explanatory reason. See Thomas Nagel, *The Possibility of Altruism* (Princeton, NJ: Princeton University Press, 1970), Chapter V.
5. Of course, we can engage in the activities of forming, coming to have, maintaining, refusing to consider objections to, and trying to get rid of beliefs. The sense of justification with which I am concerned does apply to these sorts of activities.
6. The language of *prima facie* reasons is derived from W. D. Ross, *The Right and the Good* (Oxford, UK: Oxford University Press, 1930), but I do not claim to be following his precise view about the meaning of the terms here.

7. I certainly do not intend this to constitute an argument against noncognitivism, especially not the sophisticated versions of the view that have emerged in recent years. However, there is no doubt that some noncognitivists, such as C.L. Stevenson, have been struck by the obvious 'dynamic use'—to borrow Stevenson's term—to which 'ought' judgments and other normative judgments have been put. See Stevenson, "The Emotive Meaning of Ethical Terms," *Mind* 46 (1937): 14–31.

8. The answer to this question is actually more complicated than I am here making it appear. I will address that complexity in Chapter Two.

9. See Section IV of this chapter for more detailed discussion of this aspect of reasons and of its implications for the ontology of reasons.

10. I will discuss intrinsic goodness and the agent-neutral reasons that it grounds in Section IV of this chapter.

11. The need to specify such features will play a crucial role in my argument against a constraint against killing or torturing the innocent (Chapter Six).

12. I will not discuss reasons of prudence in this book. For an interesting discussion of prudence, see Derek Parfit, *Reasons and Persons* (Oxford, UK: Oxford University Press, 1984), Chapter 8.

13. One logical consequence of S's doing p is S's doing p. So S has a derivative reason to do p if the performance of the action p is itself intrinsically valuable.

14. Henry Sidgwick, *The Methods of Ethics* (Indianapolis: Hackett Publishing Co., 1981), 432–433.

15. As I say, I am concerned with the ontology of reasons. Thus, the main division with which I am concerned is that between subjectivists and objectivists. Insofar as linguistic analysis, per se, is not my main interest, I do not discuss any noncognitivist conceptions of reasons: noncognitivists and subjectivists will generally agree on the ontological level, disagreeing only at the level of linguistic analysis. Noncognitivists have a distinct disadvantage with respect to subjective descriptivists: they have to work much harder in explaining away the surface grammar of statements about reasons. Thus, if, at the ontological level, we have reason to reject subjective descriptivism, we also have reason to reject noncognitivism. See Richard Fumerton, *Reason and Morality: A Defense of the Egocentric Perspective* (Ithaca, NY: Cornell University Press, 1990), 18–30.

16. See Joel Feinberg, "Psychological Egoism," in *Reason and Responsibility*, 12th ed., ed. Joel Feinberg and Russ Shafer-Landau, 476–488 (Belmont, CA: Wadsworth, 1978). Feinberg uses this point in arguing against psychological egoistic hedonism.

17. I am taking it to be the case that, as I have mentioned before, agents only have reason to do or to pursue some object, action, or state of affairs O if they are in a causal position to do or to promote O. So for both subjective agent-relative and objective agent-neutral reasons, the agent's being in a causal position to promote the relevant state of affairs is part of the grounds of her reason to do so. For ease of exposition, for the rest of this section, I will take this stipulation about causal position for granted.

18. It is a completely independent question as to whether I have reason to become aware of the pictures and of their content. I may have reason to become aware of that which will give me reason to believe p without its being the case that I have reason to believe p.

19. I am not adding 'and my being aware of the fact that the relevant fact constitutes evidence.' I want to allow that one can have a reason to believe p without believing that one has reason to believe p. So there remains an important sense in which we can come to know that we have certain reasons.

20. Again, I am not supposing that in order to have a practical reason that one must believe that her desire constitutes a reason: it is sufficient to have a reason that one have a desire of which one is aware.

21. Some people will think that we need not appeal to the dolphins to find a reason for me to refrain from ordering the tuna—they will appeal to the nature of the tuna themselves. I focus on the dolphins simply because more people seem to understand dolphins but not tuna as appropriate objects of moral concern, particularly if the killing of the dolphins is unnecessary and unrelated to any human consumption interests.

22. See John Mackie, *Ethics: Inventing Right and Wrong* (New York, NY: Viking Penguin, Inc., 1977), 39–40.

23. See David Brink, *Moral Realism and the Foundations of Ethics* (Cambridge, UK: Cambridge University Press, 1989), 37ff., and Russ Shafer-Landau, *Moral Realism: A Defence* (Oxford, UK: Oxford University Press, 2003), Chapter 6.

24. See Nicholas Sturgeon, "Moral Explanations," in *Essays on Moral Realism,* ed. Geoffrey Sayre-McCord, 229–255 (Ithaca, NY: Cornell University Press, 1988).

25. See Gilbert Harman, "Ethics and Observation," in Sayre-McCord, 119–124.

NOTES TO CHAPTER 2

1. As I will make clear in the next chapter, not all persons whom we call 'friends' and not all members of our families considered in the biological sense are really intimates in the sense in which I am going to use that term. For my purposes in this chapter, however, we can work with this very rough notion of an intimate.

2. This is, of course, very rough, but it will serve my purposes in this chapter.

3. I will leave it vague as to what constitutes a short-term and what a long-term desire. Nothing in my discussion hinges on making these terms precise.

4. I will leave aside any issues about whether one can actually want what one has come to believe to be impossible.

5. This distinction parallels that between private and nonprivate projects made by John Perry in "The Importance of Being Identical," in *The Identities of Persons,* ed. Amelie Rorty, 67–90 (Berkeley, CA: University of California Press, 1976).

6. Actually, it is not clear, in this case, whether any of my projects are non-self-involving. After all, what I want to have happen after my death is that my mentor finish a book that presents *my* views on reasons.

7. I am going to focus on friendship as the paradigm case of an intimate relationship. As I will argue later, those familial relationships that are genuinely intimate relationships are really just types of friendships and not a *sui generis* class of intimate relationships. Also, I will have much more to say about the nature of friendship in the next chapter. For now, I am working with, I hope, certain uncontroversial claims about the friendship relation.

8. I am assuming that Tracy exists. I am not worried about cases in which a person has desires regarding fictitious or illusory persons.

9. For a detailed rejection of a contemporary defense of Aristotelian character friendship, see my "Friendship, Virtue, and Impartiality," in which I argue against an Aristotelian view advocated by Jennifer Whiting. *Philosophy and Phenomenological Research* 57 (1997): 51–72.

10. Of course, if I have a desire to look good, and, as a matter of fact, I look good in skirts but not in trousers, I do in fact still have a reason to buy the skirt

rather than the trousers. For the purposes of the example, I am supposing that no other such subjective reasons come into play.

11. Notice that there is nothing intrinsic to the object of a desire that determines whether a desire for that object is short-term or a project. I may have a project to find the perfect gray skirt, and I may be on this mission for months or years. My examples are just illustrations of desires that are typically short-term or typically projects.

12. I will pursue this further in Chapter 3.

13. I am not going to consider a response based upon an appeal to second-order desires. Such desires differ only in that they take first-order desires as their intentional objects. Thus, the Humean has no reason to accord second-order desires any special standing amongst an agent's reasons. Even if second-order desires are somewhat more stable (and that is a big 'if'), they are still subject to all of the difficulties that face first-order desires, i.e., they are subject to all of the same shifts.

14. My claim is only a causal one about the emotions: experiencing them can lead us to ignore significant features of situations. Some philosophers have seemed to make a stronger conceptual claim, i.e., that emotions *just are,* in some sense, our dispositions to attend to or to regard as salient various features of situations. See, for example, Ronald de Sousa, "The Rationality of Emotions," in *Explaining Emotions,* ed. Amelie Rorty, 127–152 (Berkeley: University of California Press, 1980). I myself find nothing stronger than the causal claim to be at all plausible.

15. I leave aside an account of criticism according to which its function, i.e., what makes it valid, are the aims that the agent hopes to achieve by making the criticism. For more on the various senses of 'ought,' including its expressive function, see Chapter 1.

16. In the sense that those reasons are determined by facts about the agent's own psychology and nothing else, at least not on the fundamental level. I am not claiming that we are in complete control of our attitudes and desires. But if I have a second-order desire not to desire to care for Tracy, and I institute a long-term plan to alter my first-order desire, then institution of that plan is rational for me (given that the second-order desire is stronger, etc.).

17. Here an appeal to second-order desires might secure a greater range of cases in which agents maintain reasons to care for friends. However, as I noted in note 13, the presence of second-order desires, like that of first-order desires, is a contingent matter.

18. Another way of attacking (ii) would be to say that it is not, in fact, always rational to abandon a project in the ways that I have assumed that it is. But I do not think that the Humean has any ways of making this claim within the confines of her theory, because, for the Humean, there are no facts about rationality independent of the agent's short-term desires and projects.

19. Of course, one Humean line of attack involves claiming that certain attitudes, such as that which grounds what we call 'morality,' are not idiosyncratic, but are somehow essential to us as persons; for example, perhaps such attitudes have been hardwired into us through evolutionary processes. Hume himself, in the *Enquiry Concerning the Principles of Morals* (La Salle, IL: Open Court Publishing Company, 1966), seems to adopt this strategy, at least at a couple of points.

20. G. E. Moore's consequentialism is the best-known version of consequentialism according to which friendship is intrinsically valuable.

21. Actually, I do not think that this is true, at least not in all cases. However, I will not pursue this issue here.

22. I am not sure, actually, whether, for example, taking a stand between a pure sensation or a cognitive theory of the emotions really affects our commitments with respect to whether we can control our emotions. There seem to be certain obvious facts about our ability to school our emotions that are phenomenologically given. Then, if we adopt a sensation theory, we ought to conclude that there are certain sensations that we can control. Similarly, if we adopt a cognitive theory, we can conclude that at least with respect to those judgments that are emotions, we have a certain type of control over them. For a helpful overview of the different theories regarding the nature of emotions, see Cheshire Calhoun and Robert Solomon in their introduction to *What Is An Emotion?* (New York: Oxford University Press, 1984), 3–40.

23. Some of these statements about the Aristotelian view are too simplistic. However, I do think that attempts to modify the view end up really being versions of a more inclusive consequentialist strategy.

24. I do not think that such weighing and balancing is *always* inappropriate. My claim is just that the extent and ways in which the objectivist requires us to engage in such calculations in our deliberations is excessive and inappropriate for friends to do.

25. In what follows, I assume a maximizing version of consequentialism. Michael Slote, for example, has argued in favor of a satisficing version of consequentialism, i.e., a version according to which right action is action that produces *enough* value (as opposed to the most value possible in the circumstances). Putting aside any general worry about such an account, I need not address it here. Everything that I say about the maximizing version applies equally well to the satisficing version, unless we make the *ad hoc* assumption that we will always be able to produce sufficient value and also continue to care for and to maintain current friendships. Just as there is always the possibility that more value could be produced by acting in what we take to be an unacceptable way with respect to our friends, there is also the possibility that we could not produce enough value unless we did so. See Michael Slote, *Common-Sense Morality and Consequentialism* (New York, NY: Routledge Publishing Co., 1985).

26. I think that such claims are often true. If Tracy is my best friend, then our friendship will not survive any lessening of the affection and attention which I have, in the past, given to her. Once two people are very good friends, especially if they are each other's best friends, then the friendship will probably not survive being displaced to a lesser position in one person's conception of her friendships.

27. Again, I do not want to say that we are never justified in switching our allegiances. If my friendship with Tracy is, for some reason, keeping me isolated, and being friends with Emma opens up possibilities of a richer interpersonal life, then I might be justified in trading Tracy for Emma. However, my point is that we need to know more about the case in order to say that I am justified in trading Tracy for Emma: that it would be a one for two trade does not, in and of itself, make it the case that I ought to make the trade.

28. Henry Sidgwick, *The Methods of Ethics* (Indianapolis: Hackett Publishing Co., 1981), 432ff.

29. Some contemporary utilitarians such as Peter Railton, in "Alienation, Consequentialism, and the Demands of Morality," *Philosophy and Public Affairs* 13 (1984): 134–171, have argued that dispositions to benefit friends are instrumentally valuable and so ought to be cultivated. Thus, once the dispositions are in place, we cannot be criticized for acting on them even in situations where we might have done more good by benefitting a stranger or

by helping two strangers cultivate their friendship. This response has always struck me as having a far too simplistic conception of human dispositions. In fact, I think, it seems obvious that human dispositions are far more fine-grained than Railton's utilitarian defense of friendship can allow.

30. W. D. Ross, *The Right and the Good* (Indianapolis: Hackett Publishing Co., 1930), 17. (Italics are mine.)

31. The most famous deontological account of reasons of fidelity, that of Kant in the *Grounding for the Metaphysics of Morals* (Indianapolis: Hackett Publishing Co., 1981) also relies on empirical claims about what would result from persons' not keeping their promises, although, for Kant, it is not important whether such consequences are really in the offing. But it is very interesting to note that Kant, perhaps the most infamous defender of promises as absolute, does not, in fact, take promise-keeping very seriously as morally significant in its own right. Neither Kant nor the consequentialist can accommodate the Rossian idea that the fact that I have made a promise is, in and of itself, significant: the consequentialist ultimately grounds reasons of fidelity in the production of value, while Kant grounds them in the avoidance of contradiction in the will. It turns out, on both views, that we do have reasons to keep promises, but it is not as a result of the very nature of promise-making. Similar concerns with both of these views arise in their attempts to ground reasons of intimacy.

32. Kant makes a similar overgeneralization, but his has to do with failing to make distinctions between different promises with respect to their content. So, for example, Kant never distinguishes between a world in which people do not keep their promises whenever breaking them would serve their interests, and a world in which people do not keep their promises whenever breaking them would save the life of a loved one. The latter world is, after all, the real world, it seems to me, and yet we do still manage to trust one another sufficiently to have an institution of promise-making.

33. The psychology of promise-making is much more complicated than this—people often make promises to do what they, at least in some sense, do not want to do. Maybe they also make promises when, at the time, they do not want to keep them.

NOTES TO CHAPTER 3

1. In the *Nichomachean Ethics,* trans. Terence Irwin (Indianapolis, IN: Hackett Publishing Co., 1985), Book 9.

2. One could, if one thought that Aristotle was just wrong in his conceptual analysis, simply say that friendships for pleasure, for utility, and complete friendships are all friendships, but that the latter is the friendship that realizes all of the goods that such relationships are capable of realizing. Then, what actually happens in complete friendships is what ought to happen also in friendships for pleasure and utility. On this reading, friendship would not be a normative notion. After describing different friendships, Aristotle would conclude that the most valuable is the complete friendship.

3. I do not regard Aristotle as understanding the distinction between these three types of friendships as a distinction in the causal generation of various friendships. So I do not take Aristotle as claiming that friends for pleasure become friends because they derive pleasure from one another's company, but, insofar as they are friends, they do come to care for one another for the other's own sake, etc. (This alternative, idiosyncratic reading of Aristotle is defended by John M. Cooper, "Aristotle on Friendship," in *Essays on*

Aristotle's Ethics, ed. Amelie Oksenberg Rorty, 301–340 [Berkeley: University of California Press, 1980].) I understand Aristotle as making a distinction between the intrinsic character of different types of friendship, not a distinction concerning causal origin.

4. The lapse in usage of 'intimate' in this context is probably due to the unfortunate appropriation of that term to describe two people who are engaged in some form of a sexual relationship. 'Emotionally intimate' is probably the term from common usage that comes closest to my use of 'intimate.'

5. I will explain this caveat.

6. Of all of the features of friendship that I discuss, this is the one that is most likely a necessary condition: no intimate relationship of the reason-generating sort involves two parties who don't like or love one another.

7. Or, at least, they work this way for some of us. As a philosopher, I have not engaged in any extensive sociological inquiry about attitudes in friendship, because I am not concerned to defend empirical claims. I am delineating a relationship that I hope most of my readers will find familiar from their own lives, one that I am convinced grounds certain types of reasons. In fact, various kinds of popular entertainments depend, for their appeal, on a depiction of friendships in which the mutual attitudes of the parties are hard to figure out. What is the attitude of Mary to Ted, and vice versa, on the *Mary Tyler Moore Show?* I would describe them as friends, but their attitudes toward one another, while some form of concern, are not accurately described as liking. Another example of the same phenomena is the relationship between Alex and Louie on *Taxi.*

8. He may have derivatively relative reasons: given my obsession with him, he can bring me a great deal of pleasure by sending me autographed photos, or even by visiting the city in which I live. But he has no fundamentally relative reasons, unless he has a general desire to care for his fans.

9. For a discussion of the way that conditions or criteria can interact, see William Ramsey, "Prototypes and Conceptual Analysis," *Topoi* 11 (1992): 59–70.

10. It is not the case that a person's attitude toward her friend must be stronger than her attitude toward *any* other person. After all, each of us has more than one friend and we usually care about some more than others. But for all of those persons who are our friends, there is a wide gulf between the degree of concern that we have for them and the degree that we have for anyone that is not our friend.

11. What I say here depends on empirical facts about the number of people in the world, their spatial locations, etc. If there were only, say, four people in the world, then it would certainly be possible for someone to be friends with everyone in the world (as long as they were not separated by vast reaches of oceans, etc.). Certainly Adam and Eve were friends with one another, once they resolved the issues concerning the apple. I am presupposing that there are at least hundreds of people in the world, scattered over vast geographical space. So, again, I am not engaged in conceptual analysis in any strict sense, but, rather, description of a type of relationship that grounds reasons of intimacy.

12. It is a very obvious fact about human beings that we have these sorts of differential affections. I am not here making any claim about whether it would or would not be objectively better if human beings were constructed in some other psychological manner. Even if it would be better for us to be different kinds of beings, it may still be the case that reasons are grounded by the kinds of relationships that we have, as the kinds of persons that we are.

13. These sorts of facts about human beings reveal, I believe, the inadequacies of certain versions of what is known as an ethics of care. The care that we feel and/or display with respect to our intimates is of a sort that we cannot

extend it beyond a small circle of persons. Some care ethicists, such as Nel Noddings, acknowledge this fact, and, as a result, end up narrowing the realm of moral concern to an unacceptable extent. Noddings claims that we cannot care for starving children in Somalia, and so they are beyond the reach of our moral obligations. I think that such a view is one that clearly overweighs the moral significance of the type of concern that intimates have for one another. See Nel Noddings, "Caring," in *Justice and Care: Essential Readings in Feminist Ethics,* ed. Virginia Held, 7–30 (Boulder, CO: Westview Press, 1995).

14. By 'affective' I mean to be referring to a state that can be understood as a feeling or sensation of some sort. So, for example, on standard readings, Hume offered an account of emotions as purely affective (but, in opposition to this reading of Hume, see Marcia Lind, "Hume and the Moral Emotions," in *Identity, Character, and Morality: Essays in Moral Psychology,* ed. Owen Flanagan and Amelie Oksenberg Rorty, 133–147 [Cambridge, MA: The MIT Press, 1990]). I have avoided asking whether attitudes are emotions, because even if they are, we are still left with the question as to whether emotions are cognitive or affective states (or some combination of the two).

15. I am not concerned to decide between the following two positions: (i) concern is a compound state with affective and cognitive components, and (ii) concern is just a handy term to use to describe the mental set of a person who has both certain affective states and certain cognitive states. These two options really seem like the same option under two different descriptions.

16. The danger of the sort of philosophy that I am here doing is that one may end up, instead of making *a priori* plausible psychological claims, just revealing one's character flaws. In the process of taking one's own pettiness for some truth about people in general, one can be misled about the cogency of one's own claims. The author doubts that her own text could ever be subject to such difficulties.

17. This seems to me to be another objection to Aristotle's view of friendship if it is to be taken as in any way a description of how actual friendships work: we do not hold off on caring about someone until we are assured that he or she is virtuous and, according to Aristotle, thereby worthy of being loved. It takes quite a long time to assess someone's virtue. By the time that I decide that Tracy has some moral flaws, I will already be intimate with her and, I will argue, thereby have (objective agent-relative) reasons to continue to care for her.

18. Dean Cocking and Jeanette Kennett, "Friendship and the Self," *Ethics* 108 (1998): 518.

19. Cocking and Kennett, 517.

20. In *You Just Don't Understand: Women and Men in Conversation* (New York: Random House, 1991), linguist Deborah Tannen presents many examples and anecdotes concerning the ways in which men and women interact in conversation. She hypothesizes that part of the explanation as to why women and men converse differently is the result of the types of games that we play as children.

21. The best fiction, I believe, is able to mirror this process of becoming intimate with another, by slowly and subtly providing access to characters through both words and action. Fiction can, then, not only provide pleasures similar to some of those of friendship, but can also provide excellent training for real-world friendships. Of course, life is more complex than fiction insofar as our characters are not revealed in neatly ordered plots laid down by an omniscient author. Again, this explains why ambiguities make for the greatest fiction, as evidenced by the great character studies of Henry James. In

James's work, whatever we conclude about characters would probably be highly interesting both to the characters and to James himself.

22. In fact, it may be beyond empirical psychology or sociology as well. Our source of knowledge about intimacy depends, to a great extent, on our own phenomenological evidence and the reports of others. But, in looking back on a friendship, it becomes extremely difficult to trace the various steps in the development of various types of trust and in the acquisition of various forms of knowledge and understanding.

23. I am assuming that people can have concepts that they cannot fully articulate, and that two people can have the same concept and yet, to use Rawls's distinction, fill it out with two different conceptions. If one is uncomfortable with any of this, then one can simply understand concern as involving being directed toward what one takes to be the good of the other.

24. I am grateful to Richard Fumerton for emphasizing this point.

25. Again, literature can serve an important function here. Some of the greatest pleasures of fiction and the mark of a truly great author derive from the reader's being transported sympathetically into the life of a person that previously had seemed utterly mysterious or foreign to them.

NOTES TO CHAPTER 4

1. See quotation from Ross in Chapter 2.

2. By an imperfect duty, what I mean here is simply a duty to perform a certain number of acts of a certain type, or to make some percentage (less than 100) of one's acts, acts of a given type. So refraining from murder is not (as typically understood) an imperfect duty, because one must make 100% of one's acts, acts of the type not-a-murder. Promise-keeping is usually viewed as a perfect duty because no amount of promise-keepings justifies a promise-breaking (at least not in the absence of other considerations, such as competing reasons), and, thus, it seems, one must make 100% of one's acts instances of the act-type not-the-breaking-of-a-promise. (I avoid understanding imperfect duties, in contrast to perfect duties, as not correlated with rights of a particular other, because I do not think that the reference to rights is informative in this context.)

3. Of course, my promisee can justify the *utterance* of a complaint in ways that others are unable to do. My promisee's complaint-utterance might very well have good consequences that such an utterance on the part of a third party would not have. But this kind of justification is a matter of the consequences of the utterance not of the content of the utterance, considered in itself.

4. I am not going to discuss Hobbes's understanding of promises and contracts. Hobbes says that the signs that an individual transfers a right

> are either words only, or actions only, or (as it happeneth most often) both words and actions. And the same are the BONDS by which men are bound and obliged, bonds that have their strength, not from their own nature (for nothing is more easily broken than a man's word) but from fear of some evil consequence upon the rupture. (*Leviathan* [Indianapolis, IN: Hackett Publishing Co., 1994])

Hobbes's view is consequentialist but, unlike classical utilitarians, Hobbes takes the relevant consequences to be those for the promisor herself, not for all persons affected. This view makes the promise itself rationally insignificant. What is rationally significant is that, in the commonwealth, keeping of promises or contracts is one of the acts commanded by the sovereign and so is such that its breach brings in its wake severe punishment. This is simply an egoistic rather than a universalistic consequentialism. The plausibility of this account of promising depends, in part, on the plausibility of Hobbes's response to the Foole, and on whether one thinks that reasons of fidelity are dependent on a person's rationality in risking expulsion from the commonwealth.

5. I say 'a' Kantian account, because there are many different accounts that could be construed as Kantian. I am here focusing on one of Kant's own accounts.

6. I am here influenced by Christine Korsgaard's reading of Kant. See her "The Right to Lie: Kant on Dealing with Evil," *Philosophy and Public Affairs* 15 (1986): 325–349.

7. I have some not very scientific evidence to back my supposition here. I ask my Introduction to Ethics students whether they would make a lying promise in order to save a loved one, and, in every class, the vast majority do not hesitate in saying that they would. I then ask whether they would, on the basis of seeing how many people would make such a lying promise, be less inclined to lend money. Very few, if any of them, say 'yes' to that latter question.

8. Kant's case of the lying promise makes it quite clear that the making of a promise does not presuppose an intention to keep the promise. If such were not the case, there would be no such thing as a deceptive promise, and there do clearly seem to be such promises.

9. This account of promising is similar to that given by Thomas Scanlon in *What We Owe to Each Other* (Cambridge, MA: Harvard University Press, 1998), 295–317. Scanlon claims that obligations or reasons to keep promises are derived from various principles (principles forbidding unjustified manipulation and principles requiring 'due care') that could not be reasonably rejected (per his particular contractualist understanding of what such reasonable rejection involves). The contractualist details of Scanlon's account are not important for my purposes here. A good general statement of an expectations account of promising can be found in A. I. Melden, *Rights and Persons* (Berkeley, CA: University of California Press, 1977).

10. Much more could be said about the notion of a voluntary act. As I proceed, I will say what I need to say for my purposes. Hopefully, my discussion will not require any controversial claims about the nature of voluntary action. I do not intend to be offering anything like an analysis of voluntary action that could then be imported into any situation in which that concept is employed.

11. As should be clear, it is not entirely clear how the latter two cases really differ. With the former case in which Jasmine threatens Sam with the loss of future promotions, we might decide that in that case as in the latter case of moving her furniture, Sam voluntarily decides that a certain transaction is worth the cost. In the former case, however, Jasmine bargains with something that is not really hers to bargain with: she has breached her objective agent-neutral reasons in offering the option to Sam. Thus, the situation may not really be a bargaining situation at all if we understand a bargaining situation as requiring two parties who bargain about transactions of resources to which they have legitimate claims.

12. And, of course, Sam's objective agent-neutral reasons will be increased if the other sorts of consequences that are commonly referred to by utilitarians would come about as a result of Sam's failure to keep his promise, i.e., if other persons had their general trust in humankind diminished, etc. For the purposes of this discussion, I will set aside consideration of such consequences.

13. Scanlon, *What We Owe to Each Other*, 312.

14. Actually, I am not sure about any of my claims about the sorts of facts that ground obligations for Kant. Given the supposed equivalence of the two

statements of the categorical imperative, it cannot be both or either of hypothetical consequences or rational nature that grounds our promissory obligations. For Kant, these obligations are not *sui generis,* but are simply instances of the application of the moral law. So some deeper facts about the laws that rational nature gives to itself are what ultimately ground our obligations. But appeal to such facts must be mediated by application of the moral law in order to get any specific account of promising; thus, I focus on those applications of the moral law rather than on the deeper metaphysical grounding of Kant's moral theory as a whole. After all, I am here not critiquing his entire theory and its basis, anymore than, in my discussion of utilitarianism, I was critiquing the principle of utility and its basis. I am only concerned with the accounts of promising yielded by these theories.

15. Walter Sinnott-Armstrong, "Moral Skepticism and Justification," in *Moral Knowledge? New Readings in Moral Epistemology,* ed. Walter Sinnott-Armstrong and Mark Timmons, 3–48 (New York, NY: Oxford University Press, 1996), 26.
16. Ross, *The Right and the Good,* 21.
17. From *A Review of the Principal Questions in Morals,* ed. D. Daiches Raphael (Oxford, UK: The Clarendon Press, 1948), 97–98.
18. From *The Sources of Normativity* (Cambridge, UK: Cambridge University Press, 1996), 38.
19. From *After Virtue* (Notre Dame, IN: Notre Dame University Press, 1984), 17.
20. Much of Chapter 6 will be devoted to responding to the worry that intuitionism is objectionably dogmatic and fails to provide us with any kind of decision procedure in ethics.
21. To be precise, the reason supervenes upon R's awareness that he, R, has made a promise. For simplicity, I will sometimes speak about the reason supervening upon the act of promising itself, rather than upon R's awareness that he has made a promise.
22. Of course, the making of a promise presupposes certain background conventions. I am not making the implausible claim that in any possible world, if a person utters the words 'I promise . . . ' then she has bound herself. There is, of course, more to the making of a promise than the simple utterance of words.
23. If p is, or is instrumental to, the production of a valuable state of affairs, then others will necessarily have a reason to promote p—an objective agent-neutral reason. The reason that is not necessarily shared by others is the agent's reason of fidelity. Thus, if p is objectively valuable, the agent has an additional, objective agent-relative reason beyond her objective agent-neutral reason to promote or to do p.
24. In the latter relationships, the obligations are asymmetrical: the therapist assumes certain obligations toward her patient but it is not at all clear that the patient assumes obligations toward the therapist. In cases where the client does assume obligations, such as the obligations that a client has to reveal pertinent information to her attorney, the obligations are different from those that the service provider has to her client. In the former associations, members usually have reciprocal obligations unless they assume some position in a hierarchy within the association.
25. Of course, all reasons, *qua* reasons, are irreducible. What I mean in speaking about irreducible reasons of fidelity is that promising is an ultimate ground of reasons.
26. I purposely do not discuss the state as a contractual association, because I think that consent theory in the political context is unworkable. See Chapter 7 for more discussion of consent theory and political obligations.

27. Further types of crises can arise between members of a department when they are parties to other sorts of relationships beyond those of mere colleagues. In small departments where relations are generally amiable, expectations can move beyond what is strictly required on the professional level, and, again, crises arise when members have different understandings of these expectations. Also, members can become friends, even close friends, and then reasons of fidelity can become mixed up and confused with reasons of intimacy.

28. I am understanding a contract simply as a mutual promise, i.e., a case in which each promisor is also a promisee. A contract may involve more than two persons (as may a promise as well).

29. Simmons, *Moral Principles and Political Obligations* (Princeton, NJ: Princeton University Press, 1979), 80–81.

30. John Locke, *Second Treatise of Government,* ed. C. B. Macpherson (Indianapolis, IN: Hackett Publishing Co., 1980), 64.

31. I am not here pointing to any worries about time and temporal divisibility and so on. By 'instant' I mean some clearly delineated period of time that could be as long as a day. It is true that in some relationships, we can find a time that is the first 'instant' of friendship, if we extend the notion of an 'instant' to be long enough, perhaps a week or a month. But it is also true that in many friendships we could not even do that much.

32. See his "Of the Original Contract," in *Essays Moral, Political, and Literary,* ed. Eugene F. Miller (Indianapolis, IN: Liberty Fund, Inc., 1987, 465–487).

33. Then, of course, there will be cases in which biological relation alone does nothing to generate obligations. If a young girl becomes pregnant in a situation where she was deprived of full knowledge of the nature of sex and parenthood, then I think that her obligations are quite different than if an educated woman gets pregnant. (Similar claims can be made about men in these circumstances.) Also, cases of sperm donation and surrogate motherhood are not cases where the agent, as a result of playing a role in bringing a child into being, undertakes actions that she or he can be expected to know will result in certain obligations to the resultant child. Which actions represent the voluntary assumptions of obligations depends on the full and complete nature of the context, not on some biological facts about genetic inheritance or physical conception or birthing.

34. I was led to use this example by reading Carol Delaney's excellent *Abraham on Trial: The Social Legacy of Biblical Myth* (Princeton, NJ: Princeton University Press, 1998), in which she questions the assumption of the naturalness of the Western conception of paternity and fatherhood. I use the example to illustrate a different, but not, I think, unrelated, point.

35. It is important to see that I am not here endorsing any sort of cultural relativism. My point about the differences between the moral implications of certain types of actions in the Trobriand Islands as opposed to the implications of the very same action types in, for example, the United States, is no more relativist than the claim that while uttering the words "I promise . . ." to someone in the US has moral implications, doing so in the Trobriand Islands, where English is not spoken, has no such implications

NOTES TO CHAPTER 5

1. Although those who defend particularism do not always make their meta-ethical commitments entirely clear, it seems that at least most of them accept some form of objectivism about the nature of morality, i.e., they seem to

accept that moral facts are not completely a matter of human attitudes toward features of or states of affairs in the world. For ease of exposition and given the focus of this book, I will limit myself to considering particularism within the context of objectivism about morality.

2. My focus on moral properties will make it the case that the taxonomy of particularist theses that I offer is different from that offered by, for example, McKeever and Ridge, in their aptly titled "The Many Moral Particularisms," *The Canadian Journal of Philosophy* 35 (2005): 83–106. While McKeever and Ridge differentiate particularist theories on the basis of those theories' attitudes toward moral principles, my taxonomy shifts the focus to the way in which various particularist theories understand the relationship between a moral property, such as being a reason, and other properties in the world (Ontological Particularism), and, given that relationship, the epistemic status of moral agents with respect to moral truths (Epistemological Particularism). I also consider, under the rubric of Practical Particularism, the role, if any, that particularists assign to moral truths (what McKeever and Ridge are calling principles) or to rules in moral deliberation. While there is necessarily some overlap between my taxonomy and that of others such as McKeever and Ridge (which I will indicate as I proceed), my ontological/epistemological focus forces more and different distinctions.

3. In "Particularity and Principle: The Structure of Moral Knowledge," in *Moral Particularism,* ed. Brad Hooker and Margaret Little, 178–204 (Oxford, UK: Clarendon Press, 2000), 179.

4. I am here using the term 'epistemological' broadly as a way of referring to human cognitive capacities generally.

5. Not literally derived, of course, given that imperatives do not have truth values.

6. Mill also calls these "the rules of morality for the multitude," which, I think, rather than being denigrating, can be taken as Mill's way of saying that the truths of morality may only be of interest to philosophers *qua* philosophers, and that, in our everyday lives as moral agents, the secondary principles are all that we need. As I indicate in the section on practical particularism, this view that not only Mill but many utilitarians have taken sounds very much like a thesis that some particularists claim as differentiating them from generalists, where utilitarians are taken as paradigm generalists.

7. McKeever and Ridge distinguish between principles understood as standards and principles understood as guides. Standards are, essentially, truths about moral reality, whereas guides function as aids to moral deliberation. As they indicate, principles can also be understood as what they call action-guiding standards, truths about moral reality that do double-duty and also aid in moral deliberation. As the utilitarian example shows, guides, I would suggest, may not have a truth value, or, if they do, may be false. I discuss this further in the section on Practical Particularism.

8. I am assuming for the purpose of this example that it makes sense to speak of a property of being a particular person. The issue as to what is a genuine as opposed to a spurious property is, of course, a complicated and contentious one. Here I am working with a rather generous view of properties.

9. And, if the particularist were defending a claim about a more pervasive inability to know general truths, then it would not be a thesis of particular interest to ethicists. Particularists seem to think that there is something about normative properties *as such* that makes their theses plausible.

10. It is here that my focus on moral properties rather than on moral truths as such forces my taxonomy to differ from that of McKeever and Ridge. They differentiate particularists on the basis of the latter's 'attitudes toward

principles.' Thus, their taxonomy is limited to varieties of what I am calling epistemological particularism. In the next section, I want to try to understand the particularist attitude toward moral principles (truths) via possible attitudes that the particularist might take toward the moral truth-makers.

11. In *Moral Reasons* (Cambridge, MA: Blackwell Publishers, 1993), 60.
12. In "The Particularist's Progress," in Hooker and Little, *Moral Particularism*, 130–156, 130.
13. In "Moral Particularism: Wrong and Bad," in Hooker and Little, *Moral Particularism*, 1–22, 6.
14. In *Moral Reasons*, 64–66.
15. I purposely leave it vague as to whether 'people' refers to most people, all people, or some specific subclass of persons.
16. Of course, sexual intimacy is the feature that most readily comes to mind, but many nonsexual intimate relationships involve expectations of some sort of exclusivity: friends expect to be the one asked for certain kinds of help, to be the one with whom certain kinds of problems are worked out, or, on a more mundane level, to be the one that certain kinds of movies are viewed with.
17. Recent debates about whether to make chess an Olympic 'sport' were clearly attempts to make just such a decision, not attempts to do conceptual analysis the results of which would have decisively settled chess's fate with respect to the Olympics.
18. The issue as to whether romantic relationships are socially constructed is a red herring in this debate. It may very well be that this type of relationship only occurs in certain cultural situations in certain historical epochs given certain social pressures and needs, etc. But that is probably true of any sort of human relationship, if we understand relationships as being something more than just a simple attitude or feeling toward another person. Whatever the truth about the genesis and cultural contingency of romantic relationships, it seems clear that they exist and that they have distinctive features that mark them off from other types of intimate relationships.
19. I suppose that there might be some question here about the individuation of friendships. Suppose that Tracy and Diane become estranged, and then reconnect after many years. Do they begin a new friendship, or do they simply continue the one that they initiated years ago? I am inclined to say that the latter is the correct description of what happens. However, if the former is correct, then my last claim in the text would be false. I will leave this issue aside here.
20. Here, however, we could alter the normal circumstance of cleaning out the cat's litter box, and imagine several people in a large auditorium being timed as they clean out litter boxes and then being judged on how clean the litter boxes are, with prizes being awarded for cleanest litter boxes in the least amount of time. Is this a sport?
21. I myself think that all pleasure is intrinsically valuable, so I am only using this case of Dancy's as an illustration.
22. Others have made similar points. See, for example, Joseph Raz, "The Truth in Particularism," in Hooker and Little, *Moral Particularism*, 48–78, 61.
23. It is important to see that our ability to grasp a whole or a class does not imply that we can grasp every part of the whole or every member of the class and/or the relationships between those parts or members. To assume that knowledge of wholes/classes implies knowledge of parts/members would seem to involve committing the fallacy of division.
24. I leave open that some divine or alien beings could acquire knowledge in some other way. I am here only concerned about how we actual human beings can hope to have knowledge in this area.

NOTES TO CHAPTER 6

1. For a concise discussion of this issue, see Russ Shafer-Landau, "Rationality and Disagreement," in *Moral Realism: A Defence* (Oxford, UK: Clarendon Press, 2003), Chapter 9.
2. I do not mean to imply that constructivists have paid off on this particular promissory note, just that it is held out as a supposed advantage of the view that it offers more hope of dispute resolution than does, say, Platonism or intuitionism.
3. In *After Virtue,* 2nd ed. (Notre Dame, IN: University of Notre Dame Press, 1984), 17.
4. See Shafer-Landau, 223ff.
5. This case was originally offered by Gilbert Harman in *The Nature of Morality* (New York, NY: Oxford University Press, 1977).
6. There are two versions of the position that accepts that there is a constraint against killing an innocent person:

    (A) The reason not to kill the one is a *prima facie* reason, and, thus, is to be weighed against, among others, the consequentialist reason, thereby leaving open the possibility that, in certain circumstances, an agent's all-things-considered reason will be to kill one in order to save the greater number.

    (B) The reason not to kill the one is always an *all-things-considered* reason, that is, it always outweighs consequentialist reasons (and any other reasons), foreclosing the possibility that an agent ought to kill one to save the greater number.

    I will discuss only option (A). After all, if (A) is not plausible, then it does not seem that (B) would have much chance of being so. Also, (B) has little 'intuitive' support, and, since much of the motivation for defending the constraint against killing the innocent depends upon 'intuitions,' there seems little reason to pursue (B). It really does seem that only a mad person (or Kant) would say that it would be wrong to kill one to save a million or a billion or the entire human race (including the one herself).
7. From now on in this chapter, I will use 'constraints' to refer to only the constraint against killing or torturing the innocent, unless I specify otherwise.
8. See also Peter Railton's appeal to consequentially justified *motivational dispositions* in his "Alienation, Consequentialism, and the Demands of Morality," *Philosophy and Public Affairs* 13 (1984): 134–171.
9. This seems to be part of J.S. Mill's strategy in Chapter V of *Utilitarianism* (Indianapolis, IN: Hackett Publishing Co., 1979).
10. In what follows, I am attempting to characterize the sorts of arguments offered by Shelly Kagan in his excellent defense of consequentialism *The Limits of Morality* (Oxford, UK: Oxford University Press, 1989), 27ff., and by Samuel Scheffler in his equally interesting *The Rejection of Consequentialism* (Oxford, UK: Oxford University Press, 1982), Chapter Four.
11. Actually, I think that their dignity will be violated in a worse way: the one killing them does not have the desire, most likely, that she did not have to do this.
12. The reason provided in this case is a reason to refrain from performance. To be reason-giving can be either to give a reason to do or to give a reason to refrain from doing.
13. I will admit that I am very often pulled by the force of the examples in the literature that are used to defend a constraint against killing the innocent. However, after considering the various points that I have just mentioned, I am not sure that I can rationally maintain my initial reaction—I am not even sure anymore what it is to which I am reacting.

14. Michael Stocker was one of the first to raise this issue, albeit not in the context of a defense of constraints. See his "The Schizophrenia of Modern Ethical Theories," *The Journal of Philosophy* 73 (1976): 453–466.
15. In *Value in Ethics and Economics* (Cambridge, MA: Harvard University Press, 1993).
16. I have borrowed the structure of the constraint deontologist arguments from Anderson, but similar arguments can be found in many defenders of constraints. See, for example, Frances M. Kamm, *Morality, Mortality, Vol. 2: Rights, Duties, and Status* (New York: Oxford University Press, 1996).
17. In the earlier arguments, and in what follows, all reference to reasons should be understood as reference to *prima facie* reasons, unless otherwise indicated.
18. Anderson certainly seems to endorse this approach. See page 77, where she uses the language of constitution, and page 81, where she seems to equate expressing respect and acting in accordance with constraints. It is difficult to tell, however, how seriously we should take these remarks, given her overt disavowal of any ontological commitments at this point in her book.
19. I have stated the claim in terms of 'expression' just in case anyone is worried that an expressivist will be completely uninterested in anything that I have to say. An expressivist like Anderson has to be making claims about actions having properties of expressing attitudes and how those properties relate to other properties of actions.
20. For more discussion on these issues, see Chapter 3.

NOTES TO CHAPTER 7

1. A. John Simmons, *Moral Principles and Political Obligations* (Princeton, NJ: Princeton University Press, 1979), 13.
2. Of course, this might not be true in a world of only a few people. For example, Adam and Eve may very well have had special obligations to all persons. So the limited subset, in some extreme cases such as that of a highly depopulated world, might be coextensive with the set of all persons.
3. If there was a constraint against killing or torturing the innocent, it would be an objective agent-relative reason but also, it seems, a natural duty. The relevant 'status' in this case seems to be that of a moral agent. So such a constraint would cut across categories in an interesting and perhaps problematic way. I will leave those constraints aside given my argument against them in the previous chapter.
4. I am here, of course, thinking of natural-born citizens. We can renounce our native citizenship and voluntarily commit ourselves to another country. (Some people, such as those who take military oaths, commit themselves to their country of birth.) But many people think that until we do so, we have special obligations to our compatriots, regardless of the fact that we did not choose to have these people as compatriots.
5. Lindley Lecture at the University of Kansas, "Families, Nations, and Strangers." For my response to Scheffler's lecture, see my "Associative Obligations, Voluntarism, and Equality," *Pacific Philosophical Quarterly* 77 (1996): 289–309.
6. For many of us, our unchosen roles/relations play a role in determining our subjective agent-relative reasons: many of us have desires to maintain ties to family, nation, etc.
7. It is interesting that the explicit making of a promise and signing of a contract still exists in the context of monogamous sexual relationships, even those, such as gay or lesbian marriages, that do not, as such, involve a legal

contract. Doing a little *a priori* history, I can make sense of such contracts as having arisen along with the marriage institution when marriages were not primarily a matter of love, and so explicit assumption of obligations was necessary in order to bind two people who might not even have known each other prior to the marriage ceremony. In today's world, we regard the ideal as one in which the public wedding vow is merely a reaffirmation of preexistent special obligations acquired as a result of the formation of an intimate relationship. If two people were to regard themselves as not having, prior to the wedding vow, special obligations to be faithful, etc., I can only think that they are not ready to be making the vow.

8. One can promise to *try* to be someone's friend, but that is very different from actually promising to be a friend.

9. This phenomenological fact has been used by some in order to reject a voluntarist requirement (even if they do not state the requirement explicitly). See, in particular, Michael Sandel's influential communitarian critique of liberalism in his *Liberalism and the Limits of Justice* (Cambridge, UK: Cambridge University Press, 1982).

10. There are, of course, plenty of philosophers who would insist that acting for a reason is necessary or even constitutive of voluntariness. Of course, types of voluntariness will depend upon the nature of the reason upon which one acts: when I give my money to an armed robber, I act for a very good reason. While voluntary in some sense, my act is not voluntary in another important sense. I am inclined to think that the concept of being voluntary is not a unitary one, and that many of its senses are evaluative and/or relativized to particular judgments that one wants to make about the situation or the agent or both.

11. I have been motivated to respond to these sorts of worries through my writing of comments on Andrew Cohen's paper "Examining the Moral Bonds and Bounds of Friendship," presented at the April 2001 American Philosophical Association Central Division Meetings, Group Meeting of the Society for the Philosophy of Sex and Love, Chicago, IL.

12. Marcia Baron uses this type of claim to defend the Kantian account of moral motivation, in her "On the Alleged Moral Repugnance of Acting From Duty," *The Journal of Philosophy* 81 (1984): 197–220. For my defense of acting from the motive of duty, see my "A Defense of Acting From Duty," *The Journal of Value Inquiry* 32 (1998): 61–74.

13. This phrase comes from Bernard Williams's by now famous case of a man saving his wife from drowning in his "Persons, Character, and Morality," in *Moral Luck* (Cambridge, UK: Cambridge University Press, 1981), 1–19.

14. See, in particular, Michael Stocker's well-known case of Smith visiting his friend in the hospital in his "The Schizophrenia of Modern Ethical Theories," in *The Journal of Philosophy*. I discuss this case of Stocker's in my "A Defense of Acting From Duty."

15. While I think that it is extremely important to get girls involved in physical activities such as sport, I do not think that we should denigrate the value of traditionally female forms of play, for the reasons described in the text. What we want is to get both boys and girls involved in both sport and traditional female role-playing games. Simpleminded rejection of traditional female play mars certain contemporary, popular attempts to stress the need for young girls to be physically active. See, for example, Collette Dowling's *The Frailty Myth* (New York, NY: Random House Publishing Group, 2001).

16. In *The Morality of Nationalism,* ed. Robert McKim and Jeff McMahan (New York: Oxford University Press, 1997), 139–157.

17. See my "Special Relationships and the Problem of Political Obligations," *Social Theory and Practice* 27 (2001): 19–40.

18. I am excluding from this discussion of family both spouses/lovers and children. The former clearly meet the voluntarist requirement, while the latter also do, at least under certain conditions (the woman was not raped, birth control was readily available, etc.).

19. Here, the fact that common sense falsely takes biological relation to ground special obligations is also relevant: if my uncle with whom I have no intimate relationship thinks that I have special obligations to care for him, it may be easier for him to accept aid from me, thereby easing his stress and bolstering his self-esteem.

20. The classic statement of this view is offered by Socrates in Plato's *Crito*. More recently, it has been defended by A. D. M. Walker in "Political Obligation and the Argument from Gratitude," *Philosophy and Public Affairs* 17 (1988): 191–211. George Klosko responds to Walker in "Political Obligation and Gratitude," *Philosophy and Public Affairs* 18 (1989): 352–358.

21. For a voluntarist response to Rawls, see Nozick, *Anarchy, State, and Utopia* (New York, NY: Basic Books, Inc., 1974), 90–95, who essentially relies on the distinction between receiving and accepting benefits.

22. Of course, lack of special political obligations does not mean that one has no obligations to obey the laws. Considerations of objective value require us to obey most laws in reasonably just societies, and, even in unjust societies, we have reason to obey, for example, traffic laws and laws against rape.

23. In discussing the following accounts of special obligations, I will offer suggestions about how the notion of a familial connection can be conceived as something distinct from a mere biological connection.

24. See his *Liberalism and the Limits of Justice*.

25. Sandel himself offers little in the way of a positive conception of such obligations. Thus, I will use his comments to motivate a view that is not necessarily his.

26. See also, Charles Taylor, "Atomism," in *Philosophy and the Human Sciences: Philosophical Papers 2* (Cambridge, UK: Cambridge University Press, 1985), 187–210, and Iris Marion Young, *Justice and the Politics of Difference* (Princeton, NJ: Princeton University Press, 1990).

27. See Richard Brandt's discussion of cognitive psychotherapy in *A Theory of the Good and the Right* (Oxford, UK: Clarendon Press, 1979). Although I disagree with Brandt's normative conclusions, I think that the sort of cognitive psychotherapy that he describes is essential to deliberation about which commitments to take up.

28. In his "Honor Thy Father and Thy Mother and to Thine Own Self Be True," *The Southern Journal of Philosophy* 24 (1986): 149–162, 153.

29. Sandel might say that these are precisely the reasons that supervene on these young women's constitutive attachments. But it seems that understanding these reasons as derivatively relative agent-neutral reasons captures their force much better, because the reasons are not to be understood as reasons to help those who form our identity in the way that we help friends. (It is curious that Sandel follows his discussion of constitutive attachments with an illustration concerning *friendship*. He also never even considers the difficulties for his view of the sorts of concerns that I have just raised, concerns that are familiar to any moral philosopher discussing a view of this sort.)

30. This point needs to be remembered in my upcoming discussions of Scheffler and Hardimon as well. My own view has certain counterintuitive results, so it is not simply on that basis that I am rejecting these other accounts. (It is part of my argument, however: I argue that my account is better, *taken overall*.) I am primarily concerned to use the implications of these views to highlight the underlying features of their accounts that we ought to reject.

31. John Stuart Mill made this point in an extremely powerful and eloquent way in his *The Subjection of Women* (Indianapolis, IN: Hackett Publishing Co., Inc., 1988).
32. I do not mean to deny that most people will incline to the view that we have special political obligations, at least in nations such as the modern United States, Canada, Britain, France, etc. I do not think, however, that that intuition is as deeply rooted as the intuition about familial obligations.
33. In *The Journal of Philosophy* 91 (1994): 333–363.
34. See my "Families, Friends, and Special Obligations," *The Canadian Journal of Philosophy* 28 (1998): 527–556.
35. I do not mean to imply that this sort of appeal has not been used throughout the history of philosophy: Hume's moral theory seems to involve certain types of counterfactuals. I do think, however, that this strain of thought has become more standard than it ever was before.
36. Actually, this claim is only true if we understand 'used to be' as referring back to, say, the 1950s. In earlier times and places, such as colonial America, the early death of women due to childbearing led to a great many stepmothers and stepsiblings.
37. In his "Relationships and Responsibilities," in *Philosophy and Public Affairs* 26 (1997): 189–209.
38. In the course of Scheffler's discussion, it becomes unclear whether persons have to both have a reason to value the relationship *and* actually subjectively value it, or whether the former condition is both necessary and sufficient for the having of special obligations. I will leave this ambiguous, because my criticisms are the same, whichever option Scheffler chooses. (The argument that I summarize in the next paragraph leaves Scheffler's view ambiguous as well, I think.)
39. Actually, I am unsure if these are genuinely *special* obligations; after all, they are based on subjective valuings and objective value of the relationships. Why would these factors, which generate reasons of their own, in combination lead to special agent-relative reasons?
40. I am not entirely sure that this is true, but, if it is, there is an easy explanation of it: common sense has more to say about ethics than about any other area of philosophy. We all need views about how we ought to behave, whereas, in daily life, we do quite well without a metaphysical account of, say, universals.

NOTES TO THE CONCLUSION

1. See *The View From Nowhere* (Oxford UK: Oxford University Press, 1986).

Bibliography

Anderson, Elizabeth. *Value in Ethics and Economics.* Cambridge, MA: Harvard University Press, 1993.

Aristotle. *Nichomachean Ethics.* Translated by Terence Irwin. Indianapolis, IN: Hackett Publishing Co., 1985.

Baron, Marcia. "On the Alleged Moral Repugnance of Acting From Duty." *The Journal of Philosophy* 81 (1984): 197–220.

Belliotti, Raymond. "Honor Thy Father and Thy Mother and To Thy Own Self Be True." *The Southern Journal of Philosophy* 24 (1986): 149–162.

Brandt, Richard. *A Theory of the Good and the Right.* Oxford, UK: The Clarendon Press, 1979.

Brink, David. *Moral Realism and the Foundations of Ethics.* Cambridge, UK: Cambridge University Press, 1989.

Calhoun, Cheshire, and Robert Solomon. "Introduction." Pages 3–40 in *What Is An Emotion?* New York, NY: Oxford University Press, 1984.

Cocking, Dean, and Jeannette Kennett. "Friendship and the Self." *Ethics* 108 (1998): 502–527.

Cohen, Andrew. "Examining the Moral Bonds and Bounds of Friendship." Paper presented at the April 2001 American Philosophical Association Central Division Meetings, Group Meeting of the Society for the Philosophy of Sex and Love, Chicago, IL.

Cooper, John M. "Aristotle on Friendship." In *Essays on Aristotle's Ethics,* edited by Amelie Oksenberg Rorty, 301–340. Berkeley, CA: University of California Press, 1980.

Dancy, Jonathan. *Moral Reasons.* Cambridge, MA: Blackwell Publishers, 1993.

———. "The Particularist's Progress." In *Moral Particularism,* edited by Brad Hooker and Margaret Little, 178–204. Oxford, UK: The Clarendon Press, 2000.

Delaney, Carol. *Abraham on Trial: The Social Legacy of Biblical Myth.* Princeton, NJ: Princeton University Press, 1998.

de Sousa, Ronald. "The Rationality of Emotions." In *Explaining Emotions,* edited by Amelie Rorty, 127–152. Berkeley, CA: University of California Press, 1980.

Dowling, Colette. *The Frailty Myth.* New York, NY: Random House Publishing Group, 2001.

Feinberg, Joel. "Psychological Egoism." In *Reason and Responsibility* 12th ed., edited by Joel Feinberg and Russ Shafer-Landau, 476–488. Belmont, CA: Wadsworth, 2005.

Fumerton, Richard. *Reason and Morality: A Defense of the Egocentric Perspective.* Ithaca, NY: Cornell University Press, 1990.

Garfield, Jay. "Particularity and Principle: The Structure of Moral Knowledge." In *Moral Particularism,* edited by Brad Hooker and Margaret Little, 178–204. Oxford, UK: The Clarendon Press, 2000.

Hardimon, Michael. "Role Obligations." *The Journal of Philosophy* 91 (1994): 333–363.

Harman, Gilbert. "Ethics and Observation." In *Essays on Moral Realism,* edited by Geoffrey Sayre-McCord, 119–124. Ithaca, NY: Cornell University Press, 1988.

———. *The Nature of Morality.* New York, NY: Oxford University Press, 1977.

Hobbes, Thomas. *Leviathan.* Edited by Edwin Curley. Indianapolis, IN: Hackett Publishing Co., 1994. First published 1668.

Hooker, Brad. "Moral Particularism: Wrong and Bad." In *Moral Particularism,* edited by Brad Hooker and Margaret Little, 1–22. Oxford, UK: The Clarendon Press, 2000.

Hume, David. *An Enquiry Concerning the Principles of Morals.* LaSalle, IL: Open Court Publishing Co., 1966. First published 1777.

———. "Of the Original Contract." In *Essays Moral, Political, and Literary,* edited by Eugene F. Miller. Indianapolis, IN: Liberty Fund, Inc., 1987, 465–487.

———. *A Treatise of Human Nature.* Edited by L. A. Selby-Bigge. Oxford, UK: The Clarendon Press, 1978. First published 1739–1740.

Hurka, Thomas. "The Justification of National Partiality." In *The Morality of Nationalism,* edited by Robert McKim and Jeff McMahan, 139–157. New York, NY: Oxford University Press, 1997.

Jeske, Diane. "Associative Obligations, Voluntarism, and Equality." *Pacific Philosophical Quarterly* 77 (1996): 289–309.

———. "A Defense of Acting From Duty." *The Journal of Value Inquiry* 32 (1998): 61–74.

———. "Families, Friends, and Special Obligations." *The Canadian Journal of Philosophy* 28 (1998): 527–556.

———. "Friendship, Virtue, and Impartiality." *Philosophy and Phenomenological Research* 57 (1997): 51–72.

———. "Special Relationships and the Problem of Political Obligations." *Social Theory and Practice* 27 (2001): 19–40.

Kagan, Shelly. *The Limits of Morality.* Oxford, UK: Oxford University Press, 1989.

Kamm, Frances H. *Morality, Mortality, Vol. 2: Rights, Duties, and Status.* New York, NY: Oxford University Press, 1996.

Kant, Immanuel. *Grounding for the Metaphysics of Morals.* Edited by James Ellington. Indianapolis, IN: Hackett Publishing Co., 1981. First published 1785.

Klosko, George. "Political Obligation and Gratitude." *Philosophy and Public Affairs* 18 (1989): 352–358.

Korsgaard, Christine. "The Right to Lie: Kant on Dealing with Evil." *Philosophy and Public Affairs* 15 (1986): 325–349.

———. *The Sources of Normativity.* Cambridge, UK: Cambridge University Press, 1996.

Lind, Marcia. "Hume and the Moral Emotions." In *Identity, Character, and Morality: Essays in Moral Psychology,* edited by Owen Flanagan and Amelie Oksenberg Rorty, 133–147. Cambridge, MA: The MIT Press, 1990.

Locke, John. *Second Treatise of Government.* Edited by C. B. McPherson. Indianapolis, IN: Hackett Publishing Co., 1980. First published 1690.

MacIntyre, Alasdair. *After Virtue.* 2nd ed. Notre Dame, IN: Notre Dame University Press, 1984.

Mackie, John. *Ethics: Inventing Right and Wrong.* New York, NY: Viking Penguin, Inc., 1977.

McKeever, Sean, and Michael Ridge. "The Many Moral Particularisms." *The Canadian Journal of Philosophy* 35 (2005): 83–106.

Melden, A. I. *Rights and Persons.* Berkeley, CA: University of California Press, 1977.

Mill, John Stuart. *The Subjection of Women.* Edited by Susan Moller Okin. Indianapolis, IN: Hackett Publishing Co., 1988. First published 1869.

———. *Utilitarianism.* Edited by George Sher. Indianapolis, IN: Hackett Publishing Co., 1979. First published 1861.

Nagel, Thomas. *The Possibility of Altruism.* Princeton, NJ: Princeton University Press, 1970.

———. *The View From Nowhere.* Oxford, UK: Oxford University Press, 1986.

Noddings, Nel. "Caring." In *Justice and Care: Essential Readings in Feminist Ethics,* edited by Virginia Held, 7–30. Boulder, CO: Westview Press, 1995.

Nozick, Robert. *Anarchy, State, and Utopia.* New York, NY: Basic Books, Inc., 1974.

Parfit, Derek. *Reasons and Persons.* Oxford, UK: Oxford University Press, 1984.

Perry, John. "The Importance of Being Identical." In *The Identities of Persons,* edited by Amelie Rorty, 67–90. Berkeley, CA: University of California Press, 1976.

Plato. *Crito,* in *The Dialogues of Plato, Volume I,* translated by R. E. Allen. New Haven, CT: Yale University Press, 1984, 117–129.

Price, Richard. *A Review of the Principal Questions in Morals.* Edited by D. Daiches Raphael. Oxford, UK: The Clarendon Press, 1948. First published 1787.

Railton, Peter. "Alienation, Consequentialism, and the Demands of Morality." *Philosophy and Public Affairs* 13 (1984): 134–171.

Ramsey, William. "Prototypes and Conceptual Analysis." *Topoi* 11 (1992): 59–70.

Raz, Joseph. "The Truth in Particularism." In *Moral Particularism,* edited by Brad Hooker and Margaret Little, 48–78. Oxford, UK: The Clarendon Press, 2000.

Ross, W. D. *The Right and the Good.* Indianapolis, IN: Hackett Publishing Co., 1930.

Sandel, Michael. *Liberalism and the Limits of Justice.* Cambridge, UK: Cambridge University Press, 1982.

Scanlon, Thomas. *What We Owe to Each Other.* Cambridge, MA: Harvard University Press, 1998.

Scheffler, Samuel. "Families, Nations, and Strangers." 1994 Lindley Lecture at the University of Kansas, Oct. 17, 1994.

———. *The Rejection of Consequentialism.* Oxford, UK: Oxford University Press, 1982.

———. "Relationships and Responsibilities." *Philosophy and Public Affairs* 26 (1997): 189–209.

Shafer-Landau, Russ. *Moral Realism: A Defence.* Oxford, UK: Oxford University Press, 2003.

Sidgwick, Henry. *The Methods of Ethics.* Indianapolis, IN: Hackett Publishing Co., 1981. First published 1907.

Simmons, A. John. *Moral Principles and Political Obligations.* Princeton, NJ: Princeton University Press, 1979.

Sinnott-Armstrong, Walter. "Moral Skepticism and Justification." In *Moral Knowledge? New Readings in Moral Epistemology,* edited by Walter Sinnott-Armstrong and Mark Timmons, 3–48. New York, NY: Oxford University Press, 1996.

Slote, Michael. *Common-Sense Morality and Consequentialism.* New York, NY: Routledge, 1985.

Smith, Michael. *The Moral Problem.* Oxford, UK: Blackwell Publishers, Ltd., 1994.

Stevenson, C. L. "The Emotive Meaning of Ethical Terms." *Mind* 46 (1937): 14–31.

Stocker, Michael. "The Schizophrenia of Modern Ethical Theories." *The Journal of Philosophy* 73 (1976): 453–466.

Sturgeon, Nicholas. "Moral Explanations." In *Essays on Moral Realism*, edited by Geoffrey Sayre-McCord, 229–255. Ithaca, NY: Cornell University Press, 1988.

Tannen, Deborah. *You Just Don't Understand: Women and Men in Conversation*. New York, NY: Random House, 1991.

Taylor, Charles. "Atomism." Pages 187–210 in *Philosophy and the Human Sciences: Philosophical Papers 2*. Cambridge, UK: Cambridge University Press, 1985.

Walker, A. D. M. "Political Obligation and the Argument from Gratitude." *Philosophy and Public Affairs* 17 (1988): 191–211.

Williams, Bernard. "Persons, Character, and Morality." Pages 1–19 in *Moral Luck*. Cambridge, UK: Cambridge University Press, 1981.

Young, Iris Marion. *Justice and the Politics of Difference*. Princeton, NJ: Princeton University Press, 1990.

Index